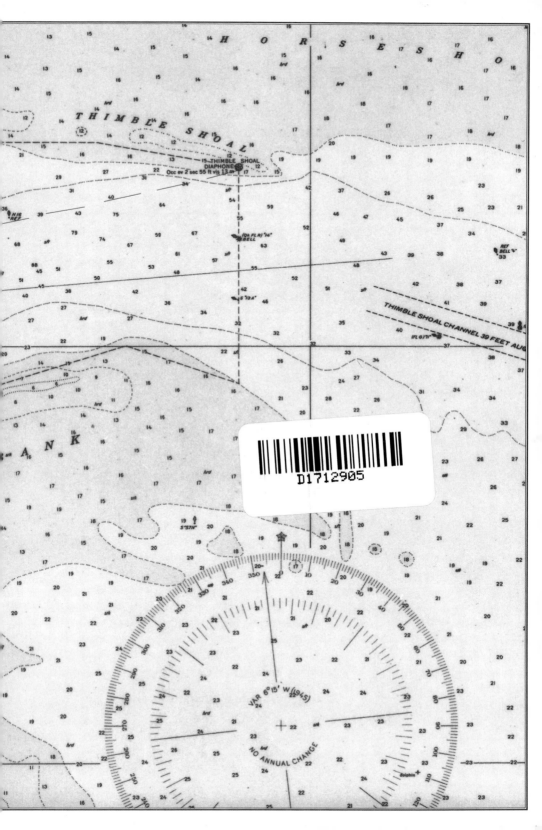

STRIKE ABLE-PETER

The Stranding and Salvage of the USS *Missouri*

JOHN A. BUTLER

NAVAL INSTITUTE PRESS
Annapolis, Maryland

Library of Congress Cataloging-in-Publication Data
Butler, John A., 1927–
Strike able-peter : the stranding and salvage of the USS Missouri / John
A. Butler.
p.   cm.
Includes bibliographical references (p.   ) and index.
ISBN 1-55750-094-0 (alk. paper)
1. Missouri (Battleship : BB 63) 2. Shipwrecks—Virginia—Hampton
Roads. 3. Stranding of ships—Virginia—Hampton Roads. I. Title.
VK1255.M5B88   1995
623.88'84—dc20   95-18391

BUTLER   1341495

Printed in the United States of America on acid-free paper ∞

02 01 00 99 98 97 96 95   9 8 7 6 5 4 3 2
First printing

For Carrie

Contents

Preface

Too often in a lifetime of seagoing have I been aboard a grounded vessel. These were not always shameful episodes. In the middle of the long river passage to the tidal port of Seville, it was a navigational requirement, as the waters ebbed, to settle an ocean-going freighter on the bottom; it was acceptable on the marshy Malay shore while taking on a final bargeload of rubber prior to the flood tide; it was excusable after ice floes pushed the Patapsco channel buoys a hundred yards closer to Baltimore. But the later strandings, when I took command of my own vessels, bent only upon pleasure, were all my own fault—napping while a midnight fog closed in off Cape Cod, poking too far into unsounded backwaters of some attractive tidal creek, refusing to recognize that local knowledge of Maryland's eastern shore took precedence over printed charts. It was in the Chesapeake that I pushed my luck too far, not with the bottom of the Bay but with my crew. Perhaps it was my fourth failure—I'd stopped counting—that caused my mate to cool abruptly to my cavalier approach. Although we remain happily married, we haven't sailed together since.

In an effort to justify my deficiencies, or at least to put these not uncommon incidents into perspective, I decided to compile a list of well-known groundings of far greater import than my trivial mishaps. The list was never produced, diverted as I was by one of the first events I uncovered, the most spectacular and once widely known stranding of an active battleship in Hampton Roads. That discovery triggered a memory of how the event had briefly touched my own life. During the winter of 1951 I was a mate on a freighter being guided up the Chesapeake by a pilot who directed our attention to the waters west of Thimble Shoal Light. It was over there, he pointed out, that he had been piloting the first steamship to pass by the hapless USS Missouri, probably within minutes of its grounding. The conversation dwells in my memory because that was the winter of the Patapsco incident, a particularly frigid one on the upper Bay. Forty years later I wondered if my recollection was more fanciful than valid. Micro-filmed newspapers containing the Norfolk shipping news proved that the years had not misled me. Not only did I find listed the 1951 arrival in the Bay of my own ship, but I found enough evidence of what I recalled about the pilot's story that I knew this was reality. His experience is related briefly in a later chapter of this book.

Soon I became absorbed in the front-page stories of the Missouri incident, fascinated by that extraordinary mishap and the nearly impossible challenges presented by it. Naval officers should have been better trained for their tasks, thought I, and the enlisted men sharper and better disciplined than their wartime counterparts. The same questions raised at the time now perplexed me. How could such an unusual accident have occurred? What circumstances could have led to it? Nothing would do but that I find the explanation. Long-filed naval reports perhaps uncovering extenuating circumstances had to be seen. A voyage across the same waters might help me understand the difficulties faced by the participants. As pieces of the story came together, it occurred to me that an account of the stranding and salvage might benefit in the retelling, there were so many people and so many angles of interest. Something about the event—not the details of what happened on board, but the tenor of the period—struck me as pertinent to current times. Perhaps there was a lesson to be drawn from the affair, but if there was I couldn't grasp it. I put the idea of writing a story out of my mind as something that would have little value without a moral, and probably little interest in itself—no sex, no violence, no intrigue. The only women involved were a few unnamed relatives left standing on the pier. It was a peacetime event; no guns were fired, and not a person was seriously hurt. As to intrigue, if there was one common characteristic through the whole story it was the naive honesty of the participants, even as they kept their private counsel. Yet I was haunted by the parallels to be seen in two periods some four decades apart, in the nation's similar trials adjusting to the end of worldwide tensions, the divided political leadership, and the contentious military environments, then and now. At that point, purely by coincidence, something happened that brought the lesson I felt was there to center stage.

Having lived in different parts of the country since high school, my brother Edmund and I are apt to converse only on celebratory occasions. In the 1950s we even sailed on different oceans. Thus it was entirely by chance that through him I uncovered the single item that changed my view on the value of the *Missouri* story. Some time after my visit to Hampton Roads, I mentioned casually to Ed that I had been in Norfolk, not far from where he lives in retirement, investigating the history of the *Mighty Mo*. At once he recalled how, during the Korean War, that incident on the Chesapeake had touched his life, more even than my own. His story enters into the final part of this book. After completing most of my research, his tale fit so perfectly into the facts, and illustrated the lesson so dramatically, that I felt obligated to include it. Lest I be accused of literary nepotism, the coincidence may be indicative of the extent to which mariners in those years discussed and analyzed the extraordinary events in Hampton Roads.

The affair was well documented, even to what people said and, sometimes, thought. If it had transpired four or five years earlier or later, at the end of World War II or during the intensifying paranoia of the Cold War, the news might have been contained. The times made the difference. More devious military minds might have expanded on an element of truth in the situation and stated that the grounding was a training exercise of little concern to most people and certainly not newsworthy. The Navy could have made it a non-event. If it was on television at all it would have been presented as old news; filmed first, replayed later. It happened to be a particularly photogenic occurrence, but television technology in 1950 couldn't improve on newspapers for current events. Few homes were equipped with TV, making costly on-site reporting difficult to justify. The news services might have treated it as something of local interest—the local papers were obligated to cover it, it was so painfully obvious. Except for those in the Tidewater area, people might have read an inch or two on an inside page, then put the paper aside with a wry comment and shake of the head. What made the event sensational was that it happened to the last and most famous of those awesome battleships, the president's own, at a most embarrassing time. Had the same problem faced the owners of a rusty freighter, or even one of the Navy's destroyers, it would have hardly been noticed.

As it was the details unfolded quite openly, giving the populace more than a month of day-to-day suspense in the midst of a dull winter. We got caught up in it, wondering how the problems would be resolved. The Navy was quite open about what had happened and fair in reporting what they were doing to recover.

As we read the stories we formulated dozens of ideas on how the stranding had come about, all of them wrong. We had plenty of suggestions on how to overcome the principal salvage problem as we perceived it. None of them were pursued. It was one of the worst days in the history of the peacetime Navy, but it took months for a handful of people, more perceptive than most of the naval leadership, to identify the cause. By then the public didn't care. The excitement was over. While it made front-page news we asked the wrong questions, and when it was over, when there were no more photographs and little mention of the ship in the papers, we went back to following collegiate basketball, the possibility of Communist subversion, and descriptions of Detroit's new cars. We seemed more fascinated by portholes on the fenders of Buicks than by anything to do with the military. It was only then that the significance of the circumstances leading to the event emerged, but the Navy kept its classified observations to itself, rivalries between the armed forces being intense. Within six months, what was learned would be put on the shelf to be forgotten as attention centered on the new Korean War. Now, nearly a half century after the embarrassment that put a spotlight on naval weaknesses and strengths, the major lesson derived in midcentury cries out for recognition. It focused on what was then the mightiest vessel afloat in the world, the battleship *Missouri,* America's symbol of strength and righteousness, and its nearly unrecognized, tragic weakness.

The salvage problem overlapped the mystery of the event's cause. At first reading it looked like the Navy's approach to saving the ship was to throw admirals at it, wrapping it in gold braid, a Keystone cop exercise with the uniformed chasers elevated to flag rank. I thought of admirals as blustery elder men of slight substance, enjoying their amenities but contributing little in the way of wisdom or sleeves-up production, as they were often caricatured. Again, like most others, I was wrong. The men who saved the ship, physically and politically, were energetic, meticulous in detail, bright, loyal, and dedicated. They provided the contrast of characteristics that ties the lesson together.

This story concerns the making of men in a time of peace, and in that respect it is a parable for today. No glory in warfare or quavering enemies; the sea battles were over, and the enemies were what men, good people with predictable strengths and weaknesses, made for themselves. The message that emerged from the event is as pertinent nearly fifty years later as it was then. If heeded it could be the *Missouri*'s greatest contribution to the nation, exceeding its successes in battle and fame in Tokyo Bay.

There are many people and organizations I would like to thank for their aid in putting this story together. The trove of newspaper clippings maintained by the Mariners' Museum in Newport News was a most valuable source. What is no longer available in the National Archives, specific transcripts of testimony given in the hearings, can be found verbatim in the reporting of several newspaper columnists, chiefly the papers of the Tidewater area. Archivist Tom Crew and Trish Allen, Mariners' Museum library assistant, were especially helpful. The photos in the Ted Stone Collection and over a hundred pages of news clippings in the Alexander Crosby Brown collection covered the events thoroughly. Recognition must also go to Peggy Haile, custodian of the Jim Mays photo collection in the Norfolk Public Library, donated by the *Norfolk Virginian-Pilot*.

I had the cooperation of several Naval Academy graduates as soon as they learned of my pursuit. Capt. William S. Busik, USN (Ret.), head of the U.S. Naval Academy Alumni Association, arranged to provide detailed information on the careers of several officers in this account. I am especially thankful to Allan E. Smith Jr. for sharing his father's personal papers. From those, and from direct conversations with Allan Smith, I hope I have captured something of his father's personality and done justice to the late admiral, who is the focal point of much of the narrative. Insight into Admiral Smith's writings would not have come about were it not for the support of Comdr. William E. Campbell, USN (Ret.), a USS *Iowa* alumnus, and submariner Capt. Joseph Fitzpatrick, USN (Ret.), both of whom encouraged Allan Smith Jr. on my behalf.

It was essential to get the feel of what it is like to take the conn as skipper of an *Iowa*-class battleship, something difficult to do so long after the events being described. Capt. Larry Seaquist, USN (Ret.), former skipper of the *Iowa,* provided excellent technical advice and enthusiastically recommended that the story be told. It would not have happened without Larry's backing, for which I am most appreciative.

Enlisted men play a large role in this tale. I am indebted to Angelo Goffredo, president of the USS *Missouri* Association and electronic technician on the *Missouri* from 1946 to 1950. "Guffy" arranged my meeting with several members of the association who were aboard at the time. I can't recall when I have met such loyal, exuberant, and energetic people. At first I was skeptical about relying on the memories of men in their late sixties about events forty years in their past. Would they differentiate fact from fancy? I soon had no concern, so vividly did they recall their experiences, while independently and inadvertently corroborating each other's stories. Before long I felt I was inside the skin of a *Missouri* bluejacket, handling stores, racing across the deck, living the forlorn life aboard the stuck ship. I salute the men of the *Mighty Mo,* stalwart themselves.

To Master Chief Fire Controlman Steven Skelley, USN, of the Naval Surface Warfare Center, Dahlgren, Virginia, a battleship advocate and former crew member of the *Iowa,* I owe thanks for checking the accuracy of my limited knowledge of fire control centers. I am grateful to William E. Smith, CPO, USN (Ret.), recently deceased, former signalman third class aboard the USS *Guam,* for his recollections and for sharing the account of the kamikaze attack on the *Mo.* My story does little justice to the knowledge, experience, and dedication of the backbone of any ship's crew, the chief petty officer, and for that I am sorry. It happens that they entered into the events with a very low profile.

I had to see the great ship for myself, even in its idle state. Don Gillikan of the Naval Sea Systems Command in Portsmouth, Virginia, arranged my visit to the Naval Inactive Ships Maintenance Facility in Bremerton, Washington. Thanks to Peter Galassi and Gunnar Watson for their support, and most certainly to Jim Cole for his two-hour guided tour, stem to stern, through more than a dozen decks of the *Missouri*'s interior.

Thanks go also to Dave and Anne Blair, owners of the trawler *Andante,* for the informative cruise through Hampton Roads along the route taken by the *Missouri.* It was not difficult to simulate the tension one might feel in the strangely marked waters east of Old Point Comfort, and quite rewarding when we found the exact spot from which the ship was finally pulled free.

There were many locations at which I spent extended time reviewing microfilms, turning the pages of fifty-year-old texts, studying charts and diagrams. All the people were courteous and helpful, and to them my gratitude. Mark Werthheimer, curator at the U.S. Navy Museum Library in Washington, was particularly cooperative in guiding me to sources of battleship lore. Comdr. R. N. Fiske, USN, Deputy Assistant Judge Advocate General, Navy Office of the Judge Advocate General, provided the important Report of the Court of Inquiry, on which much of the testimonial detail is based. Archivist Richard von Dorenhoff, in the Military Reference Branch of the National Archives, patiently aimed me in the right direction. Even then I found myself turning to private libraries. James D. Hanlon, former classmate, licensed chief mate, navigator, naval officer, and admiralty lawyer, deserves thanks for the use of his library, as does Don Robertson, whom I have only met electronically but who kindly provided me with a copy of a valuable out-of-print source.

Writing is a long and arduous task that comes to nought without the guidance of a publisher. I am grateful for the patient support of the following people: Allan B. Lefcowitz, Ph.D., artistic director of The Writer's Center, for his early direction; Paul Wilderson, executive editor at Naval Institute Press, for his encouragement; and Jonathan Lawrence, for his sensitive editing.

Finally, the relatives. I am blessed with a loquacious brother and sedate wife. Ed's story of his evening on the USS *Mount Olympus* lit the match that fired my enthusiasm. Elinor's patience with my unaccompanied travels and long hours at a word processor more than offset her earlier distress as we sat too often and too high above the waters of the Chesapeake.

What I relate here is true. If imagination intrudes anywhere it is to provide a sense of the times and the environment, and then in but minor details. Here, then, is a modern parable, the story of the stranding and salvage of the *Mighty Mo.*

STRIKE ABLE-PETER

1

Last of the Best

Heavy steel has a subtle smell— dank, vaguely evocative of its fiery birth, its aura persistent under layers of paint. Combine steel with the tang of sea air and it takes on the power to invigorate, to encourage the timid and strengthen the weary. Men thrive in the presence of steel, in shaping it, joining it, moving it, living in its protection. In September 1950 the men of the USS *Missouri* urgently needed that bracing feeling. These were not fainthearted sailors. In the preceding month they had wrestled the battleship through a damaging Atlantic hurricane, then dodged a mid-Pacific tropical storm, only to encounter a typhoon off the east coast of Korea. Whatever strengths had been sapped by those struggles, youthful resilience had amply refreshed.

This was the dispirited crew of the most powerful warship in the world, a floating monument that had once stirred the heart of America. The *Missouri* was still a popular icon, a patriotic reminder of a two-ocean war well fought, ranking with the welcoming symbols of the Golden Gate Bridge and the Statue of Liberty. During the past year the men of the *Mighty Mo* had achieved new peaks of spirit and efficiency. They delighted in General MacArthur's recognition when all hands formed on deck at the fourth-anniversary celebration of the Japanese surrender. Theirs also was the glorious moment at the close of the 1949 summer maneuvers when the Atlantic Fleet's commander in chief awarded the prized Navy "E" to the ship for the excellent performance of three of its departments. Now at sea off Korea, twelve months later, while sailors watched the high-line transfer from the deck of the destroyer *Maddox* of the new commander of Task Force 95, many thought his presence would open old wounds. Rear Adm.

1

Allan E. Smith was already familiar to many of the crew. Six months ago it was he who had written of personnel failures in the *Missouri*. The vessel itself, now to be his flagship, was well known to him, for he was also the one who had saved it from a shameful fate. The admiral understood the crew's ennui better than anyone. But he knew also of their earlier reputation and had advocated the use of their ship in this new Pacific war. He could, if he chose, restore the proud feelings these men lost during the troubled weeks he had been with them earlier in the year. Or he could put the broom to the masthead, raise the long commissioning pennant, and make this the final tour of duty for the world's last active battleship.

They were magnificent vessels, the battleships, once the focus of the fleet in preserving the century-old "line-of-battle" tradition. Designed for ocean warfare in the protection of sea-lanes, they did the job well until submarines and air transport made those very routes indistinct. By midcentury no one questioned that fast carriers made battleships strategically obsolete. During World War II their roles were reduced to carrier escorts and floating gun platforms for shore bombardment. Willingly they took up that work, yielded their dominance, and gave not an inch of pride in the transition. It was their near indestructibility that kept them from obsolescence. No other ships so well combined the ability to withstand intense punishment with speed and fighting might. Often their weaponry was more powerful in its presence than in its use. Their very existence influenced foreign policy, conditioning the attitudes of friends and enemies. They became symbols of America's search for peace through strength, the *Missouri* even taking its place on foreign postage stamps. The battlewagons fought the good fight, captured the peace, and in the process built men.

Fighting ships go back to the Vikings, to the ten-year Trojan War, to Xerxes and Alexander and Caesar's approach to Britain. When brass cannons replaced spears, seagoing gun platforms soon became effective tools of war. The most exciting characteristic of battleships—the broadside, rows of midship cast-iron cannons belching fire and shot at close quarters with the enemy—was a sixteenth-century development. The English frigate *Mary Rose,* the first with this capability, carried several guns below decks behind hinged side ports, each rigged with tackle enabling it to be hauled inboard for cleaning and loading. After years of fighting, the *Mary Rose* came to its end in action with France when water streamed through open gunports and the ship swamped and sank, all in the dismayed view of Henry VIII.[1]

By the end of the eighteenth century, the height of the great age of sail, fast frigates became more useful than their larger, more powerful but unwieldy counterparts. Given such robust agility, nothing was to be feared, hence "dreadnought," a name initially given to a frigate. The first *Dreadnought* sailed with the loftier classes in the British fleet to drive out the Spanish Armada.[2] In time the term would apply not to these smaller, handy vessels but to the largest of ships, commercial and naval. Frigates came as an evolutionary step. So that they would prevail in battle, their firepower was increased—more guns, heavier shells, longer range. In turn they needed thicker armor to resist hits from similar ships, and they gradually grew in size. One frigate remains in service to this day, the USS *Constitution,* pride of the American navy of 1812 and current flagship of the U.S. Navy's First Naval District.

Following the American War for Independence, technical advancements shifted back and forth across the Atlantic. The fifteen-minute history of the French *Pyroscaphe,* in 1783 the first ship to navigate under steam power, has been well documented. Considered unsuccessful, it was still enough to start development in the New World. American John Fitch's initial effort made little improvement. Doggedly learning from his first trial, he demonstrated a fully operational steam vessel on the Delaware River in 1787 and became widely known as the first American inventor of the steamboat. Fitch's efforts were eclipsed by several others, among them an American Leonardo, Robert Fulton. A painter well recognized in Europe, an engineer and inventor, Fulton produced the commercially useful *Clermont,* with steam-driven paddle-wheel propulsion, in 1807. Like da Vinci, Fulton spawned more creative ideas than he delivered. He produced plans for submarines, underwater torpedoes, and, perhaps of more direct consequence, a steam warship. That idea simmered for a half century, untried while sail flourished.

Then in 1840 a Swede, John Ericsson, developed the first ship with a screw propeller, aptly named the *Archimedes.* The propeller was vastly superior to the paddle wheel and earned wide recognition for Ericsson's engineering prowess. With the onset of the American

Civil War, the erratic Ericsson found himself working for the Union. The genesis of the battleship would soon be marked by the shift from sail power.

When the Civil War started, ten oaken ships of the Union fleet, carrying twelve hundred cannon, stood ready in the South's largest shipbuilding and repair facility, blockaded by Confederate vessels lurking off the Virginia capes.[3] Hampton Roads was commanded by Union forces in Fort Monroe on Old Point Comfort* and in a small gun emplacement on Rip-Rap, a fortified pile of rocks across from the fort in the midst of the passage. The Roads remained in Union hands, but the fleet inside had nowhere to go. The steam frigate *Merrimac,* forty guns and eight hundred sailors and marines, stood embattled in the Gosport yard, engulfed in flames. Virginia seceded and its militia took over the shipyard, putting Hampton Roads largely in Confederate control. A battle line was drawn there between North and South.

The *Merrimac*'s hull survived to be rebuilt, covered like an armadillo with iron plate, renamed CS *Virginia,* and sent out to destroy the Federal fleet. The Union soon lost its prize warship to the *Virginia*'s fire, as two other Federal vessels, *Minnesota* and *St. Lawrence,* grounded beyond the range of the *Virginia*'s guns, south of the Newport News channel. Fort Monroe's cannons provided protective guard until help arrived from the north.†

The U.S. Navy's first metal warship, Ericsson's *Monitor,* was built in one hundred days in response to the blockade and to rumors circulating in the north that the rebels were building a ship of iron. It had only one gun and fought for a total of four hours in but one battle, a contest that most would judge as being without victors. Unseaworthy from launching to loss at sea, it lived for just eleven months. The vessel displayed no advances in design, its only innovation being that it employed all the recent ones—steam power, screw propulsion, armor of iron, and a revolving gun turret. It revolutionized naval warfare and struck the death knell for wooden warships.

In 1861 the USS *Monitor* made Hampton Roads famous. It arrived

---

* Originally called Old Point, it was the site in 1619 of the introduction of African slaves into the English colonies. A hospital was later built there and the name changed to Old Point Comfort.
† Named for Pres. James Monroe, the six-sided structure is the only Army fort built within a moat. After the Civil War, Rip-Rap, the off-lying fortification, was renamed Fort Wool, for Gen. John Ellis Wool, who commanded Fort Monroe during the siege.

on the scene in darkness to stand by the *Minnesota* while steam tugs attempted to free it. Later that morning the two ironclads did battle off Sewell Point. At one moment the *Virginia* grounded in twenty-two feet of water, becoming a sitting duck for the *Monitor's* single cannon. Building extraordinary boiler pressure, the Confederate ship succeeded in backing off, thereby establishing the first lesson in self-powered salvaging techniques. The two ships continued firing at each other at close range but did little harm. Then, as the tide ebbed, the shallow-draft *Monitor* attempted to draw the *Virginia* onto a shoal. The weary crew of the *Virginia* withdrew into the safety of the Elizabeth River, ending the battle in a draw.

These were the waters that so often came into the conversations of the 1950 crew of the *Missouri,* in the wardroom and in the sailors' mess, even as they crossed the Pacific. They could describe the contours of Hampton Roads in detail, from Sewell Point across to Fort Monroe and outward to the light near Thimble Shoal. They knew the shallows and the flow of tide. They had a sense of what it felt like to be aboard the stranded *Minnesota,* and the struggle faced by the beleaguered *Virginia.* Day after day, certainly not within earshot of Admiral Smith, they would refer to their own distressing days in January, agonize over what had caused them, and, with youthful spirit, occasionally laugh at their own miseries.

The nature of navies changed, worldwide, following the encounter of the ironclads. A new class of warships arose, and the intense arms race that followed would continue for 130 years. The news of Hampton Roads initiated development of the ninth British *Dreadnought,* the modern battleship. Open-hearth fusing of carbon and iron started the industrial era and enabled the first truly steel ships. Built in secrecy and launched in 1906, HMS *Dreadnought* had ten 12-inch guns able to fire 850-pound projectiles. Gone were the traditional reciprocating engines, replaced by steam turbines, quieter and with less wear and loss of oil and steam. The ship traveled at seventeen knots but could achieve nineteen. Speed, according to the designers, was a good substitute for armor, yet it carried five thousand tons of armor on its turrets. It had sealed compartments without horizontal access, so the crew climbed in and out of each through a main deck hatch. Officer country and the captain's quarters were placed in the forward part of the ship, ending the long tradition of living aft with a stern view from a windowed cabin. The only ship the *Dreadnought* ever sank was a German submarine it rammed in the English Channel in 1915, yet it influenced major warship design prior to World War I and gave its name to the modern battleship.

With the characteristics of speed, armor, and armament at cross-purposes, these were the steps by which warship development escalated through four centuries. Ships got bigger, faster, and more maneuverable. During the first thirty years of the twentieth century, six nations competed for ocean dominance. Italy and Imperial Russia followed Great Britain's early start in steel warship development, fomenting an armament drive culminating before World War II in the German *Bismarck* and the Japanese *Yamato,* the latter the mightiest warship in the world. The first of two in its class, the *Yamato* carried nine 18-inch guns, a size that has never been equaled. In response, plans for the American *Iowa*-class battleships were drawn up in 1940.

By custom America named its battleships for federal states. A class of ships takes the name of the first of the group to be constructed. Each ship's hull number, assigned prior to construction, is prefaced by initials designating the type (BB for battleships). Ships' names have been used multiple times, chosen through the combined forces of precedent, tradition, emotion, and a large measure of politics. With minor variances, hull numbers are useful in dating each ship and associating it with its class. Two battleships were planned during World War I that would have deviated from the naming convention, the *Lexington* and *Saratoga.* The convention prevailed when the two were completed as aircraft carriers, an early recognition of the rise of airpower.

In the 1930s, as the threat of a new war grew, the U.S. fleet looked newer on drawing boards than it did on the sea.[4] It was not until then that the brutal work in the stokehold came to an end. The oldest battleship to remain active through World War II was the coal-burning *Arkansas,* one of two in the *Wyoming* class.* Oil finally replaced coal, and the fleet learned to refuel while under way, thereby extending its range far across the waters, dependent no longer on coaling ports.

The United States had seventeen active battleships prior to its entry into the war: three were obsolete, twelve well armed and pro-

---

* See appendix B, table 1, for a complete list of American battleships of World War II.

tected, two modern. More were on the way, either proposed, in construction, or engaged in sea trials. Of eight ships in "battleship row" on 7 December 1941, two were sunk and the other six suffered medium to heavy damage. (The *Arizona* remained where it sank; the *Oklahoma* was declared a total loss.) The American battleship force was completely immobilized, out of action for months while other forces were reconstructed to join the fleet with more powerful armament. That immense damage called for the quick delivery of salvaging skills. At the time the Navy had no contract for salvage work in the Pacific and lacked even a salvage school.

The losses at Pearl Harbor stimulated a drive to build the *Iowa*s as rapidly as possible.* Keels for five of these ships were laid between 1940 and 1945. Keels were also laid for the wider, *Montana*-class ships in 1943, only to have construction canceled with the launching of the *Iowa*s in the following year. The *Iowa*s would be better suited for task force duty, and the countdown to their final days was put on hold. The message emerged, to be denied by many for years, but the days of the battleship were numbered. Four hulls—*Iowa, New Jersey, Missouri,* and *Wisconsin*—were launched from 1942 to 1944, to be commissioned in 1943 and 1944, and recommissioned again and again. They became survivors in military strategy as much as they were survivors at sea.

Assigned hull number 63, the *Missouri* was the newest battleship of World War II, third of its class and last to be launched, following the *New Jersey* down the ways by a week. On a cold, blustery January day, before more than twenty thousand people gathered on both sides of New York's East River, a sprightly young lady swung a bottle of champagne against its forefoot and gave the name USS *Missouri* to America's last battleship. The hull, its prime yellow coat still visible, delayed its response. Margaret Truman fidgeted while her doting father continued to beam with pride. Launch time had been advanced by five minutes to meet the tide. Senator Truman had raced through his speech to meet the schedule, and now the great ship seemed reluctant to move. Finally, to the cheers of the crowd and the shrill screams of tugboat whistles, the hull broke loose from its bonds and slid gracefully down the ways of the Brooklyn Navy Yard.

---

* See appendix B, table 2, for a history of the four *Iowa*-class battleships.

Prior to the war, the classical seagoing organization was the battle-ship division (BatDiv), a tactical unit typically made up of three to four ships of one or two classes. Keeping similar ships in a division allowed a unit that maintained the same speed and range of action, one that could be jointly administered, supplied, and used for training. The continual process of overhaul and refitting could be staggered so that the division could remain in operation. One week after the attack on Pearl Harbor, Japanese aircraft sank the British *Prince of Wales* and *Repulse* in the British Eastern Fleet. The concept of fighting BatDivs suddenly became obsolete, to be replaced by task-oriented organizations. Task groups assembled according to planned operations included auxiliary ships, minesweepers, transports, and multiple classes of capital ships either detached from units or in complete divisions. Task groups were elements of task forces and could be subdivided into task units. During the early phase of the war the task group was the typical operational unit, usually with a rear admiral as group commander. Later it evolved into a task force unit, under a vice admiral. Task forces operated in an area designated as a fleet, commanded by an admiral. That organization prevailed after the war, and divisions of similar classes were retained only for administrative purposes.

After 1940 Japan launched no more battleships. Even with the losses at Pearl Harbor, within six months the United States began to outclass its enemies in capital ships. The new *Iowa*s brought major improvements in ship design. Equipped with immensely powerful engines and longer hulls, they could outpace nearly anything afloat. Their length would barely fit on three football fields. They stood as high above the water as a twenty-story building, and were a tight fit in the Panama Canal. Limiting their beam to that requirement gave them a sleek, almost sensuous look. If a destroyer could be lowered onto the deck of an *Iowa,* only sixteen inches would be added to the battleship's thirty-seven-foot draft.

Four fifty-seven-ton propellers drove each vessel at up to thirty-five knots. Twin rudders, larger than barn doors, turned the *Iowa*s in a tighter circle than their own destroyer escorts'. They carried enough fuel to float a Liberty* ship, adequate to cross the Pacific three times

---

* Wartime freighter of 7,176 registered gross tons, able to carry 10,000 tons of deadweight cargo.

LAST OF THE BEST

without refueling; that is, if they didn't run out of coffee, the crew's normal wartime consumption being over three hundred gallons a day. With wartime complements in excess of twenty-five hundred officers and men, these ships were floating villages. Their generators could produce enough power to illuminate the city of Tacoma. They had a post office, barber shop (two hundred haircuts a day), cobbler, printer, a store dispensing nine thousand gallons of ice cream per month, a fifty-six-bed hospital with two operating rooms, and a two-chair dental clinic. Long before multiplex theaters, they ran as many as seven separate shows per night. At midcentury, when less than half of American homes had telephones, the eleven-hundred-phone systems of the *Iowa*s provided the nerve-ends of this seagoing community. Twelve levels above the main deck of an *Iowa*, "sky control," standing two hundred feet above water, looked down on nine 16-inch guns. Each could hurl a projectile the weight of a staff car more than twenty miles, and the electromechanical fire control equipment could put the payload ashore at an intersection before the light changed. These were the first computers out of development labs, designed to remain useful throughout the life of the ships. They had to last. Removal would have required structural alteration of the armored decks and bulkheads.

By sheer fate, the *Missouri*'s name would sire its fortune. A $100 million investment, it was described by the *New York Times* as the "world's greatest warship . . . a study in superlatives." The first crew came from the weary warships of the Atlantic Fleet at Norfolk and Charleston, fresh from training at Great Lakes and Sampson, from Annapolis, and out of ROTC programs around the nation. Many faced their first seagoing experience. They assembled in Newport, soon to go aboard as "plank owners." Following by a few days its sister ship the *Wisconsin,* the *Missouri* was commissioned on 11 June, within a week of D-Day, in public ceremonies with Secretary of the Navy James Forrestal in attendance. After sea trials in the Chesapeake, it headed to the Pacific and joined Task Force 58 for battles at Honshu, Nansei Shoto, Iwo Jima, and Okinawa.

The long-predicted value of airpower in sea warfare was confirmed in 1941 when aircraft from the British carrier *Ark Royal* finally pursued and sank the destructive *Bismarck.* But lone carriers are too vulnerable a target, requiring escorts for accompanying support. Battleships could deliver the necessary fighting power. The four *Iowa*s operated briefly as a high-speed BatDiv, but their speed made them more suitable in providing surface protection for carrier groups. As the war progressed they developed a symbiotic relationship with the dominant carriers. Carrier-based aircraft provided a dome of fighter protection for the force, overcoming the operational limitations of scout planes. Should enemy craft bent on bombing the vulnerable carriers penetrate the combat air patrol, they would encounter the immense antiaircraft firepower of the battleships.

Though no vessel larger and more powerful than the *Yamato* has ever been built, it met its end in March 1945 at the hands of Task Force 58. When it sank under carrier-based air strikes, a clear message again emerged concerning the fate of the battlewagons. But air strikes worked both ways. During the last months of the war the Pacific Fleet faced a new threat—bomb-laden suicide planes. In desperation Japan had taken to sending young flyers in old single-pilot planes loaded with explosives and enough fuel for a one-way trip to their targets. Before the war's end the kamikazes would strike 398 Allied ships.[5] No capital ships were lost, but in such an encounter the *Missouri* had its most harrowing experience. In midafternoon on 12 April 1945, it cruised in battle formation off Okinawa with the light cruiser *Guam* nearby, fighting off vicious and sporadic single-plane raids. Spidery black clouds of flak crawled across the sky while plumes of near-miss bombs lined the sea's surface. Of more than a dozen approaching suicide planes, two found a hole in the task group's fighter protection and skimmed low over the water, one headed for the stern of the *Guam,* the other for the side of the *Missouri.* The *Missouri*'s attacker was the first to come within range and dove toward the hull in a stream of tracers, finally taking an explosive hit before it crashed near a 40-millimeter emplacement on the ship's starboard quarter. Its right wing tore off, lodging next to a midship 5-inch mount. A sheet of red flame enveloped the after superstructure as great clouds of black smoke leapt into the air. The second kamikaze was blasted in midair off the fantail of the *Guam.* The *Mo* sailed on unperturbed, with no casualties and only slight damage. The crew pried the remnants of the plane's wreckage off the ship and dumped it into the sea. The next day they buried the top half of the pilot's body—all that remained—with full military honors.[6]

During that campaign, in the heat of battle, the *Missouri* lofted a 5-inch shell that struck one of its accompanying destroyers, the *Trathen,* inflicting minor damage. In 1950 the destroyer's skipper would find himself assigned to the *Mo,* a central figure in the troubles of Hampton Roads.

Battleship sailors track major events and trivia in the lives of the big ships like baseball fans trade statistics on familiar players. During the fall of 1950 there may not have been many in the *Mighty Mo's* crew who could recount details of the long and glorious warship tradition, but to a man they knew the particulars of the Japanese surrender. It was more familiar than the Articles read to them monthly. There was not a man aboard who hadn't paid a reverent visit to the Surrender Deck, where the memorial plaque was ensconced. They couldn't miss the further description in bronze on a nearby bulkhead. Those details remained their ship's very reason for being.

Five years earlier, after the enemy had capitulated on 15 August, the *Missouri* was operating off the coast of Japan as Adm. William Halsey's flagship. They were waiting orders to proceed with the occupation while a large fleet and air support was being organized.[7] As a nod to the new president, the *Missouri* was selected over the more senior *Iowa* and *New Jersey* for ceremonies that would formally conclude the war. On 27 August the ship took aboard an advance contingent of Japanese emissaries and a youthful pilot and proceeded into Sagami Wan, Honshu, anchoring the next day, where thousands of the vanquished could look on its overpowering presence. Minesweepers moved up the harbor, followed by picket boats clearing away capsized boats, wreckage, and floating bodies, the final flotsam of war. Early on the morning of the twenty-ninth, the ship got under way within its screen of destroyers, entered Tokyo Bay, and anchored off Yokosuka Naval Station at 0925. There it remained until 2 September, again in full view of the citizenry. At the *Missouri's* launching nineteen months earlier, before the senator from Missouri was elected as vice president, before the invasion of Europe, before Roosevelt's death, Admiral Halsey had sent a prophetic message: "We have a date to keep in Tokyo." No one could then have forecast the events that would bring about its fulfillment, but the *Mighty Mo* was about to become an American icon.

Admiral Halsey, Commander Third Fleet, moved his flag from the

Missouri to the *Iowa*. Fleet Adm. Chester W. Nimitz boarded the *Missouri* at 0805, and his flag was broken. Officers and men assembled in formation on deck, the officers in dress khakis. The word was passed that General MacArthur had insisted on undress uniform, and hastily the officers removed their coats and ties. Master of dramatic entry, MacArthur arrived forty minutes after Nimitz's flag was raised. He was followed up the steep gangway by the formally dressed Japanese delegation, the military aides being required to check their ceremonial daggers and samurai swords in flag quarters. A mess table covered with decorated green baize had been placed on the forward quarterdeck. With the *Missouri*'s crew in undress whites looking on from every vantage point, the Japanese officials signed the surrender documents, witnessed by the leadership of the Allied forces. Within thirty minutes, the dignitaries departed and everyone went back to work. The mess table was returned below, unidentified, a lost relic. The battleship remained at anchor until 6 September, when it departed for Guam and Pearl Harbor, arriving at the latter on 20 September. After the ship's heroic return to New York, a circular bronze plaque was embedded in the teak of the starboard O2 deck, roped off and referred to thereafter as the Surrender Deck.

U.S.S. MISSOURI
LATITUDE 35° 21' 17" NORTH — LONGITUDE 139° 45' 36" EAST

OVER THIS SPOT
ON 2 SEPTEMBER 1945
THE INSTRUMENT
OF FORMAL SURRENDER
OF JAPAN TO THE ALLIED POWERS
WAS SIGNED
THIS BRINGING TO A CLOSE
THE SECOND WORLD WAR

———

THE SHIP AT THAT TIME
WAS AT ANCHOR
IN TOKYO BAY

The ship became Harry Truman's favorite. In the fall of 1945 the new president boarded it in the Hudson River following the commissioning of the new carrier *Franklin D. Roosevelt*. The *Missouri* provided the platform from which he reviewed the largest display of armament in the nation's history—fifty warships steaming by as twelve hundred planes flew overhead, the *Missouri* in the center of it all.[8] Two years later it served the president again, bringing him and his family back from Rio de Janeiro, his first trip by sea since the cruiser *Augusta* had brought him back from the Potsdam conference. Truman returned in December 1948 to present the warship with a magnificent silver service as a gift from the people of his home state. He vowed then that the *Missouri* would not be inactivated while he remained in office.[9] Within eighteen months, war broke out in Korea and the Navy sent the *Mo,* its only active battleship, to serve.

It would take a year of service in the Far East Fleet off Korea before the power of steel underfoot would overcome the malaise tormenting the men of the *Mighty Mo.* The cause lay in two troublesome weeks early in 1950, perhaps more in the months that preceded them. It festered among the men, officers and enlisted, without their awareness. The shame they suffered in that fortnight would highlight a problem that would take much longer to define. Yet that period may have generated the *Missouri's* greatest contribution to the nation and its armed forces; not the victorious battles of World War II or the fact that it provided the venue for its end, but the lessons learned from what the Navy saw as its greatest humiliation.

2

The Wedge

At the time of the Japanese surrender, over 5,000 ships made up the active fleet of the United States, including 98 carriers, 23 battleships, 72 cruisers, and some 700 destroyers and escorts.[1] Demobilization began rapidly, following plans that had been in place for months, but not without a few moments of splendor for the victors. The U.S. Navy had its time in the spotlight with the Hudson River display of power occasioned by the commissioning of the carrier *Franklin D. Roosevelt.* Then, as the Navy cut back its fleet—mothballing valued vessels, scrapping some, delivering others to Bikini for the 1946 nuclear tests, hastening discharges of reservists, and reducing enlistment periods to two years—the leadership undertook a refurbishing program. The nation's postwar economic boom stretched to the end of the decade, pausing only to tighten its belt under defense cutbacks and an influx of newly graduated veterans into the job market. But the administration, reflecting the attitude of a war-weary public, focused on a peace to be preserved through nonmilitary means and turned its back on military interests.

The Truman Doctrine, announced in March 1947, initiated a costly three-year series of formal commitments to Europe. United Nations relief efforts were extended by an aid program quietly introduced in the summer of 1948. It helped stabilize Europe and build Western resistance to threats of Soviet expansion. Through production of foodstuffs, supplies, and building materials, the program known as the Marshall Plan served to stiffen the shaky American economy, which was potentially faltering under demobilization. Eighteen months later it was evident that the programs were an overwhelming success in revitalizing the European economic community,

14

while the American merchant marine flourished on busy European sea-lanes. During the spring of 1949 the North Atlantic Treaty Organization (NATO) was formed, to be approved by the U.S. Senate in less than four months. It was virtually certain that the Soviets were building new, more powerful submarines, equipped with German-developed snorkels enabling extended underwater operation. Preservation of the ocean passages to Europe became a naval priority, and the Navy's demobilization pace slowed while it implemented its peacetime plans.

The armed forces were placed under the control of a civilian bureaucracy by the National Security Act. The Department of Defense was formed, subordinating the Secretaries of Army, Navy, and Air Force under a new cabinet post, Secretary of Defense. Congress charged the new Joint Chiefs of Staff to consolidate their forces by eliminating overlapping fields of endeavor and unnecessary duplication. Without a major conflict, the structure could be tested only in war games, the first joint series being scheduled for the spring of 1950 in the Caribbean. Among the issues they could resolve was the contention between seaborne power and airpower in landing support. Yielding their autonomy reluctantly, each of the services independently undertook planning for what was internally referred to as World War III.[2]

In June 1949 the last Soviet and American occupation troops debarked from Korea. That arbitrarily divided nation's two governments were left with a handful of military advisors as they contested for control of a tenuous peace. The United Nations, stating that civil war in the Far East peninsula was likely, expressed its concern from its recently dedicated New York headquarters. Inexperienced in what would become known as Cold War tactics, it asked for no peacekeeping forces. Continued peace in the Pacific depended on the presence of American naval forces centralized in Subic Bay in the Philippines.

Meanwhile, the nation's level of paranoia elevated as Congress and the public gradually became aware of the extent to which Communist sympathizers lurked in the shadows of government. Revelations of wartime penetration intensified fears of Soviet action.[3] Political opportunist Joseph McCarthy soon questioned the loyalty of a number of public figures, claiming that the nation was faced with ongoing espionage in government and public manipulation via the arts. Communists, it seemed, prowled everywhere. An undeclared contest between the Soviets and the West—the Cold War—crystallized to hang specterlike over the future of the free world. Military leadership was disturbed that there existed no commitment to defend Europe or the United States against Soviet aggression.[4] Congress was more interested in reduction and unification of the armed forces and was not open to alternatives. At this point a storm burst over the naval establishment.

The first appointment to Secretary of Defense was heartening to naval leadership. Former Secretary of the Navy James V. Forrestal, a World War I naval aviator, understood the importance of naval strength. But he was a sick man, and he resigned his office in March 1949, less than two months prior to his self-inflicted death. President Truman's nomination of Louis Johnson as replacement was quickly approved. Johnson, a determined advocate of military cutbacks, proceeded to unsettle the Pentagon. He canceled construction of the new $186 million supercarrier *United States,* a major component of the Navy's peacetime refurbishment program, without consulting either the president or Secretary of the Navy John Sullivan. Sullivan resigned in protest. The following month Johnson slashed an additional $1.4 billion from the military budget. Accused of weakening the nation's defenses, he claimed the United States could subdue Russia "with one hand tied behind our back."[5] In the opinion of many in the "old boy" network of Navy admirals, Sullivan had contributed to the termination of the supercarrier project through his own inept politics within the Joint Chiefs. They felt he had overestimated his ability in naval matters and failed to listen to advice that ran contrary to his own ideas, becoming needlessly involved with Air Force proponents of strategic bombing. In that circumstance he was destined to lose. Johnson's decision on the supercarrier, they felt, was conditioned by Sullivan's blunders.[6]

In Norfolk, construction on the missile-carrying battleship *Kentucky,* the uncompleted fifth ship of the *Iowa* class, continued sporadically. Until the *Kentucky*'s completion, the *Missouri* would remain the nation's only active battleship. Truman's enthusiastic promise that it would not be inactivated as long as he remained in the White House lingered in the air. The beleaguered Johnson wasn't about to test that vow. The mighty warship had a stay of execution.

Shortly thereafter, newly appointed Secretary of the Navy Francis P. Matthews sent a report to the president stating that it had been "evident to me that there was definite resistance on the part of some naval officers to accepting unification of the armed services notwithstanding the fact that it was established by law."[7] In the midst of the furor, the outspoken Chief of Naval Operations, Adm. Louis Denfield, expressed before a congressional committee his dissatisfaction with the cutbacks, claiming that the Navy's attack power was being chopped away under policies set by Army and Air Force interests in the Pentagon. Upset by these candid views, Truman unilaterally removed Denfield from office. Whether such action was proper and whether there then existed a vacancy was subsequently questioned in Congress.[8] The issue was solved by the proper nomination and appointment in the following month of Adm. Forrest P. Sherman. By midyear, the top men in the Navy held a very dim view of their civilian leadership, and the public was forming an equally disapproving view of the Navy.

In September the president made public what he had known for some months, that the Soviets had already tested an atom bomb. Tensions grew in both hemispheres, and stability remained elusive in a world pressed between opposing nuclear powers. Meanwhile, naval leaders struggled to preserve territory in the face of public criticism for failure to cooperate with their rival forces. Rear Adm. Allan Smith, Commander of the Atlantic Fleet Cruiser Division (ComCruLant) and an advocate of guided-missile cruisers, spent much of December contacting friendly members of the press, university heads, and other opinion makers to explain the Navy's position. Smith was a politically adept spokesman, not one to overstep his limits, careful but determined in expressing his views.

During the last year of the decade, the turmoil in the American military was little more than an element of the nation's own dilemma. Factionally split under a marginally popular president and plagued by mixed signals of lasting peace and threatening conflicts, the American populace lacked focus in its search for security. A stronger Europe had emerged under the Marshall Plan and the formation of NATO, but with one war still fresh in memory, the prospect of another in a nuclear age gave pause.

The turnover of military leadership was of course in full public view. Things were no better among the rank and file. During demobilization a substantial number of experienced reserve officers, having found a rewarding lifestyle in the Navy and uncertain as to what they might encounter in civilian life after four years' absence, opted to become regulars. They brought their wartime habits with them, tendencies ingrained under the reduced training and often relaxed discipline of those wearying years. Lacking the attitudes fostered by a long naval tradition, their legacy was an exposure of at most four years to a single purpose: winning the war. Facing the pressures of battle, they had paid little attention to regulations or superficial discipline; in the view of these suddenly converted civilians, many of the traditional rules were considered to be contrived—"chicken shit" in the vernacular. Peacetime operations took on a different tone. There was no war to be won, no external motivating force. Training and performance became paramount while shipboard crews were reduced to nearly half their wartime strength. Among the youngest regular officers— those who had joined since the war, many of them Naval Academy graduates—disillusionment with the peacetime Navy sent their resignation rate to the highest in the century.[9] By the end of the decade, 65 percent of the officer personnel were current or former reservists. Good young leadership was lacking throughout the fleet. Could this newly adopted life engender anything for them but languor and a narrow sense of responsibility?

Enlisted men, more likely to make a career of military life, shared much of the same lassitude, partly due to the example set by young officers, more due to their own postwar formation. Given that a peacetime term of enlistment was limited to two years, a sailor on his second hitch would typically be less than twenty-two years old. The war to him was a glamorous memory in which he had romped through adolescence, danced to the music of the big bands, and learned to smoke and drink like the movie military heroes. Blithe to the earlier depression years, he was a product of wartime prosperity curtailed only by brief and explainable shortages. Quite likely he had more money and less parental supervision than his older brothers, while holding those returned veterans as role models. He came of age in an era of full employment and was healthier, better schooled, and more adept at learning, but he knew little discipline except what he had shockingly encountered in boot camp. Even there he was more aware of his rights than his responsibilities. This stereotype was symptomized in December 1948 when the Navy's absent-over-leave rate soared. Excuses were rampant—last bus blocked by snow, mother took sick on the final day of leave, return funds in short supply. The truth was, responsibility was in short supply.

Into these crosscurrents of controversy and concern steamed the Navy's shining star, the *Missouri,* returning to Norfolk at the end of September 1949 for a long-scheduled refurbishment.[10] Known widely as the floating stage on which World War II ended and the president's favorite ship, it was the Navy's subtly accepted anachronistic leader. As the decade came to a close, training and preservation of a state of readiness were the major roles of capital ships. In June the battleship had steamed up the Chesapeake to Annapolis, boarded a contingent of midshipmen for a summer cruise to England, and later gone to sea for combat exercises. Under the command of Capt. Harold Page Smith, the *Mighty Mo*'s well-trained crew earned awards in the battle drills. Now, while its engines were overhauled for the first time in three years and it was fitted with new experimental radar, its crew would take extended schooling and long-sought leave. H. Page Smith had done exemplary work in his ten-month cruise. Under current practice he was ready for relief, fast turnover of captains being the norm. The principal concern at the top was that after a warming-up period for a skipper there was little time for contribution, so efforts were focused on accelerating the warm-up rather than lengthening the term of command.[11] Few saw frequent shifts in command as detrimental to morale. Crews on the larger ships hardly got to know their skippers; to them commanding officers were nearly as remote as flag officers and staff admirals.

Shipyard work neared completion in early December; the *Missouri* was expected to be ready for sea duty within two weeks.[12] Thereafter it was fully scheduled through the next year: a midwinter cruise to Guantánamo Bay in preparation for the joint Army–Navy–Air Force effort planned for the spring, then a midshipmen's cruise to Portugal and Nova Scotia, further maneuvers in the Caribbean to follow. The springtime Portrex exercise was to be the largest schedule of peacetime war games ever conducted by the United States, an intense program to aid in unifying the activities of the diminishing armed services.[13] The Navy's only battleship was designated as flag.

Fig. 1. Map of Chesapeake Bay area, with principal cities identified.

Rain had been forecast for 10 December, and the *Missouri*'s plan of the day was revised.[14] In lieu of all hands forming on deck, selected divisions were called to muster in the mess hall, where a microphone had been rigged to broadcast the award and change-of-command ceremony throughout the vessel. Rear Adm. Allan Smith, ComCruLant, was introduced by the skipper. Short in stature, hair the color of polished pewter, narrow of jaw, and speaking with often excited inflections, the admiral appeared enthusiastic about the occasion. He commended the *Missouri*'s communications, combat operations, and gunnery departments and then presented plaques to Captain Smith (no relation). Captain Smith took the opportunity to recognize his crew, saying he could not recall one unpleasant day on board, and then read his detachment orders. Capt. William Drane Brown stepped up to the microphone, read his own orders, and assumed command from his Naval Academy classmate. With handshakes all around, the battleship gained its ninth skipper. Rear Adm. Homer Wallin, representing the Norfolk Naval Shipyard and a compatriot of Admiral Smith, beamed on the exchange. Three of the four officers participating in that brief ceremony would be together soon again in much less jubilant circumstances; the fourth would continue as an interested observer.

At age forty-seven, Captain Brown was the image of the classical commanding officer. Tall, trim, with close-cropped, dark hair greying at the temples and a firm, tight jaw, he looked like he might have attained Eagle Scout early in life and never given it up. Well tanned under arched eyebrows, his was the seasoned appearance of a long-time mariner. A native of Florida, class of 1924 from the Naval Academy, he would complete thirty years of service in 1950. With a splendid performance record behind him, standing in the top 22 percent of nearly eighteen hundred line officers in his grade, Brown had a good chance of being considered for flag rank in the next year. Completing submarine and destroyer duty early in his career, he had assumed his first command in 1940 as skipper of the light destroyer *Gregory* and spent the subsequent war years at sea. In 1943 he took command of the destroyer *Nicholas,* being promoted to the rank of captain in June of that year. In 1945 he commanded a destroyer squadron off Okinawa. After the war he was assigned command of the Naval Mine Countermeasure Station in Florida, a post he held until ordered to the *Missouri.*[15]

The new assignment was Brown's first seagoing billet in over five years, and the *Missouri* was his first large-ship command. As a squadron commander in his previous sea duty he had delegated most ship handling and piloting to individual ship captains. After a six-year hiatus from direct control of highly maneuverable vessels, he could expect to be rusty, yet his taking fifteen hundred men to sea aboard a vessel now assessed at $114 million troubled no one.[16] The skipper, on a routine career path for warship command, had the support of an experienced operating group. Page Smith's route was similar: destroyer commands, shore duty, then command of the big one. Matters of morale and discipline were more on Admiral Smith's mind as he conferred with this new member of his cruiser team. Recently, the admiral had written about and been giving talks on dwindling morale, discipline, and sense of responsibility in the Navy, troubles he attributed to poorly developed young officers and the influx and lax attitudes of reservists. It was this that he emphasized with Brown in preparation for the new command.[17]

The captain inspected the ship, escorted by his executive officer, Comdr. George E. Peckham. Those who sailed with Peckham said he was humorless, driving, but fair.[18] In short, he was tough, what any skipper would appreciate in an executive officer. Seven years behind Brown at Annapolis, with over a year aboard as XO, Peckham was the *Missouri*'s most experienced ranking officer. The exec's responsibility included the organization, training, readiness, and overall performance of officers and men. Peckham, like his CO, was well suited for his position. Most of his war duty had been aboard destroyers in the North Pacific, including participation as operations officer of a destroyer squadron in the longest sustained naval battle of the war. For that work under heavy gunfire he was awarded the Silver Star. Later he took command of the destroyer *Selfridge,* which lost its bow to torpedo action in a battle off the Solomon Islands. Given another command, the destroyer *Waldron,* he took it into Japanese home waters without casualty before the war ended. Postwar he was assigned to the Atlantic Reserve Fleet, with personnel responsibilities in the laying up of over a thousand ships on the Atlantic Coast.

Next in line of command was the operations officer, Comdr. John R. Millett. Also a Naval Academy graduate, he received his commission in 1936—twelve years later than the captain, five after the exec.[19] During the war he served as navigator and executive officer on destroyers and was given command of the destroyer *Trathen,* which he took into action in the Pacific during 1944 and 1945. Millett first reported aboard the *Missouri* as engineering officer under H. Page Smith; later he was shifted to operations officer, a position he had held for nearly a year when Brown took command.[20] Millett was not lacking in political skill. Early in his meetings with Captain Brown, he carefully made sure his CO was aware of his command experience. Ironically, it was Millett who had been skipper of the *Trathen* when a 5-inch shell from the *Missouri* struck the destroyer during the Okinawa campaign. The two men got on well from the start, Millett finding Brown to be warm and congenial, the captain, drawn to his ingratiating manner, quickly taking Millett into his confidence.

Even the reduced complement of a capital ship makes up a large community to be structured into several command departments: navigation, operations, gunnery, deck, and engineering, supplemented by supply, medical, dental, and repair departments. In turn, each department is made up of from one to nine divisions, the men organized by watch and by skill. Only two people report directly to the CO—the executive officer and, on matters of navigation, the navigator, who is customarily associated with the operations department for other duties.

Even before the wartime advent of electronics, the operations department held crucial responsibilities, vying for shipboard primacy with engineering and gunnery. All departments report directly and equally to the executive officer, but operations, overseeing all phases of training and ship operation, combat information, and radio and visual communications, is often the first to know plans and to recommend and evaluate action. It serves as alter ego to the CO and exec. The gunnery divisions become heroes in battle, at highest risk of life and limb, performing in the hottest, noisiest, and least-protected environments and dependent on intelligence delivered by operations. When facing the enemy, their success or failure often decides the fate of the ship, but those moments are few in relation to the lifetime of the ship—a few hours or days spread over fleet duty of months or years. The entire crew stands with them at general quarters, as lookouts, ammunition handlers, damage control parties, messengers, sharing the tensions of battle with the ordnance workers. The engineering "black gang" and the "deck apes" of the deck division are usually taken for granted in doing their day-to-day jobs, albeit the ship could not operate without either for more than a few minutes.

Commanders Peckham and Millett, Brown's fellow Naval Academy graduates and destroyer men, were the two the captain would have to rely on as he undertook what Admiral Smith called the warm-up period. There was ample technology for him to absorb after a six-year absence. Submarines, seaborne airpower, radar, sonar, electronic navigation, guided missiles, and nuclear power were bringing warfare, real or practiced, into a new technological era.

Radar was among the top concerns in the overhaul of the battleship's array of advanced equipment. The *Missouri* was to be fitted with new, heavier antennas, the SR3, an experimental search radar intended for screening the latest fast carriers. Carriers could not carry it on their limited islands, and the *Missouri* had been designated as the first ship to experiment with it.[21] Electronic ranging equipment, more than a quarter century in development, was still in gestation, and optical sighting was regularly used to verify electronic fire control. If not always as far ranging, it was often found to be more accurate. Microwave antennas made up an extraordinarily heavy and complex portion of a ship's top hamper. Below, electronic vacuum tubes, victims to vibration and rapid changes in temperature, were prone to failure, and shortages in tube inventory presented a continuing problem. Couple the motion of a ship with the complexities of antenna rotation and microwave return and the practice of calibration with visual sightings becomes frequent.

The emerging primacy of airpower made advanced radar essential to the fleet. It was generally considered the greatest single scientific development contributing to the success of the Allies in World War II.[22] More than fifty thousand radar sets of sixty-four different types were manufactured during the war years. Masts bristled with antennas while below decks multiple radar screens tracked air and surface activity. Position plan indicators (PPIs) provided eyesight in darkness and distance vision in the air, giving early warning of approaching aircraft. Although searching was the major purpose of the continuously rotating antennas atop the masts, their echoed signals were also used in combat operations to correlate the ship's position with the running plot developed in the conning tower.

Extended use of radar initiated the ascendancy of the operations department in shipboard organization. Its focal point was the combat operations center (COC),* often considered the brains of the ship. A

---

* Most people, including those on the ship, refer to this location as the "combat information center" (CIC). However, "combat operations center" was in use at the time and appears consistently in the official 1950 documentation.

well-armored, narrow, but heavily equipped facility three platforms below the *Missouri*'s main deck, it was the central source of all reconnaissance information. Here combat plans were drawn up, and from here battle orders were issued.

The multiple applications of underwater sound formed another long-lived technology with a prolonged infancy. Passive sonar, listening, had been sufficiently effective during World War I that the German Navy relied on it almost exclusively, hydrophones picking up targets over nine miles distant.[23] Reliable use of sound ranging for the determination of depth was well established before World War II. Flashing lights circling the face of the fathometer tended to obsolete the use of leadsmen swinging weighted lines from the forward chains, but *Navy Regulations* continued to require that practice, putting seamen to the task in coastal waters. While some might be more comfortable with a voice report of dry tags on a wet lead line, the fathometer's readout was continual once on soundings and lent itself to position determination. Sonar had other possibilities that were hardly exploited at midcentury: underwater messaging, vessel identification, targeting, even the possibility of ship silencing by masking underwater sound. Experimentation with such hoped-for advances had started, were held highly confidential, and would soon involve the *Missouri*.

Months before, arrangements had been made with the Army for use of space at Fort Monroe* to support a sonar research facility.[24] By midyear the Navy established a special passage marked with range buoys to seaward of Old Point Comfort and within the wide shipping channel leading between Hampton Roads and Thimble Shoal Light.[25] The specific purpose and full structure of the range was secret. Commercial pilots and naval commanding officers would be told of the markers' existence and requested to run the route at normal operating speeds in either direction. The newly refurbished *Missouri* made a splendid candidate for the experiment during its forthcoming January sortie.

Long-range navigation, loran, was a later wartime development. First conceived in 1941, by the following year some fifty ships in the North Atlantic had receivers, and by 1949 loran transmission covered

---

* In 1946 Fort Monroe had become the headquarters of the U.S. Continental Army Command.

most of the main shipping lanes of the world.[26] Prior to these developments navigators needed a clear horizon, visible sun or stars, and accurate time to determine their position in midocean. Now, day or night, with specially drawn charts and reliable equipment, a person could determine the ship's location at sea, unmindful of the weather. This was particularly useful under the North Atlantic's wintry grey skies. But loran, like radar, had inherent problems. Shipboard operation was cumbersome and, similar to nautical astronomy, required reference to mathematical conversion tables. Long before navigational computers were developed, still in the days of vacuum tubes and complex electronic wiring, the equipment required skill in its use and technicians in attendance for maintenance; even then it didn't always perform as desired. The results of loran fixes, while generally accurate, had to be prudently considered tentative. Reception in proximity to the baseline between loran towers, such as along coastlines, was the most accurate.[27] In such areas, both day and night, visible sightings often afforded as much or more accuracy.

With the new importance of the COC, there was bound to be contention between traditional navigation and electronic functions. No one claimed ships could be directed entirely from the interior of the COC, yet it could be said that many Navy people failed to take visual navigational responsibilities as seriously as they should. A few factors contributed to this. First, ships frequently traveled in squadrons, sharing navigational information. Second, the continuing importance of fire control, itself making heavy use of electronic search and sighting, brought navigational combat charts into the COC. These activities subtly contributed to a downplay of the navigator's traditional role. Many officers considered navigation a necessary duty, tedious at best, and not career enhancing. Such a view is unsupported by *Navy Regulations*. Fourteen articles outline the navigator's responsibilities to the commanding officer, and four others put detailed piloting responsibility directly on the CO himself. While radar and loran were certainly a boon, prudence dictated their cautious use. Good navigational procedure called for verifying the accuracy of each by other methods whenever practical. In the meantime, electronics officers practiced their arcane mysteries deep in the protected innards of the ship, advising skippers on matters the COs themselves were hardly expected to fully understand.

On 22 December, with shipyard personnel aboard and the customary assistance of a docking pilot, Brown eased the ship away from the Portsmouth Navy Yard and proceeded through generally poor visibility on the start of a two-day post-repair run.[28] The trip took the ship through Hampton Roads and out to sea for trials, the purpose of the cruise being to reach agreement with the Navy Yard that the *Missouri* was ready to return to the fleet in full service.

Commander Peckham reviewed policies with the new skipper as they had been carried out under Brown's predecessor. They discussed Page Smith's practice of shifting the conn (navigational control center) to the executive officer on the lower navigation level once the ship had cleared the strait at Fort Wool. The cultures of the upper and lower bridges are as disparate as the difference between a crowded elevator and the lobby from which it rises. The conning officer on the open, upper bridge gets a high perspective and full-circle visibility, helpful in congested waters. But the multitude of people within the compact facilities on the O8 level often makes direct communication between opposite sides difficult, while movement from one side to the other entails awkward sidestepping around those standing between. The O4-level enclosed bridge, a minute or two away by ladder, is the customary conning location at sea, where stern views are not immediately needed; commands are passed easily, and a more open, relaxed atmosphere usually prevails. By some naval standards, shifting the conn at midpoint in Hampton Roads could be considered premature in view of the long run remaining to the open sea. Captain Brown's early destroyer commands in the Atlantic Fleet had given him familiarity with the Hampton Roads channels. He was aware that the passage across the lower Chesapeake opened up once one was beyond the Fort Wool strait. Considering Peckham's performance record, there was little risk in shifting the conn as it had been done, and Brown had no objection to his predecessor's practice.

In the vicinity of landmasses, radar's navigational use was often suspect, showing false shorelines, shadows, and misleading sea return in heavy weather, compelling corroboration with other sources. Interpretation of the glowing green screens, refreshed every twelve seconds, was not always easy, even by people with considerable experience. Beam width, pulse length, and the state of recent mechanical adjustment had to be factored into the readings. Even then, charts did not always give the necessary information for correlation. As part of the COC, this was Millett's responsibility. Although fully equipped, the COC, under combat operations officer Lt. John A. Carr, was understaffed. Along with Carr's radarmen, technicians under the ship's electronics officer, Lt. (jg) Harold B. Gibbs, were needed in constant attendance to keep the heat-producing arrays of tubes and circuitry reasonably reliable. During this short cruise, the *Missouri*'s search radar equipment was found to have a two-hundred-yard range error. Operations department personnel had intended to calibrate and adjust it, but poor visibility prevented coordination of radar readings with appropriate navigation marks. Ironically, while low visibility hampered the adjustments of one electronic facility, it justified the use of loran, however marginal some might have considered it.

If uncalibrated radar was a disappointment to the commanding officer, it wasn't his foremost concern. What vexed him more in his initial observations—as he discussed with his operations officer—was the new navigator's approach to his job. It wasn't a major issue. The skipper merely felt piqued by things he had observed. Perhaps it was the classic conflict of crusty, old-guard attitudes with the allure of new technology to younger men. Brown may have had Admiral Smith's adjuration in mind. Perhaps it was Naval Academy elitism in dealing with a ninety-day wonder. In the captain's view, the navigator, Lt. Comdr. Frank G. Morris, was too reliant on loran for fixing the ship's position. The towers on the Virginia capes had been sighted and could have been used in the traditional way to take a final fix as they departed from sight of land. Morris preferred a loran fix in support of his dead-reckoned position.

A source of further vexation was a small, uncorrected error Captain Brown had observed in a gyrocompass repeater on the primary conn, putting Morris's competence, or at least his attitude, in shadow. The captain's discussion with the operations officer about these concerns remained casual. Millett was a good listener, and he was available when the skipper had the need to work out his annoyance.

Morris, younger than Millett by four years, had the self-assurance of a surgeon. Dark hair, glancing blue eyes, sharply cut features, and a spare frame gave him an eager and energetic appearance. One of the few in the top staff of the *Missouri* who was not a Naval Academy graduate, Morris had started as a reservist in the V-7 program.[29] Completing boot camp after the summer of 1940, he was promoted to midshipman and commissioned ensign in December of that year. His wartime assignments included instructor of navigation, commanding officer of a World War I destroyer escort, and then command of the flush-deck destroyer *Babbitt*. Signing over to the regular Navy in 1946, he was assigned to the Bureau of Ships as an oceanographer, and following that to the *Missouri*. He had held the navigator position for two months when Captain Brown came aboard—two months in the shipyard.

Sea experience in the navigation department lay more among the quartermasters than with the officers. An assistant navigator's request for flight training had been approved earlier in the month, and just before the two-day cruise Morris temporarily appointed Ens. Elwin R. Harris to the assistant's job, assigning him duty as plotter on the primary conn during the periods of departure and arrival. At twenty-three, Harris was the youngest officer in the *Missouri*'s regular bridge complement. Enrolled in the Naval Reserve Officers Training Corps at Villanova College,[30] he received his ensign's commission upon graduation. In spite of his limited experience, the new assistant did his job well enough on the December voyage that he would be retained in that role.

There was a camaraderie among Naval Academy graduates that long outlasted their careers. Most wore their gold class rings proudly. Upon meeting they quickly observed the year of graduation embossed on the side, this often a better means of assessment than stripes on the sleeve. Each class had its own identity and reputation. Mix Annapolis graduates among a larger group of naval officers and they soon coalesced in school loyalty, trading stories of familiar graduates, career paths, contacts, and accomplishments. Reservists-turned-regular were a mixed breed. Naval Academy men knew who were the chosen ones. But if Morris was a pariah in the wardroom among the Annapolis "ring-knockers," it wasn't evident and didn't disturb his self-assurance.

Navigation was on Brown's agenda frequently during his first cruise—more, it seemed, than adjustments to the radar. During the return run to Norfolk the executive officer went over several navigational matters with the skipper—the practice of shifting the conn after clearing Fort Wool, the small error in the gyrocompass repeater, the pros and cons of using loran along the coast, the capabilities of the shorthanded navigation group. The specifics weren't recorded and didn't require follow-up, but it played on Brown's mind until the end of the voyage. It was then that he brought up the earlier discussion with his exec.

"George, I know the advice you gave me this morning was meant well and was a result of your experience on the *Missouri*. However, let's have it understood that I am the skipper and you are the executive officer and administrator and I expect the operations officer and navigator to keep me advised on navigational matters. Do we understand each other?"[31]

The reproach took the executive officer by surprise, and he acquiesced without comment. Later he related the incident to Millett and Morris. Stern-looking as always, Peckham told them how Captain Brown had bawled him out.[32] That bit of gossip was destined to travel. Very little remains secret when men live and work as closely as they do on a naval ship. The crew quickly learned their new skipper didn't take kindly to unsolicited advice. Not that he would get much anyway as commanding officer of a battleship. The captain customarily ate in his own mess, rarely joining the wardroom informally, thereby shutting himself off from even the carefully structured gossip of his senior officers. He would learn only at his own request and hear only the formal and reserved discussions of the men on duty around him.

Upon return to the yard, a large portion of the crew were about to start on Christmas leave. They tucked away their copies of the two-bit best-seller, Mickey Spillane's *I, the Jury*. They went off singing a catchy new tune about *Rudolph the Red-Nosed Reindeer*. They watched *The Goldbergs*, TV's first situation comedy, and live Texaco commercials starring Milton Berle. In Manhattan they might have enjoyed a pricey new show glorifying the lives of Seabees and Navy nurses, Rodgers and Hammerstein's *South Pacific*. But radio was the common man's form of entertainment, and there were always the Lone Ranger, Sergeant Friday, and Groucho Marx. Christmas parties were held in Norfolk, and Midnight Mass was planned aboard the

Missouri. These were the last weeks of rest and relaxation before the winter training began, and the onboard crew thinned out.

If Captain Brown were to assess his situation as he headed homeward he might have concluded that, on balance, he was in fortunate circumstances. Battleship command was the traditional route to admiral, even as the battleship era neared its end. Training was the major purpose of the only active battleship in the U.S. fleet, and the *Missouri* was well suited for it, fully equipped with the largest in gunnery, modern electronics, and immensely powerful engine rooms. It had ample accommodations for visiting contingents and a two-year history of introducing midshipmen to foreign shores while sharpening their skills. Countering ongoing talk about military cutbacks was the president's promise to keep the *Missouri* active. Being in its command was an unquestioned honor.

The ship was short of crew, no different from any other ship in the fleet, since the Bureau of Personnel kept complements close to minimum level under the Pentagon's continuous demobilization efforts. The crew would need drilling at sea after their long period in the shipyard. The skipper could say the same thing for himself. He knew that his seaman's perceptions were not as sharp as they had been six years earlier. Current plans for the ship couldn't have been better suited for corrective action. The cruise to Guantánamo would give them the chance to sharpen up before the intensive exercises in March. Those should give the Navy an opportunity to impress the Joint Chiefs with its efficiency in shared combat operations. As a short-term goal, Captain Brown could do worse than striving for another "E" pennant to match the one his predecessor left flying from the foremast. A return to Norfolk in the spring with another commendation would be a sure way to impress his superiors.

It was time to wrap up the shipyard work, load stores, and get on with his command. For Captain Brown the seas had never looked calmer or a voyage more prosperous. But clouds lurked on the new skipper's horizon. By the separate conversations he had held with his two top officers, Brown had positioned a wedge over his officer team. Peckham's subsequent discussion with Commander Millett and Lieutenant Commander Morris was the mallet that drove it home. The operations officer could readily have concluded that his own position with the skipper was enhanced, based on Peckham's inadvertent report. And from what he heard, the self-assured navigator had no reason to believe that he too wasn't highly respected in the eyes of the captain. It remained to be seen whether the top men of the *Missouri* would function as a team.

3

Raise Able-Peter

Much of the battleship's complement of close to fifteen hundred men came from east of the Mississippi, with a large contingent living in the Tidewater area, chiefly those with dependents. During the three-month overhaul period, a third of the crew took annual leave. Others hustled eagerly to nearby electronics and gunnery schools, and less eagerly completed the predictable tedium of classroom training.[1] As the weeks passed, damage control and fire drills alongside the dock wore thin. Activity increased in the loading of stores and ammunition, heavy work not fondly regarded. Nor was Norfolk highly ranked as a liberty port. Nestled between locker clubs, pool halls, and tattoo parlors, waterfront taverns with televised wrestling matches held little allure. The ten-block length of East Main Street, sailor town, alternated sandwich shops with strip joints and the last traveling burlesque acts in the nation. When sailors took the ferry to Hampton, where the main attractions were tiny clam bars run by fish packers and an art deco movie house with Wurlitzer performances between films, their recreational adventures were near exhaustion. The men of the *Mighty Mo* were bored. Enough of schools, chilly days, and dingy bars. Tomorrow the blue waters of the Gulf Stream; next stop the Guantánamo naval base; then the big guns firing off Vieques, with liberty in Havana or San Juan. Tropical skies, rum and Coca-Cola, and Caribbean beaches beckoned.

The new CO generated the usual curiosity among the crew. Distant as he was from the enlisted men's daily lives, his leadership would set their shipboard lifestyle. Could Captain Brown restore their competitive edge and lead them to the capture of another "E"?

Portrex, the ambitious series of joint Army–Navy–Air Force maneu-vers, was scheduled for March off Puerto Rico. The program would conclude with the *Missouri* as flagship during a simulated attack on the small island of Vieques. Top military men expected Portrex to demonstrate that the armed forces could overcome contentions and work effectively together.[2] In the process the Navy was determined to reaffirm that the battleship had fully evolved from obsolete guardian of sea-lanes to vital provider of landing support, more essential than air cover. Lacking the new guided-missile technology, high perfor-mance was critical if the men of the *Missouri* were to champion shore bombardment as their contribution to land-sea operations. New fire control equipment had been installed, and the January cruise would give them time to work with it.

On Pier 7 at the naval base, yellow cones of light cast indistinct circles on the pavement extending alongside the battleship. A forklift laden with a stack of empty pallets maneuvers toward a nearby shed, leaving a pungent trail of diesel smoke in its wake. Torrents of cooling water pour from the ship's engine rooms into a dark void between the hull and the pier. Eclipsing the lights on the superstructure, the high wall of grey armor spreads a shadowy rim along the pier's edge, bro-ken only by two brows leading to the quarterdecks.

Local leave-takers are among the last to return, often accompanied by women, some with children in tow. Lingering on the pier, they are caught in shafts of light beaming along the lengths of the brows. A few officers stand stiffly with their spouses near the approach to the forward quarterdeck. Enlisted men, pea coat collars upturned under white hats, drop their duffels to cluster in greater numbers aft, extending their last moments ashore. For most of the women, depar-tures and arrivals are routine events interspersed with weekly com-missary runs, pediatric trips to Portsmouth, quickly called parties to celebrate news of a promotion or of an immanent return, mostly to break the boredom and share the loneliness. Young mothers are among them, newlyweds and those soon to be, and girlfriends. A few parents gather, proud to see a sailor son off to sea. People come from "Navy town" neighborhoods bordering Norfolk, from Portsmouth across the river, from Virginia Beach. Entire closely knit families travel up from Chesapeake City, home to the largest Filipino popula-tion on the continent, a community whose lives center on the U.S.

Navy. A dark or Oriental face is likely to be that of a cook, baker, or messman. It is an honored profession, a way to become part of America. Most steward's mates are Filipino, often aliens recruited directly for fleet duty.[3] Some, very few, are black. Truman had issued an executive order for full integration of the armed forces. The Navy saw continuation of a practice dating from the end of the Spanish-American war, that of recruiting Cubans and Filipinos for food services, as meeting that requirement.

After the war most families owned a car. A thousand dollars would buy a good year-old model in 1950, a heavy but necessary expense as suburban sprawl pushed available homes further from the seaport. When leaves expire wives drive their men to the ship, even if it means tugging children out of warm beds an hour or so before dawn in the absence of a fifty-cent baby-sitter.

Gulls waken, fluttering among the shoreside groups to settle at pier end, searching for an easy meal along the musty waterside. Aboard ship wisps of vapor drift from vents between the masts; soft clouds billow from the after stack. An elongated chirp of a boatswain's whistle from somewhere in the superstructure precedes the mechanical burble of the morning call for sweepers to man their brooms. The scent of fried sausage issues from an open hatch. Never fully at rest, the ship now stirs into visible action as men gather on deck, arranging lines, running out hoses, circuiting idlers poised at the railings. Women on the pier edge closer, searching the decks for the faces they recently kissed. Now and then a voice rises above the murmurs—"There's Daddy," "Take care," "Write soon"—someone on tiptoe waves, silently mouths a few words and forces a smile for her distant observer, protocols of farewell on this long-planned departure day.

There seems to be no haste. Every man's task is fitted to a predetermined schedule, all part of long-practiced drill as the workers grow in number. Oblivious to the small talk being whispered to shipmates above him, a sailor with a quartermaster's "crow" on his arm strides the length of the pier, focuses a flashlight near the water at bow and stern, jots down draft readings, and casually climbs aboard. A half-dozen laborers in black woolen caps and dungarees arrive, distancing themselves from those who came to watch the departure. They hover near the bollards, waiting to cast off the sagging hawsers.

Tugboats steam into the slip, assertive puffs alternating with watery growls as they ease along the outboard side to make fast lines lowered from chocks near the high prow. A grating voice blares from a shipboard speaker, interrupting the subdued babble on the pier. The last crew members hasten their good-byes, shoulder their seabags, and return to their ship.

Thus, early on this mid-January Tuesday morning, an enlivened crew musters aboard. The men rejoin their shipmates and eagerly greet those they haven't seen in weeks, excitement apparent in their renewed energy. There are new tales to relate, jokes to share, freshly learned lessons to apply, but more than anything, once again they face the thrilling prospect of taking the mightiest ship in the world to sea.

First light, and a boatswain's call pipes the special sea and anchor details. Lookouts, signalmen, talkers, line handlers, electricians, quartermasters, radarmen, and the chiefs and officers who would lead them—a quarter of the crew—hasten along corridors, up and down ladders, and out on deck, buttoning up jackets to report to stations. The decks bristle with activity under a gloomy grey sky. A lookout high in the conning tower discerns a moderate chop driven across the Bay by a northerly breeze. The wintry air is clear, visibility soon stretching halfway to the Virginia capes.

Four days earlier, on Friday the thirteenth, the officer of the deck had received a manila envelope for Captain Brown with detailed orders for the training cruise. Engaged in the seemingly endless paperwork of clearing a ship for sea, the captain surveyed the contents of the package briefly and passed it to Commander Millett for implementation. The bundle included a separate packet with a routine-looking mimeographed request from the district commandant that the *Missouri* run a sonar range during its planned departure. Compliance, it noted, was optional. With no further examination, the ops officer handed the packet to navigator Morris. Later that day Morris reported to Millett that the departure course had been charted according to instructions in the envelope.[4]

The next day, Captain Brown had held an hour-long planning conference with the two officers to discuss the forthcoming cruise. Late in arriving, Millett found Morris explaining to the captain the route they would take through Hampton Roads to the waters off Little

Fig. 2. Profile of *Iowa*-class vessel, with key locations identified.

Creek, a distance of some fifteen miles. The ops officer interrupted to discuss with Brown the request for running the range. According to Millett and Morris, five privately maintained buoys should be found in the channel, although the navigator expressed confidence in the existence of only two. "Here is the range," he said to his seniors, pointing to the red north and south markers on a chart that had been included in the packet.[5] How were the buoys labeled? The instructions, with little explanation, used two differing conventions—alphabetic identification (cited as A, B, C, D, and E) and, for two of those buoys, the compass points N and S for labels. In spite of his belief that only two markers existed, B or N, and C or S, without written authority to ignore the others, Morris refrained from removing the A, D, and E buoys from the chart. The diagram in the packet showed those three in pencil, whereas the other two, referenced as B and C, elsewhere as N and S, were marked in red. Thus, lacking contrary evidence, the joint understanding of the three men in that pre-departure meeting was that five buoys identified the range. Would two of them bear physical markings N or B, S or C? No one knew for sure. But these were small matters. Feeling they had ample information, the three took but a few minutes to wrap up that topic and turn to details concerning the run to Guantánamo.[6] Soon after getting under way, shore bombardment was to be simulated off Little Creek, an amphibious training facility on the beaches east of Norfolk and some eight miles inside Cape Henry. Ships could assemble offshore in deep and relatively protected water to practice bombing runs, experiment with underwater demolition, and stage troop landings. New radar on the *Missouri,* still uncalibrated fire control equipment, and gunnery crews who had been idle for three months would all be exercised before heading south. The gunnery crews could start to shape up with nonfiring gun drills. Beacon tracking, the setup of fire control mechanisms, and simulated firing were on the morning plan of the day. This was the *Big Mo*'s work, and it was time to get to it.

The chart work that Lieutenant Commander Morris had reported to Commander Millett, and what the officers discussed briefly with their skipper, did not yet include the plot of a danger bearing. Dutton's *Navigation,* the classic Navy publication on navigation and piloting, used as a textbook in the Naval Academy and found aboard nearly every seagoing naval vessel, describes its use:

> A danger bearing is a limiting bearing (either maximum or minimum) of a fixed object on shore which may be used to insure safe passage of an outlying shoal or other danger to navigation.
>
> Danger bearings should be used by a navigator to keep his ship clear of an outlying danger. . . . The value of this method decreases as the angle between the course and the danger bearing increases. Unless the object is nearly dead ahead, the danger bearing is of little value in keeping the ship in safe water as the danger is approached.
>
> Danger bearings should be plotted on the chart, in advance, at every point where they might possibly be used.[7]

Quartermaster First Class (QM1) Richard Wentz* must have delighted his teachers. He was that kind of person. A portly lad, quiet, confident, and meticulous in his work, he spoke sparingly but with a remarkable degree of self-assurance. Among the *Missouri*'s quartermasters, he was admired as one who had well earned his rating. When Wentz did something he did it carefully, thoroughly, and correctly; his work on the bridge could be trusted. On Monday, laying out charts to be used the following day, he had marked a danger bearing in red on the Hampton Roads chart that would be used to keep the plot. A printed line on Chart 400 extended from Old Point Comfort Light to Thimble Shoal Light at an angle of 080° from true north. Below that he drew a red line to Thimble Shoal Light from the plotted position of acoustic range buoy B, the danger bearing of 075.5°. By maintaining a position such that the actual ship's bearing taken on Thimble Shoal Light would remain less than that angle, the ship would steam safely in deep water. Along the plotted courses, that

---

* Findings and contemporary newspaper reports give differing first names to Wentz. The *Pilot*, 15 February 1950, included a photograph and detailed profile of the quartermaster, identifying him as "Victor Wentz." Finding 44 of the court of inquiry identifies him as "Richard (n) Wentz, quartermaster first, U.S. Navy." The name ascribed by the Navy is used here.

sighting lay nearly dead ahead. Steering through the channel to keep the light bearing less than 075°, thereby holding to courses south of Wentz's danger line, the ship would remain comfortably within the mile-and-a-half-wide passage.

The quartermaster had plotted both the actual and questionable buoys on the chart to be used in secondary conn on the O4 level. Lieutenant Commander Morris transcribed that work to a similar chart that he and the assistant navigator would use on the O8 level. Combat charts with similar navigational marks and with overlaid grids for naval use were spread out in the COC. In that electronic facility an officer would track the vessel out of Hampton Roads to Little Creek by radar bearings, thence to a suitable position for the bombing drills.

Earlier, Lieutenant Carr, combat operations officer, had asked the XO if the bridge would need radar-based navigational advice after getting under way. Commander Peckham had replied that they would ask for it only if the visibility proved poor on the morning of the sortie. Radar, in both of their views, did not match visual observations for navigational accuracy.

All these matters were tidied up before Tuesday, when all divisions mustered aboard and reported readiness to the exec. The special sea detail was set. The civilian docking pilot, Capt. Roland McCoy, reported to the officer of the deck for an escort to meet the skipper, and the last shipyard officials hustled ashore.

The primary conn is a lozenge-shaped compartment on the O8 level, as wide as the conning tower itself, shorter in its fore and aft dimension, affording about as much room as a cluttered one-car garage. Standing in the narrow passageway between chart room and wheelhouse, all one can see is sailors and the gear they use—dials, levers, switch boxes, headphones. If any open space remained on a bulkhead, someone would have fastened a bracket to it and hung a battery-powered battle lantern there. There is little headroom and just no walk-about space. The sailors aren't there to hold a square dance.

One after another, the watch standers step up from the sloping ladder centered through the conning tower's decks and file to posts in the primary conn, unhurried, using the time to test their equipment before getting under way. Seamen Arden Field, John Watson, and Oscar Hood take their telephone talker positions near bulkhead-mounted jacks, Field attaching headphones to the JA voice-powered circuit beneath portholes forward of the steering console, the other two near the bulkhead partially separating the pilothouse from the chart room aft. Seaman Hood, radarman third class striker, having trouble with the circuit that normally enabled him to converse with the COC, switches to an alternate circuit to establish a suitable connection. Nearly every function on the battle-ready ship has a redundant counterpart.

Standing near the chart table, Seaman (SN) Arthur Cole writes the date into a bearings notebook and plugs himself into a telephone circuit connected to the wings of the secondary conn, four decks below. There, at alidades on each side, Quartermasters Ward Folansby and Robert Hess plan to take minute-by-minute sights on Chesapeake navigational marks, reporting the identity of each, its compass bearing, and the time of observation. Cole will then record the reports for use by the plotting officer. Familiar with the intensity with which these are usually called out, he has devised his own shorthand for writing them into his bearings book. Deployed on two weather levels, as well as in combat operations, three decks below the main, these men function like a well-drilled infield supporting a pitcher. One checks another as they observe, report, record, plot, and verify; visual bearings on both sides of the ship called in from O4, further sightings made on O8, time-labeled markings quickly penciled onto the plotting chart and compared with radar-based plots in combat operations, the ship's position dynamically portrayed in three separate locations like stop-action films.

A sailor looks to the engine order telegraph fixed at shoulder height near Field's telephone station. Pointers on two small dials are positioned at "Stop," the last orders sent to the engine room nearly a month ago. Now chatting idly with Field, he will soon be relaying commands to main control more than a dozen decks below by turning handles on six-inch dials.

QM2 Bevan Travis, one of the ship's more experienced helmsmen, takes his position behind a stainless steel wheel in the center of the pilothouse. Below chest level, its diameter is no greater than the steering wheel of a car. Under the seasoned eye of Chief Quartermaster Reams, standing beside him, he checks the wheel's connections and responses to its turns. These are displayed on a circular rudder angle indicator in a waist-high console a few feet before him as he applies experimental left and right twists to the wheel. Giant twin rudders driven by stern steering engines swing in parallel under control of his nearly effortless turns. Built-in resistance to the wheel's motion dampens its effect, giving the steerer a feeling of effort. His view of the waters ahead will be limited as he stands some four feet aft of a row of portholes, several obscured by lookouts and talkers. Travis's skill lies in his attention to the console before him, sensing at the same time the behavior of the hull as it responds to his touch on the wheel. With one hand he can cause this 57,000-ton juggernaut, 888 feet in length, steaming at fifteen knots, to turn in a circle tighter than that cut by a destroyer. More important, with eyes focused on the gyrocompass repeater before him and the rudder angle indicator, he can maintain the vessel on a fixed course, leaving behind a mile-long, arrow-straight wake. He has little need to see beyond the wheelhouse itself.

QM3 Harry Kimble, quartermaster of the watch, who will later take his duties to the O4 bridge, joins the men in the chart room, bringing to eight the number of those now crowding within the armor-encased wheelhouse. Ensign Harris, on his second voyage as assistant navigator, sits at the chart table to starboard of the partially separated chart room, assembling his instruments. Also equipped with headphones, he has the task of maintaining a running plot of the ship's position, listening to the quartermasters' reports from the O4 wings and those issued from the primary conn. This is his territory, and he is ready to slide a combination protractor–parallel ruler over the charts of the Chesapeake that navigator Morris has spread out. Harris or anyone looking over his shoulder in the closet-sized space can discern where the ship is positioned at any time, where it is heading, and then quickly estimate when it will be at the next way point.

Communications officer Lt. Paul Bland, a casual observer at this time, eases himself into an out-of-the-way position on the port side of the wheelhouse. He is responsible for the work of the signal bridge five levels below, so he has to keep aware of the ship's activity. Capital ships take particular pride in flag handling, promptly shifting the union jack and ensign as the vessel gets under way, raising appropriate signals to the yardarms, and recognizing ship seniorities for the exchange of passing salutes. The *Missouri,* likely to prevail as senior on any encounter with other naval vessels, stands ready to respond with spirit.

The junior officer of the deck for the morning watch arrives, followed shortly by his superior, now intent on the removal of the brow below. Lt. Roland Hatfield, assigned first duty as underway officer of the deck for the morning watch, is to be relieved by Lt. Edward Arnold at 0800. A tingle of excitement fills the air, readiness for action, as Captain Brown and his entourage climb the narrow ladder into the chart room. There Brown reviews the plotted courses with Morris, who points out shoal waters north of the range, ample searoom to the south, and the subsequent route to Little Creek. Under an overcast sky, good visibility continues, and they can expect little shipping traffic—in short, splendid circumstances for an easy run to the exercise grounds. Brown's orderly steps gingerly out of the way, hovering near the ladder between upper and lower decks, ready for messenger service. Hatches on each side of the wheelhouse open to the outer bridge. A narrow walkway encircles the conning tower, exposed overhead to the weather but surrounded by a solid chest-high dodger of armored steel. As the skipper steps out the navigator checks for the logging of the departure drafts: thirty-five feet, nine inches, forward, a foot deeper aft. Earlier in the battleship's life a chart table had been rigged on the weather deck, tucked inside the high dodger. Exposed as it was to wind and rain, and interfering with anyone's limited passage, it was found impractical and was subsequently removed. Plotting could be readily reviewed at the table maintained by the assistant navigator, within a few feet of the starboard hatchway.

Captain McCoy accompanies the skipper, engaging him in friendly conversation about the morning's plans. McCoy is well known in the Navy Yard, one of the big-ship pilots responsible for moving them in and out of their Elizabeth River berths. Guiding a ship out of its slip into the stream is a highly specialized, demanding task. Docking pilots direct as many as six tugs in maneuvering larger vessels within these tight quarters.[8] Expert ship handlers, these men hold the highest master's license. While pilots rarely find themselves more than an hour or two away from the dock, they take on a high-risk task in disengaging the ship from the shore and putting it on its way. Poorly handled lines can break or drag too long in water near the churning propellers, wind and current can take more control of the ship than its own gathering propulsion delivers. The pilot acts only as the captain's advisor, but his guidance is routinely sought and heeded.

The two men are followed by Commanders Millett and Peckham, officer of the deck Hatfield, and finally by navigator Morris. Five officers in navy blue caps and jackets and the civilian pilot lean over the high rail, surveying the ship, dock, and waters of the Elizabeth River. Two-thirds of the way to the topmast, they are the equivalent of some fifteen stories above the water. McCoy, equipped with a sports whistle, signals briefly for the attention of the tugboat skippers below. On the main deck, fore and aft, deck gangs take positions near the mooring lines. Winch handlers test the power on the drums, and the men in charge signal the bridge with a wave and by voice telephone that all is in readiness. Captain Brown and Lieutenant Hatfield check through open portholes that everything is set within the pilothouse. More than eighteen men are now on duty in or near the primary conn, with a half-dozen more taking up duties in the O4 secondary station.

Primary conn, pilothouse, and chart room make up the bridge. In that compact space, complex equipment jammed within seventeen-inch-thick bulkheads, suspended from a densely wired overhead and fastened to nearly every bit of vertical space, there is a position and a task for everyone. Half the men present are tethered to telephone jacks. The bridge crew makes up the nerve ends of the ship—its eyes, ears, and, almost entirely, its ship-handling brains. The weather deck with full compass visibility becomes the operational focal point in restricted waters or when traveling in tight formation.

Visibility is far less from within the wheelhouse of the secondary conn, four decks below. The roomier, enclosed bridge around it is suitable only for cruising in open waters. The steersman sees beyond his station through an aperture the size of a mail slot opening through thick armor to the bridge deck. It's comforting in times of attack—those within could probably survive a direct hit—but not for the claustrophobic. Larger windows surround the outer bridge, affording a splendid view of the main deck and forward turrets, a fair perspective of the waters ahead, and an obstructed view aft.

Function dictates the manning of any ship, and the layout and crew of any pilothouse says much about the vessel's priorities.

Freighters need few; three on the bridge—an officer, a man at the wheel, and an ordinary seaman as lookout and helper. Modern American cargo carriers now operate with a full crew of twenty-one, three to five per watch covering deck and engine room, that more than twice what many foreign ships carry. Fishing boats are often maneuvered during the harvest by one man poised on a stool rigged to one side, handy to the tackle. Engine controls are within reach of the wheel, and the skipper communicates by shouting. By contrast, merchant ships have a roomy wheelhouse, all but the wings protected from the weather, affording a view of half the ocean from just about any position. A single voice-powered telephone connects the bridge, one location at a time, with rarely used open bridge above, bow, stern, and engine room. The engine room telegraph, often encased in brightly polished brass with a two-foot signal lever, takes a nearly central position, standing at waist height near to the wheel and to large, rectangular windows along the forward bulkhead of the pilothouse. It would be difficult to miss it, unlike the small dials fixed close to the overhead of a battleship. A midcentury freighter's spoked wooden wheel, three feet in diameter, dominated the center of the pilothouse, positioned behind an equally large magnetic compass, quite evident with large iron compensating spheres standing sentry on each side. Ships rely almost exclusively on gyrocompass repeaters, keeping two magnetic compasses for cross-reference in locations least influenced by the ship's iron. The *Missouri*'s magnetic compass remained uncompensated after the shipyard overhaul and would remain out of commission until after arrival in Guantánamo.

The topside crew of the *Missouri* was light by normal standards, while an average number of men stood at stations on the bridge. Combatant crews can easily grow geometrically. The more men needed to do the job, the more staff needed to support them—storekeepers, cooks, barbers, bookkeepers, medics, chaplains, and bandsmen join boatswains, quartermasters, gunners, enginemen, radarmen, and electricians. Shipboard complements increase and diminish with the tenor of the times. At its wartime peak the *Missouri* carried 134 officers and 2,400 enlisted men;[9] under the constraints of military reductions, its strength was now reduced to half of that. In both war and peace a man-of-war must be able to stay at sea for extended periods and maintain battle-ready redundancy in personnel and equipment. It carries technicians capable of making emergency repairs and deck crews able to replenish ammunition and supplies and to refuel while under way. Frequently traveling in convoy, warships require rigorous attention to station keeping. Often there is just more to be done—gunnery, signaling, air and sea lookout beyond navigational needs, training, governmental record keeping, of course, and plenty of metalwork, cleaning, and painting. The Navy does more onboard maintenance than its commercial counterparts, keeping its ships in fighting trim. It trains its specialists broadly, then segments their tasks to the nearly irreducible and often duplicated. That practice may stifle initiative, but specific duties could go uncompleted, as in battle conditions, and the ship can carry on. If the price paid is restricted individual responsibility, the recompense is the glory of teamwork smoothly and successfully accomplished, which the sailors on the *Missouri*'s bridge were about to prove.

Deckhands fore and aft respond quickly to the command to single up the mooring lines. The remaining brow is carried off and the watch transferred to the bridge. Tension grows; the men stand taller as Captain Brown gives the order to cast off. Captain McCoy signals his tugs. A long, ear-shattering blast sounds forth in a jetting cloud of steam, followed by three shorter blasts as the ship moves astern, sailors hauling aboard the last heavy ties to shore. Down comes the blue union jack from its staff on the bow. Down comes the ensign on the stern. Up flies a larger red, white, and blue to the truck of the aftermast. An invariably thrilling moment is marked by the majestic transition from shorebound stillness to independent motion. Piers, pilings, bollards, long fixed adjacent to the ship, slide forward. Seamen smile at their buddies and beam with pride. It moves, their faces seem to say, as if motion were unexpected.

Astern, disturbed gulls lift from their pilings, glide close to the water swirling in lazy arcs beneath the counter, and scream objection as they head for new territory. Captain Brown and his staff peer aft over their high railing, intent on the ship's backward progress as it eases its hindquarters into the Elizabeth River. Quartermaster Kimble makes an entry into the log for 17 January 1950: 0725* underway Pier 7, Norfolk Naval Base.

---

* Twenty-four hour military time will be used for events aboard ship, while twelve-hour civilian time will be used for land-based incidents.

On the pier, the Navy families step back against the shed, dodging the last of the vehicles clearing the area. Drawing away like a stage curtain, the long hull seems endless in its slow passage along the edge of the dock. Finally the big ship swings into the stream; for the shore-bound, loneliness swings into action as the sailormen's adventures resume.

McCoy watches tugs push the towering bow to port, surveys the river, and gives Travis a wheel order to bring the ship, now moving forward, to the left of a black buoy moored off the pierhead.* The captain trades information with the pilot, ready to take direct control as the ship clears the docks and the tugs are cast free. His procedure is to keep the conn until in open water. There he is expected to turn it over to the exec, who will set regular sea watches in routine fashion. Normally that is done when the ship, fully clear of land, takes a departure—a position determined in final relation to the shoreline it puts behind. Beyond Hampton Roads the routes to the Virginia capes are in generally open water. Based on the practice discussed in December, Commander Peckham will take over from the skipper after the ship has passed Fort Wool, a kidney-shaped island in the middle of the Roads.† They had done that on the December shake-down, and Peckham expected it would again be the practice today.

Hampton Roads lay ahead, bordered on the north by low-lying Old Point Comfort, with its distant water tanks, tall brick hotel, and diminutive white lighthouse. The curving passage through Hampton Roads to Thimble Shoal channel is not commodious if its three-thousand-yard width is to be shared in a passing situation. Momentum, the forward motion of the 57,000-ton battleship, slows its response to changes in course or speed. Any ship's center of effort tends to keep its direction such that a sharp turn has a sallying element, a lingering sashay that may need correction to track the changing course line. To stop in twice its length the *Missouri* would still cover nearly a third of a mile. Sensitive ship handling required the skipper to relay timely steering orders through an open porthole to

---

* The United States didn't align its buoyage system with most of the world's maritime nations until the late 1980s. Prior to then the right side of channels upon departing from port was marked with black buoys; the current convention, more common worldwide, calls for green buoys on the right.
† Since construction of the Hampton Roads Bridge-Tunnel, started in 1950, Fort Wool marks the point where the Hampton tunnel connects to the Norfolk bridge, obscure but intact.

Quartermaster Travis. At the conn, he would take reports called to him by Seaman Field, the talker standing within, positioned between a porthole and the steering console. Those stationed on the open bridge and standing in the pilothouse could readily monitor the skipper's limited dialogue with steersman and talker, assuring that orders quietly given were quickly carried out, giant forces serenely ruled.

Captain McCoy turns the conn over to Captain Brown at 0749. Accompanied by a junior officer, the pilot hurries below to the main deck and then climbs down a Jacob's ladder to a waiting tug. Word is passed to the bridge that the tugboat has pulled away, and Brown gives the order "All engines ahead two-thirds." The Navy seldom seeks pilotage on the route to the open sea, and no harbor pilot is aboard the *Missouri* as it heads for Thimble Shoal channel. From where he stands eight levels above the main deck, Captain Brown has a commanding view of his ship, the mighty cannons of the two forward batteries aiming over a circular antiaircraft mount above the prow where lookouts are stationed, the anchor watch standing near paired heavy, black anchor chains stretching over the long, teak-planked foredeck. It is a picture of power straining for release.

At the maneuvering board behind the wheelhouse, Ensign Harris labors over the primary source of tracking information. Controlling the 4JW circuit, he tells the quartermasters on the lower bridge wings which navigational aids to sight, asking for a mark on specific bearings every minute. Seaman Cole, also on the circuit, scribbles each report into his notebook, and Harris plots the bearings along the ship's course. The first position is on the chart a minute after the last tug pulls away.

A call goes out to relieve the watch, accompanied by the high-pitched strain of a boatswain's pipe. *Ting-ting, ting-ting . . .* sounds shortly from a small clock in the chart room, a nearby bronze bell echoing . . . *clung-clung, clung-clung,* eight bells starting the forenoon watch.

In the COC, duty officer Carr faces demanding work as he glances at the time on an electric clock. A round-faced, scrappy-looking fellow, one of the more experienced officers in combat operations, it has fallen to him to be the first to work with newly installed radar, evaluating prototype equipment for *Iowa*-class ships. Although it has not been fully tested and calibrated, its first application will take place shortly during the exercises at Little Creek. Until then they can do no more than skeptically compare the output of their displays to visual fixes, matching plots derived on the navigation bridges, attempting to gain a sense of their reliability. Technical problems plague the radar-men. Electronic technicians are frequently called to replace short-lived vacuum tubes. Random "noise" on the displays is often difficult to distinguish from pips reflected by small craft or buoys in the middle distance. Landforms, particularly low-lying sandy shores, inaccurately match the detailed charts. Bearings taken off the PPIs are known to differ from concurrent visual observations. Within the dimly lit compartment, the intense faces of Carr's operators reflect an eerie green glow from the phosphorescent screens. At each station a radius of light, synchronized with a matched rotating antenna at mast top, converts microwave reflections into a vaguely understandable monochrome map of the surrounding land. Five times per minute a full sweep causes amoeba-shaped figures to ease downward within a circle centered on the ship's position—to the left a large landmass, to the right a bean-shaped island. The ship approaches the mile-wide passage between Old Point Comfort and Fort Wool. The course swings right to 053°, and the green figures on the scopes shift counterclockwise. Watches change at 0802, and the talker in combat operations is establishing connections with talker Hood on O8 and radar-man Gene Jensen on O4, chattering about which of multiple circuits is appropriate for each to use.

The Bluejackets' Manual is the enlisted man's basic training guide. Republished almost annually, it is issued at enlistment as part of each new recruit's seabag. It tells him everything from how to take care of his feet and teeth (in that order) to how to send semaphore messages, fight shipboard fires, and survive adrift in a small boat. If a sailor has read only one book throughout his naval career, it would be this one. It covers in detail the critical duties of talkers:

> In nearly every case, the information regarding activities in one part of the ship which is needed in other parts is sent from station to station by means of sound-powered telephone circuits. This means that the information must be spoken by an officer, repeated by a telephone talker at the sending station, heard by the talker at the receiving station, and then repeated correctly to the officer concerned. . . .
>
> The job of the talker is an important one. The talker and his equipment are the nervous system of the ship. If the message is not relayed, or is

RAISE ABLE-PETER

incorrectly relayed, the ship may be helpless, and her entire crew may be placed in danger by a talker who does not use his voice and his phone well. Almost everyone in the Navy will make use of sound-powered phones. . . .

. . . Talk in a loud voice. . . . Articulate clearly. . . . Talk slowly. . . . Use ship's terms with great clarity.[10]

The *Missouri* had more than eleven hundred phone terminals connected on multiple circuits, each for a specific purpose—daily routine, the special details of arrivals and departures, battle conditions, damage control. Simple in design, voice-powered circuits are crucial in shipwide operations. The transmitter controls the wire at the depression of a button; all others listen. The talker's behavior is critical. Checkpoint procedures help avoid error. Everyone on the circuit hears everything spoken; anyone can plug in a set of headphones or pick up a handset and listen in. In the quiet of a night watch in mid-ocean, sailors have been known to break the boredom by sharing gossip on the circuit, trading opinions and lurid stories, sometimes even trying a little two-part harmony, softly sung. They do so at risk of being overheard by a raspy-voiced chief threatening to report them for skylarking. Lookouts with headphones are given directions to report everything they see on the surface of the water. Beginners will do just that. The recipient of the report on the bridge, usually more experienced and aware of the flow of information, may exercise judicious editing until the young lookout learns to filter his observations. "Not the grapefruit rinds, you boob!" may be all the kid needs to hear across the circuit, just once. The telephone talkers' work is taken for granted, much of it indeed superfluous. Yet everything spoken should be acknowledged under clearly defined protocols—all commands repeated, an officer's simple "Very well" in response to information delivered. As men work together they may unconsciously develop abbreviated repartee—a nod toward the onlooking talker, "OK," or a salty expletive sometimes reduces tension and does the job as well. Improper, but effective.

Telephone talkers make up but one element of shipboard communications links. Signalmen handle intership communication, using code flags, blinker, and, on occasion, semaphore. These are vital to ships operating on station in convoy. If alone, as the *Missouri* was, the watch is at least prepared to trade primitive whistle signals with non-naval ships and to fly code flags according to international rules to explain purposes of mutual interest.

Lieutenant Carr, a wartime graduate of the Naval Academy, hovers at the table near the radarscopes. Considered an old hand at the job, he has spent four of his six commissioned years in COCs. After wartime submarine service and tours as executive officer and skipper of smaller naval craft, he was introduced to battleship life aboard the *Iowa,* serving there until it was decommissioned. After eighteen months on the *Missouri,* his top priority has just become the new radar installation. How much, the lieutenant wonders, can he trust it?

Fore and aft on the main deck, sailors finish stowing mooring lines and secure the ship for sea. A few linger near the lookouts and leadsmen watching the passage through the Roads. The Navy maintained the long-standing practice of stationing men equipped with sounding leads in the chains, platforms once suspended by chains from the sidestays of the foremast. After use of the platforms was discontinued, the term was retained because of the station's proximity to the anchors. Standing at deck's edge, they are prepared to swing a weighted line forward into the water, watch it slacken as it comes abeam, and call out the depth by noting the last mark on the line near the water. It's a tough task even from a small boat moving at four or five knots, particularly when the gunk of the Chesapeake lessens the feel of the line losing its weight. It would be practically useless from the foredeck of a warship plowing now at twice that speed. Except in fog, leadsmen did their work chiefly for practice. Seaman Apprentice (SA) John K. Williams, with a partner to aid in hauling the wet line aboard, stands ready for the order. As it happens, there is no better way to determine the depth this morning. The fathometer in the COC is on the fix list. SA John Beeman knew it before the *Missouri* left the dock, but in eighteen months on the ship he had yet to be asked for readings. Earlier, Chiefs Reams and Rice had discussed the fathometer's functioning with Chief Andrew Vargo, who said he thought it hadn't been adjusted correctly. At any rate it wasn't designed to register depths within a fathom or two of the ship's draft, so they generally considered it a useless device. Setting off near shoal waters, there seemed to be no practical means of measuring depth short of peering over the side. Keep a good lookout, stay in deep water at moderate speed, and don't worry about it. Would that have been the position of the men in charge, if asked how they would handle the situation?

It is not of much concern to ops officer Millett that these problems—suspect radar and a little-used fathometer that may not function well—are chiefly in his department as the ship heads toward the ill-defined range buoys. Standing on the open bridge beside the captain, Millett puts more priority on assisting him to complete the deepwater passage through the Navy's experimental sonar range.

The battleship's prow drives forward on even keel, carving a swath through white-flecked waves. A fresh breeze quickly clears the ship of the port's oily atmosphere. Renewed scents of the sea invigorate the men on deck. No rolling motion has set in, but the increased engine thrum makes it evident that the great ship is driving into open waters. Much of the thrill of departure lies in the last look at familiar home shores. Over the bow to starboard the low-lying brownstone fort slides aft, sandy Willoughby Spit behind it. Norfolk's skyline, dominated by masts in the Navy Yard, remains visible on the starboard quarter. On the afterdeck, as gulls soar in pursuit, sailors watch the wake of four powerful propellers curve in a wide-churning arc, reflecting a change of course. The big brick hotel and low white tower on Old Point Comfort will soon slip by to port. Take a deep breath; open seas, the Gulf Stream, and sunny skies beckon.

The *Missouri* comes up to ten knots steering through Hampton Roads, in the face of little current as it approaches the strait inside Fort Wool. Lookouts report sighting a buoy on the starboard bow, off the rocky pile surrounding the century-old bulwark on the right of the channel.

0805. On the open bridge, Lieutenant Hatfield looks at his watch, waiting for his relief, Lieutenant Arnold. Scanning ahead he picks out two spar buoys at some distance, not significant to the current situation. Beyond them he looks for Thimble Shoal Light, clay red and standing above the water like a fifty-five-foot saltcellar. Lt. (jg) Lawrence Body, the relieving junior watch officer, joins Hatfield, who tells him to stand over to starboard and "maintain a lookout for objects moving in the water."

No one seems edgy in this shoal-bordered water. An alert state of tight control prevails, confidence perhaps that someone else is responsible. Everyone knows his job. Yet there is ample reason for anxiety. The correct and only acoustic range buoys are the two that had been identified in red. They were described in one document as having been flagged, but, unknown to the officers, the flag on the southern buoy is missing.

No sooner has Hatfield spoken to Body than Captain Brown tells him to take over the conn while he goes inside to check the chart. A minute later navigator Morris gives the captain two courses to follow after passing fast-approaching Old Point Comfort. Left to 032°, curving around the southeast shore of the peninsula, then right to 053° toward the range. With precise tracking and moderate speed, that gradual path requires no extraordinary ship-handling procedures, no maneuvering with engines. There is no traffic ahead. The route through the range, as yet not clearly distinguished by the buoys, might be snug, but the ship has an unimpeded passage.

The captain soon returns to the open bridge. Commander Peckham joins him to ask whether he wants to shift the conn routinely, once the ship had passed Fort Wool. After the range has been run, replies Brown.

Range? Not more than ten minutes before the event, this is Peckham's first clue that a range is involved in the passage. The XO hastens back into the pilothouse, pushing his way past Chief Reams, who is engaged in watching Travis at the wheel, and goes to Morris, standing at the chart table. Ensign Harris had yielded his space at the table to the captain, only to find himself preempted by Peckham and Morris. Bearings are coming in regularly, more than Harris can handle with curtailed access to the chart. He is getting fretful.

"What's this dope about us running the acoustic range?" Peckham asks. Morris calmly confirms the plan.

Equally calm, Peckham, leaning over the table, says, "Well, where is it?" Morris points to the buoys he has marked on the chart. Peckham observes a line appearing to him to be safe, points to it and asks, "Is this supposed to be the track?" Morris confirms that it is.

Inside less than two minutes before his return to the outer bridge, Captain Brown resumes the conn with the words "I have it." The ship passes between Old Point Comfort and Fort Wool, and the channel widens. The range is distant by perhaps three thousand yards; they should be on it in seven or eight minutes. Lieutenant Bland, also now aware of the plan, heads below to the communications deck to attend to the setting of the signal to indicate the ship is running a range.

At Fort Monroe, personnel in the Naval Ordnance Laboratory start taking cross bearings on the battleship's foremast as it passes east of them, headed toward their underwater hydrophones. Its position in relation to the recording of the generated sounds is critical to their studies.

0808. Lieutenant Hatfield, on the open bridge, has not yet been relieved. Captain Brown, peering intently ahead, tells him to keep a sharp lookout for the acoustic range. As the captain glances toward him, Hatfield's expression reveals that he doesn't understand. Brown asks, "Do you know what the acoustic range buoys are?"

Hatfield's face suggests that he doesn't.

"Get yourself informed." With that the officer of the deck goes inside to the chart room. There ops officer Millett, now at the plotting table, points to the penciled crosses. Hatfield sees where they are marked, northeast of Fort Wool, just about due east of the tanks on Old Point Comfort. He has a sense of the route but gets no description of the buoys' appearance. They will be small and should be flagged, but no one has raised that question.

At 0810, on his return to the open bridge, Hatfield turns the watch over to Lieutenant Arnold. The spar buoys had completely slipped his mind. Once relieved, he goes below to the wardroom. Arnold lifts his cap, strokes his thinning hair, and reviews the situation. The watch officers, for the first time aware of the planned range run, had discussed it briefly while looking over the chart. In Arnold's view, all seems in order. Neither of them has studied the Hampton Roads chart in detail. It's been crowded around the chart table, and between the skipper, XO, operations officer, and navigator, those people should know what they are about.

Commander Millett leaves the chart table. After making a calculation, navigator Morris adjusts the planned course for the effect of current. He then tells the CO through a porthole that the new course should be between 058° and 060°. The captain sets the course to 058° as Kimble makes an entry in the deck log.

Meanwhile, the men in combat operations continue plotting radar bearings on the bombardment chart. Transitory pips show up on the scopes but cannot be confirmed as buoys marked on the charts. Three fixes based on the irregular landforms of Old Point Comfort and Fort Wool do not conform precisely to the visual bearings being repeated by the talkers. These landmarks are close, and their bearings change rapidly as the ship passes between them. Considering that a time lag between visual and radar bearings exists, they could assume they were looking at a vaguely reliable plot. Good enough for radar work. Navigation is often understood to be more art than science; radar navigation, some might say, is closer to witchcraft.

0811, according to the navigator's watch. The light on Old Point Comfort has passed abeam to port. Speaking through a porthole, Morris tells the captain that the ship should soon come right to 075°. A discussion follows about speed through the range. Millett's first impression is that it should be five knots. Morris says that no specific speed is required as long as it is steady. Millett advises that there is sufficient water to steam at fifteen knots.

Commander Peckham has the captain's approval to go below to the secondary conn. At 0812, Quartermaster Kimble makes his last logbook entry from the O8 level as he prepares to accompany the exec below. Entering the wheelhouse again, Peckham passes by the plotting table. Addressing Morris, he says "For God's sake, watch it," then turns to the ladder, Kimble following.

Morris now joins the others on the open bridge—the captain, Millett, and Arnold. The officer of the deck has sighted the B buoy nearly dead ahead at fifteen hundred to a thousand yards. This would bring them to it in about eighteen seconds.

The captain has sighted the spars and sets standard speed. The man at the telegraph rings up the engine order. Addressing the skipper, Millett says that the spars "may mark the range." Arnold reports the buoy at a thousand yards, and the captain acknowledges his report. Studying the object further, Arnold says he can distinguish a B, hears no comment from the others, then turns to check on his watch standers.

Brown, with Millett beside him, picks out the reported buoy bobbing in the water dead ahead—small, spherical, topped with a red flag. Millett also sights it, saying to the captain, "We could pass it to the starboard." Millett's suggestion is to put it to their right, south of their track. B or N is the northern buoy, on the shoalward side of the channel. It is now several seconds past 0813. According to Commander Millett, "there's plenty of water" on the north side of the buoy.

Further ahead, the two sighted spar buoys stand in eighteen feet of water, marking the entrance to a passage through Horseshoe Shoal fishing grounds. The captain, in the company of the navigator, the operations officer, and the officer of the deck, asks "whether all three buoys were not part of the range."

He is met with silence.

"Does anyone know if the spar buoys and this other buoy are part of the range?" Brown asks in a more demanding voice. The wind is in his face as he squints across a choppy sea. Failing to sight the second and unflagged acoustic range buoy somewhere to his right, he concludes that the spars ahead are part of the acoustic range.

"I assume I can leave this buoy on either side," he says, referring to the fast-approaching B sphere. Thinking this marker identifies the southern approach to the range, he gives an order to Travis at the wheel to come left to 053°. The danger bearing hasn't been discussed among the half-dozen people pacing between the chart table and the lookout positions on the open bridge.

Buoys E and D, plotted in pencil on the chart according to the original Naval Ordnance Laboratory plan, are not in place. Buoys N and S, plotted in red and possibly labeled B and C, are the only ones that actually mark the range. The captain's steering order has just put the B buoy to starboard.

Commander Millett, thinking all five buoys are in place and unclear as to new or old labeling, assumes that B is buoy E and that they are tracking the route between the pair Morris had drawn on the chart. The turn to the left, intended to move the ship more in line with Millett's vision of a five-buoy range, aims the vessel shoalward. Next, he mistakes the two black-and-white-striped spar buoys for range markers. More than a mile northeast of the actual range, and differing in type from the spherical range buoys, the two sets should be difficult to confuse. They "may mark the range," Millett says to the captain.

The shapes and colors of navigational markers define the waters in which they are placed. Multiple publications carry ample reference material on the American buoyage system, Dutton's *Navigation* among them. Mariners should know that spar buoys are positioned in shallow waters, the striping indicating the sides or junctions of channels. Chart 400 clearly shows the Back River channel through fishing grounds, spars 53N and 46N marking the left and right sides of the approach. Chesapeake markers are notorious for scanty labeling, many of them intended for small-craft operators and their labels subject to frequent revision, but it is difficult to understand how one would associate pole-shaped buoys delineating fishing grounds with the spherical range markers. Brown and Millett have both had ample command experience; Morris once taught navigation. Lieutenant Arnold suspects the stakes mark fishnets. But standing near Brown and overhearing the ongoing discussion between the captain and the two senior officers, Arnold doesn't think the captain intends to steer for them.

At 0814 the executive officer and Quartermaster Kimble join Ens. Francis Kelly, an assistant navigator like Harris, standing watch in the secondary conn. The ship is due east of Old Point Comfort Light. Peckham takes little time for formalities as he sights the northern buoy of the range dead ahead. He asks the captain, four decks above, if the northern end of the range has been sighted. Brown answers in the affirmative. Standing on the O4 outer bridge, the executive officer mulls that over until he observes the two spar buoys fully a mile ahead and sees the bow of the ship swinging left. He orders the seaman on the primary maneuvering circuit to recommend a right turn to the bridge. This is relayed from O4 to O8, but the message is not acknowledged. Concurrently the JA talker on O8 informs the COC that the ship is "passing buoy A to starboard." The men looking at the bombardment chart showing the plotted range buoys assume the reference is to buoy C, unidentified on the scopes at the time.

Peckham and Kimble take a minute to look at the plot. At once the situation becomes evident to both men. Peckham steps to the intercom connecting to the primary conn and says firmly, "The executive officer recommends that we come right immediately. The ship is standing into shoal water." On the O8 level telephone talker Field relays the message through the open porthole to the captain on the outer bridge. That word, too, goes unacknowledged. Field responds to O4, recognizing Peckham's second call. The circuit they use connects the bridge with the forward and after engine rooms, the forecastle, fantail, after steering station, and several mooring stations. Everyone on that 1-JV wire is now aware of the situation. Field is a soft-spoken lad, perhaps a little intimidated by all this brass scurrying about. Nevertheless, he attempts to relay to the captain the advice he has just acknowledged. The captain is standing forward of the porthole, and Field talks mostly to the back of his head. The wind, coupled with the ship's speed, gusts through the opening at some sixteen knots, full in Field's face. Brown gives him no acknowledgment, and the talker doesn't shout it, doesn't repeat it, listens only for the next message.

Navigator Morris has sensed that Peckham's warning is right. He tells the captain, "The bearing is getting high. We should come right now." Finally sensitive to the danger bearing, Morris has been keeping that responsibility to himself, but now he sees what is happening.

Brown replies, "We can't come right now or we'll spoil the run."

By now buoy B is close aboard the starboard bow. The bearing on Thimble Shoal Light moves precariously to the right as the ship swings to port. It bears 075° when Morris waves his arms and, with alarm in his voice, counters, "We must come right."

Brown then orders 10° right rudder and addresses himself to the operations officer. "The navigator does not know where he is; go find out."

By 0816 Ensign Harris has regained control of his plotting table. Meanwhile he has been getting more bearings through his headphones than he can acknowledge and lay down. Even Cole, the bearing recorder, is becoming confused. The last good plot had followed the planned track closely, putting the ship some six minutes from the shoal. Again Millett preempts Harris at the table. The quartermasters continue calling in their sightings. Overloaded with information, Harris stiffens. Perhaps ninety seconds remain to get clear, and he is no longer certain of the exact position. He has tried without success to get three workable figures from his bearing recorder during the flood of continuous reports. Too often he has been crowded from the table by other officers inspecting the chart.

The Third Repeater, flag signal for running the range, is aloft as the communications officer returns to the O8 level.

From the open bridge the captain points out a mark to the steersman and tells him to steady on 058°. Travis has no difficulty hearing him, repeats the course, and steadies on it. He focuses on the compass, not on the stakes that could be seen irregularly through the midship porthole. "Come left," orders the skipper, explaining, "I'm coming left because I have to steer a steady course for the data on the range." Travis repeats and executes the order, then reports that the rudder is sluggish. No one acknowledges his comment.

Brown issues an order to come right, following this almost at once by "hard right rudder." Travis thinks he knows why the ship isn't responding, but in acknowledging and executing rapid steering orders he says nothing—not to Chief Reams, who has heard him report the sluggish rudder, not to the captain.

It is 0817. No one on O8 has seen the C buoy. Talker Watson has heard from lookouts who have sighted the range marker, by now on the starboard quarter, but in the confusion on the bridge he doesn't report it.

Two men on O4 pick out C some distance off. Seconds after Peckham calls in his second warning, the one acknowledged on 1-JV, he looks to starboard and sees the B buoy close abeam. With that he opens the loudspeaker system and says, "The executive officer recommends back full or twist the ship to the right."

Topside, this third warning is heard broadly, the squawk box bypassing the process of the telephone talkers. Chief Reams, standing in the pilothouse, hears it loud and clear. He knows "twist right" is an emergency maneuver to put the ship into its tightest turning circle. That calls for engine maneuvering, putting the rudder hard over while backing full on the two starboard propellers. Forward propulsion on the port ones would drive the ship sharply to starboard, countering its momentum and turning it nearly within its own length. There is no return acknowledgment; no wheel or engine orders suggest its acceptance. A sailor at the intercom on O4 reports to the XO that his message is acknowledged.

Messages now come to the bridge from the engine room reporting loss of vacuum and breakdowns as the ship glides onto the shoal. Sand is filling the condensers. The much ignored Field, his head in the porthole, attempts to relay this to the captain, who turns, frowning at him in response, saying nothing. More messages come to Field from the fantail and from an after lookout on the O6 level, that the propellers are "kicking up mud." He reports this in the midst of growing alarm. Finally the engine room comes on the 21-MC squawk box to repeat its trouble report.

Brown now responds in rapid succession with "Right fifteen degrees rudder . . . right full rudder . . . stop starboard engine . . . starboard engines back two-thirds . . . all engines back two-thirds . . . all engines full astern."

Following the 21-MC reports, officer of the deck Arnold gives an order to the leadsmen to man the chains and commence taking hand soundings. In the confusion, that order never gets through to Williams on the foredeck. Small loss; at the speed of the ship over the ground it is sliding across no one would have believed lead line readings of something less than the ship's draft. Within seconds the bow is cleaving the bottom, moving at more than twelve knots, and still swinging left. Arnold sends another order to the forecastle to stand by to release the bow anchors, then waits for the captain's orders to let go.

In the chart room, Seaman Cole continues recording bearings while the ship is almost motionless. One bearing appears to have changed by some 100°.

In combat operations Lieutenant Carr is convinced they have radar equipment failures. Four radarmen agree. They have been observing widely divergent fixes and have felt it would be unwarranted to send such navigational reports to the bridge. QM1 John Spooner, becoming suspicious that something else is wrong, says to Carr, "Do you think we should come right?" Carr replies, "Yes, I think we should." He wonders aloud "what we were doing up there headed for shallow waters," then turns to the telephone talker to recommend a course change. Suddenly the talker sings out "right full rudder," reflecting the order that had been relayed on the bridge.

Peckham calls up to Harris at the plotting board to report continual bearings to him. Hearing that, Chief Rice tells the quartermasters on the wings to keep the bearings coming without regard to time.

Down in main engine control, Lt. James N. Forehan has rung up "All engines stop" on the annunciators, signifying that the propellers are no longer turning. Arnold relays this to the captain, who has been called to the intercom by Comdr. R. A. Zoeller, the engineering officer. Talking directly to the captain, Zoeller explains his plight in the engine room. Suction has been lost, and it is necessary to shut down all of the ship's four engines. Brown replies, "I understand; stop all engines."

It is 0823. The ship plows ahead for another ninety seconds. There is nothing the men on the bridge can do but stand silently and wait, wait for what seems like a week, until it gracefully comes to rest, hard aground. Again in the chart room, Commander Millett hears the mix of orders, fully understanding the situation.

Men in the enclosed radio shack feel a shudder and guess that the watch on deck has kicked the ship into flank speed.[11] Not far from the upper reaches of the engine compartments, Hatfield, having his coffee in the wardroom, hears unusual noises sounding like diesel generators cutting in. It strikes him that this familiar sound is untimely. With no view to outside, it takes a few minutes for him to realize that the ship has grounded. Well below the main deck, a cook lying in his bunk feels a jolt and hears the hull scraping bottom.

During this distressful period the communications officer quietly takes up an intercom and calls the signal bridge. Down on the O3 level a signalman, responding to the comm officer, opens *Hydrographic Office #87,* the book of international flag signals. He then tells the sailors at the flag bag to break the Code flag and below it raise Able-Peter—the international signal for "I am aground."*

High tide at Sewell Point occurred at 8:20 A.M. Five minutes later the *Missouri* was 1.7 miles east-northeast of Old Point Comfort, plotted from the station at Fort Monroe, more than a half-mile north of the normal shipping lanes, and headed north of Thimble Shoal Light. Charts of this rarely frequented neck of the harbor showed shoal water with depths of twenty-four to twenty-eight feet, sloping to sixteen feet on Horseshoe Shoal. The ship was making 12.4 knots when it grounded, plowing some twenty-five hundred feet into mud and sand—three full ship lengths—before coming to rest. In the process its own force lifted its 57,000-ton deadweight over six feet as it glided

---

* The military phonetic alphabet used in World War II continued in use until after the Korean War. It was then revised to adapt better to the dialects and accents more broadly understood by English-speaking military organizations within NATO and the United Nations. The revised signal flag designations for Able-Peter would be Alpha-Papa.

over the bank and plowed a canyon in the midst of the shoal. Sand, grit, and mud entered its condensers, clogging tubes and causing overheating with high risk of fracture. All but a few emergency generators were out of action. At the stern the thirty-one-foot draft mark was above the surface of the water, where its logged draft of thirty-six feet, nine inches, should have appeared.

4

A Magnificent Sight

In the conning tower's highest fully enclosed compartment, Spot 1 on O11 (see fig. 2 in chapter 3), Seamen John Williams* and Jimmy Happenny were perplexed. They had applied the bearings given them to focus a fire control range finder on Thimble Shoal Light. The field of view of the 25-power scope in the Mark 38 gun director is small enough that it helps to train it in the approximate direction first, just as one would position binoculars prior to sighting through them. An electric motor usually rotates the heavy equipment, bringing it to bear on the target, but the men seemed to have lost power, and the lighthouse couldn't be found through the sights. Happenny was disgruntled that he had to crank the unit by hand. Williams opened the sky control hatch to see for himself why the lighthouse was lost, found it bearing far to the right of the range finder's direction of sight, and realized at once that the ship was on a shoal.[1]

Astonished sailors on the foredeck looked from the waters to leeward, flat as a plate, to the towering bridge, and above it to the motionless radar antennas. Gulls, normally in pursuit through the harbor, circled above the masts. No alarm bells or whistles sounded, no shouts, and an eerie murmur had replaced the heady rush of bow waves. Time shifted into slow motion. A minute passed before anyone spoke, and then with words muffled in disbelief. Within the housing, the customary hum of ventilation begged for recognition of its absence. Dead air hung heavily in half-dark compartments. Adding to

---

* There were two enlisted men named John Williams aboard. The leadsman referred to in the previous chapter as John K. Williams was in the deck division. The sailor whose experience is described here was in the gunnery division.

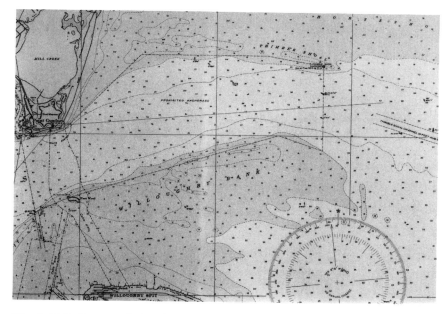

Fig. 3. U.S. Coast and Geodetic Survey Chart Number 400, Hampton Roads, dated 28 November 1949. On the front endsheet, dotted circles identify locations of acoustic range buoys B and C. The *Missouri*'s two final courses prior to grounding have been plotted, as has the danger bearing between Old Point Comfort and Thimble Shoal. Triangles identify the ship's estimated positions on the track, based on fixes recorded at Fort Monroe and aboard the battleship. Note the two spar buoys northeast of the battleship's final position.

the funereal atmosphere, the dim glow of battle lanterns supplanted normal illumination. A pair of yeomen paused in their duties and rushed to the open deck. Leaning over a railing, they saw waves gently lapping at the waterline, six feet lower than usual.[2]

Bob Marks, electronic technician (ET) striker on watch in Radio 2 below the main deck, felt a tremor a few moments earlier, wondered what had happened, and went on deck to find out. ET3 "Guffy" Goffredo, said he thought the ship had been put into flank speed. Marks saw that it was steaming along at normal speed, discounted his experience, and hastened below to his watch station. It was only then that he found the ship was helpless.[3]

Warm, soundless air rose through the platform gratings of the

engine rooms. The steam turbines had expired, and the four propeller shafts beyond them were idle. Lighting remained in the firerooms, supplied from an auxiliary source, as the men hastened amidst
early confusion to clear the saltwater cooling pumps. At the time
there was little they could do, but in an hour or two they would begin
the first of many twelve- to twenty-hour workdays.[4]

On the long "broadway" corridor below the main deck, a comforting exception to the shipwide pause in activities emerged. The damage control officer occupied a small compartment near the number
three engine room, where divisional damage crews reported, compartment by compartment, on the status of the hull. Watertight
integrity—frame to frame, deck to deck—was established and veri-
fied, the condition of each area discussed among the men in confident, low voices. A comforting sense of control prevailed, even as
they realized there would be no pressure for the fire mains without
the assistance of other vessels. Readiness condition Yoke had been in
effect, so all compartments with hatches below the waterline were
closed, to be opened briefly only for necessary passage through.
Within minutes, readiness condition Zebra—no passage between
closed compartments without permission—was set on and below the
third deck. The smoking lamp was out.

The shuddering hull around the lower sleeping quarters had
shaken many of the night watches awake. Sleepily, they rose from
their bunks to poke about near-dark spaces. Pat McGough, radioman
third class (RN3), slept through the short-lived noise until he was
called from his sack to report to Radio 1. He thought he was being
kidded until he arrived at his station, where he, too, started on a
series of long watch duties.[5]

The languid period ended abruptly as officers assessed the circumstances in brief conversations. Peckham hurried to the upper bridge
to meet with the CO. Within minutes of the grounding, Captain
Brown called for an orderly to transmit a terse message to the naval
base, stating the situation and requesting assistance. Motionless
silence was eerie and unwelcome, unexpected of a man-of-war except
in its last moments of life. On the starboard signal bridge the insistent
flutter of flags climbing to a yardarm broke the hush; under a red-
white Code pennant spread two flags of blue and white—swallow-
tailed Able and blue Peter, "My ship is aground." The foredeck crew

roused into action; a boatswain's mate hoisted a spherical, black object above the anchor windlasses, universal indicator of a ship fixed to the bottom. Rumors started at once. A sailor entered one compartment to shout, "We ain't going to Gitmo, we're grounded."[6] The situation was similar throughout the ship. On every deck and platform men stopped what they were doing in stunned surprise. Shortly after the accident the executive officer's voice was heard on the loudspeakers in the firerooms, "Attention all hands. Attention all hands. Now hear this. The ship is stuck in the mud."[7] That terse announcement wasn't heard everywhere, power being lost throughout most of the ship. Many would claim they were told nothing official for most of the day.[8] In those first, tranquil minutes, not more than fifty crew members, those in combat operations and on the navigation bridges, knew exactly what had happened.

On the bridge, Ensign Harris's chart became a focal point, officers and men shuffling around it to review the situation. More fixes were taken and compared, binoculars trained on the waters to the south; the locale offered little choice of marks. Forward in the chains, SA John Williams finally lowered the lead. Officers on the foredeck and bridge discussed between them the possibility of letting the anchors go. Reduction of three or four tons might allow the bow to lift. But the anchors could not be retrieved without power, and if the vessel should float it could not be maneuvered to take a strain. Swinging loose, it would soon ground again. Concluding that nothing would be gained, they rejected the idea. They were unaware that even this extraordinary measure would not float the ship. Proximity to Norfolk would be a mixed blessing. They could expect ample assistance, quickly delivered. But they also knew they could expect the immanent arrival of a cadre of Navy brass. In effect, the great ship was no longer theirs to control.

Morris, with Millett beside him, testily thumbed into the tide tables. They looked at each other, cross-checked their calculations, examined their watches, and glumly admitted they had lost any tidal advantage. The water would only get lower through the day; in the evening it would not return even to its present height.

If a vessel is moving at moderate speed when she goes aground, or if the tide is at a low stage, she will probably be able to get off through her own efforts or with the help of vessels in the immediate vicinity. If she goes aground hard and fast, especially near high tide, it is probable that the services of professional salvagers will be required. . . . If there is a chance that help will be needed, no time should be lost in communicating with shore and making such arrangements as the situation calls for.[9]

An encyclopedia of unknowns could have been compiled at this point. Powerless in their responsibilities, waiting for direction and assistance, the officers began a list of known facts and of questions to be resolved.

Location: through bearings taken forward and aft and proximity to nearby buoys, the unflagged southern range buoy had finally been identified. Unknown were the shape of the path astern of the ship, the shortest distance to deep water, and the extent to which shallows limited the approach of other ships to render aid. Tugs and lighters could come alongside, but restricted depth might rule out the aid of larger vessels.

Draft: computed from the logged departure draft and readings on a sounding line, the conclusion was disturbing—a lift of six to seven feet had occurred. The extent to which weight would have to be reduced for flotation was yet to be charted; fuel and water, possibly anchors, chains, and ammunition (with the associated hazards of transfer), but then what? They waited for preliminary reports from damage control. How much of what, and how fast?

Damage: none reported, except from engine room main control; watertight integrity in all living compartments below the waterline was assured. Unknown was the state of the propellers or the bottom plates of the hull's outer skin. Nor could they predict the extent of stress on the framework of the hull when attempts would be made to tow it off the bottom.

Power: the engineering officer insisted that the main engines were rendered useless until shipyard work could clear the cooling water intakes. Technicians had set to work immediately to provide auxiliary power beyond that supplied by batteries and emergency generators. That would improve living conditions, but an external power source was needed to drive machinery required for heavy pulling. Manila hawsers or steel cable strong enough to take the strain could not be manipulated without the use of the powerful deck winches.

Tidal prospects: tidal range was predicted to diminish over the next ten days. Lightening operations might offset the difference. The damage control officer said that every 150 tons removed would gain them the equivalent of one inch of freeboard in rising waters. Clearly, hasty and heavy work lay ahead, but unknown was the probability of beating the tide.

Weather: unthreatening for the present. Midcentury weather forecasting was largely empirical, far short of the scientific collection of data now taken for granted. Pilot charts, based on past records and distributed monthly, were as reliable a source of weather forecasts aboard ship as anything else. According to those, they could expect routine winter weather for the mid-Atlantic coast. They would gather reports, read the barometer, relate its changes to simple observations, base everything on experience, and make a judgment about the next twelve hours. Better yet, they would listen to the radio. Broadcasts reported mostly on local conditions; the future was limited to the next half day.

Next action: prepare to work with those coming out to give assistance. Then they would meet with the next in command, ComCruLant. Trained to plan and prepare for nearly every contingency in war, weather and worse, Navy men are uncomfortable facing unknowns they lack the power to influence. There was little speculation on Rear Admiral Smith's next move.

In Norfolk and Portsmouth the news traveled fast among the Navy's upper echelons. The Pentagon was notified within minutes. Reactions were universally grave, particularly in the vicinity of the office of Adm. William H. P. Blandy, Commander in Chief Atlantic Fleet (CinCLantFlt). "Spike" Blandy was more to be honored than feared. He had established an early reputation as chief of the Bureau of Ordnance by pushing the development of 20- and 40-millimeter antiaircraft weapons, which were widely used in the war. Later he commanded amphibious groups in the battles for Saipan, Iwo Jima, and Okinawa, and postwar was named to his present position.[10] It was an unfitting time for the sanguine Blandy to be told that his principal capital ship was out of service. His planned retirement from naval service had been announced. Sometime before the second of February, sixteen days hence, prior to closing out his naval career, he was to turn over command of all ships afloat in the Atlantic Fleet. It appeared there might be one less vessel on the transfer list.

67

Blandy immediately called Rear Adm. Roscoe Good, Commander Atlantic Fleet Service Forces, to request the help of Capts. W. L. Ware and Henry Treakle. Ware was port captain and Treakle the senior pilot in charge of towing operations at the naval base. They dispatched fleet tugs to the site within minutes of receiving Brown's message. Tugboats, little noticed until needed, soon swarmed from crevasses along the shore, hastily heading for Thimble Shoal.

Rear Adm. Allan E. "Hoke" Smith, among the Norfolk flag officers the one most familiar with the battleship and its staff, was in conference on the second floor of his headquarters when he was interrupted by a phone call requesting information about a report that the *Missouri* was aground. Upon receiving the word, shortly after 9:00 A.M., he stepped to a window in the rear of the building from where he could see the motionless battleship in the distance. Like others, for a moment he refused to believe what he saw. Realizing it was no mirage, he faced his staff. "Gentlemen," he said, "the USS *Missouri* has just gone a half mile inland."[11]

Meanwhile, shipping traffic continued on regular passages through Hampton Roads. The British freighter *Magdapur,* arriving from Philadelphia, passed Thimble Shoal Light and steamed west a half mile from the battleship. Training glasses on the motionless ship to starboard, the mate could not help but wonder what such a large naval ship was doing so far off the channel. The flags suggested a grounding, an unlikely event for a battleship in this American naval port. The signal was an international requirement. These were inland waters where local rules took precedence. Perhaps the American Navy was carrying out some unique procedure of its own.

At Buckroe Beach, a mile-long strip of sand running north from Fort Monroe along the Chesapeake shore, the recreation area afforded a close-up view. The haze-grey color of the stately vessel stood out sharply, clean and fresh from the shipyard, newly polished brass glinting as the sun broke through a dull winter sky. Quietly poised high and alone in the water, a monochrome scene but for a colorful daub of signal flags at the yards and ensign at the stern, it was a magnificent sight. You could almost wade out to it, some felt, perhaps reach it with a boat hook, nearly touch it, it seemed that close. People living in the area, accustomed to the routine passage of ships a mile offshore, were unsure at first of what they saw. Speculation centered on the motionless vessel being a mock-up. Perhaps it was intended as a target for Navy training exercises and now waited at the edge of the Bay to be towed seaward. Sailors could be seen gathered along its railings, looking over the side with seeming curiosity. It was hard for onlookers to tell what engaged them, awe or action. Throngs assembled along the seawall, and soon the truth was evident. The pride of the Atlantic Fleet was showing too much of its bottom; it was most certainly stranded on a sandbar.

The windows of the Army Officers Club at Fort Monroe looked directly on the *Missouri*'s stern. Few if any of the observers were aware of the Naval Ordnance Laboratory associated with the Army fort, the prime cause of the events leading to the accident. Morning conversation centered on the strange situation, coupled with a good deal of callous joking about the ludicrous disposition of the rival service.

By midmorning, news of the incident was being broadcast on local radio stations. Aboard ship, sailors with portable radios picked up a newscast to hear that there had been "no casualties reported as yet." The words were aggravating and worrisome, considering there was no way to get in touch with those they had left on the pier only a few hours earlier.[12]

Mariners are as consistent in their knowledge of the tide as landsmen are about phases of the moon. If you need to know it, you check it out. Tides vary too much to track like the time of day. Their characteristics differ according to location, especially in the river-bordered Chesapeake. Navy tugboat skippers, streaming converging wakes of white water across Hampton Roads, glanced at their clocks as they scanned the tide tables. They would be working in ebbing water. High tide at the Navy Yard followed by fifteen minutes that which occurred at Sewell Point, a reference point at the mouth of the Elizabeth River, a quarter-mile north. Going seaward from there, the closest measurement point to the grounding was at Fort Monroe, where the times of high and low water were thought to occur twenty-five to thirty minutes before those at Sewell Point. A thirty-minute differential could probably be applied to the listings to predict the state of the water at the battleship. The *Missouri* had departed from Pier 7 an hour before listed high water at the Navy Yard. On turning into Hampton Roads the ship had traveled seaward against a nearly completed flood. By the time it reached the approach to Thimble Shoal channel, the waters had slacked, turned, and ebbed for no more than twenty minutes. That gave the tugboat fleet poor prospects for early success.

The situation was worse than that. Twice a month the moon aligns with the sun, the combined pull of the two bodies causing the largest tidal ranges in the lunar period. These are spring tides; spring as in "leap"—waters that spring higher with both full and new moon. The new moon, on the same side of the earth as the sun, draws a higher daylight tide than the dark-of-night tides before and after. Such was the case on the morning of 17 January. It would have been difficult to pick a less opportune time than that of the daytime spring tide for the period. This one was thought to have been unusually high for the Chesapeake. Much ocean would go out from around the ship before the same amount or more would wash in to lift it.

Hasty action continued at the Navy Yard. The fleet oiler USS *Chemung* was dispatched to the site with empty tanks, even as more tugs were called into service. On board the tugs the air crackled with metallic radio chatter, a babble of brief, almost overlapping conversations as they approached the ship. The Navy operated its own talk-between-ships (TBS) frequencies for easy communication with nearby vessels, similar to what today's mariners call VHF. Each tug skipper in turn contacted the battleship to identify where his vessel would pull alongside to take up a towing position. The *Missouri* had adequate power to respond.

"Baker Baker Six Three. This is Able Tare Fox Nine Seven. We can put ten tugs aft of you, and one on each side of your bow. If you don't have docking lines ready we'll send up some of ours. Over."

"Roger, Nine Seven. We are rigging six hawsers on bitts on each side. There is no power on the winches. Over."

"Baker Baker Six Three, this is Able Tare Fox Seven Two. Send down a heavy messenger as we bring our stern to your port quarter—we'll need to take aboard a ten-inch hawser."

On the battleship's bridge, the last logbook entry at 0825 put the ship at a point bearing 266°, 1.6 miles from Thimble Shoal Light on a heading of 053°.[13] This fit with bearings logged by the observers at Fort Monroe, 1.7 miles astern of the *Missouri*. High tide was recorded that morning as 3.3 feet above mean low water, some eight or nine inches higher than predicted. The warship's special sea and anchor details remained on duty, readying hawsers that only minutes before had been stowed to secure for sea. Within a quarter hour of the grounding the crews of a dozen tugs began hauling aboard heavy towing lines lowered from the warship's after quarters in a hastily coordinated effort against the falling tide. Draft marks—twenty-nine feet at the bow, a foot more near the stern—were plainly evident. The tug operators had to do what is required to come to the aid of a stranded vessel, although they were virtually certain the work would be futile. For the moment, it was better for Captain Treakle and his skippers to prove that the task was beyond normal efforts. The world would be watching.

How then could they succeed in hauling that deadweight off the beach? On the ship's bridge an inclinometer showed 8° of starboard list, placing the hull on a gradually sloping bottom. Large-scale charts supported that, positioning the fully loaded ship a half mile from water deep enough to float freely. Some suspected that the tidal state around the ship differed enough from that at Fort Monroe that some lift might remain. The Chesapeake occasionally delivers fortunate variations if rain or winter runoff has swollen its tributaries. Any possibility was worth exploiting.

Hampton Roads is formed by the confluence of three rivers at the southwest corner of Chesapeake Bay. The Bay is among the world's largest and best natural harbors, and its deep channels remain virtually ice free. It is embraced by a pair of low peninsulas, crab-claw shaped, and further divided from the Atlantic by two outlying Virginia capes, all serving to hold back the Bay's water supply. Chesapeake Bay itself is the submerged bed of the Susquehanna River, running down from the Appalachian Mountains and the farmlands of New York and Pennsylvania. In 444 miles the Susquehanna drains more than twenty-seven thousand square miles of land, supplying the Chesapeake with half its fresh water and much of its silt. Over eons, clay carved from the cliffs of the Bay's western shore, sand from the lowlands to the east, and silt from a dozen rivers slowly spread a hospitable carpet of mud on the bottom of the Bay. Rocks were unknown near Thimble Shoal, such that simple groundings rarely troubled local watermen. A generous flow of water might do for the stranded ship what it often did for smaller craft in similar circumstances— deliver an unpredicted lift off the muddy bottom. Fluid dynamics might accomplish what engine power could not.

Brown and white water churned in great arcs around the battle-ship as twelve tugs applying full power strained to haul the ship free. A military plane flew out of the Patuxent Naval Air Station to observe, but the pilot gained no better perspective than people on the surface. Good landmarks were lacking for suitable cross bearings from the *Missouri*'s bridge. Thimble Shoal Light and the nearby trou-blesome spar buoys lay almost dead ahead, the white lighthouse and checkered water tanks on Old Point Comfort nearly right astern. Detection of even slight movement aft would be difficult. On any movement of the vessel, no more than a fractional shift in bearings could be anticipated. Hope sprang from limited knowledge. The tugs strained for a full hour as sailors peered through alidades, looking desperately for a shift of bearing on any mark. Nothing changed.

> When measures have been taken to prevent the ship from being set far-ther up the beach . . . the work of lightening her may begin—ballast tanks pumped out, cargo shifted, lightened or thrown overboard. . . . A man of war, with a large crew and plenty of boats should be able under these circumstances to get rid of several hundred tons of easily handled stores within an hour or two. . . . All water in tanks should be pumped overboard.[14]

With the ship lacking electricity in the galleys, the midday meal was sparse—cold-cut sandwiches and an apple. Bread and baloney had to be sliced by hand.[15] The coffee was stale and cold, except for those who contrived to heat it with a blowtorch. Scuttlebutts were losing pressure, and for an hour or so the heads wouldn't flush. Following the report of power loss, the USS *Kittiwake* joined the rescue fleet, arriving alongside in midafternoon. A submarine rescue ship, it car-ried enough generating capacity to satisfy most of the battleship's immediate needs. A fleet repair ship, the USS *Amphion*, joined it and anchored off to the side as guard dog, providing logistical support. Meanwhile, men of the *Missouri*'s engineering division restored the first of two emergency turbo generators to augment the single diesel engine that had been supplying the only power for lighting. Before long they found a means to bypass the inoperative saltwater pumps. Potable water would be shifted to naval water lighters, to be held for subsequent return. Freshwater use was unrestricted, but even a ship full of thirsty men at the scuttlebutts wouldn't gain an inch per day of potential freeboard.

When a Navy plane surveyed the sight shortly after noon, the empty *Chemung* was made fast to the *Missouri*'s starboard side, heavy hoses rigged between the ships. Aerial photographs were released to the press by midafternoon. The acrid stench of black oil again permeated the air. They would buy buoyancy with fuel, leaving one question for the warship's sweating oil kings. Would ten hours of greasy work, shifting grimy black hoses from tank to tank, result in enough added lift to counter the diminishing tidal effect? Captain Brown had called for a second pull-off attempt on the next high tide, one expected to be a foot lower than that of the morning. Without a dynamic means to measure the result of reducing deadweight, the tantalizing prospect of sliding the hull across a flat and slippery bottom encouraged their efforts. In Brown's view, it was worth trying.

The *Kittiwake* arrived to begin delivering enough of its own generated power for the idle warship to resume most internal operations; lighting was back to normal, blowers running again. The galleys would be in operation for a hot evening meal, liver and onions.[16] Meanwhile the *Chemung,* helped by a fleet of smaller Navy oilers, like piglets around a sow, gulped off tons of fuel. While the tugs returned to port to replenish fuel for the evening pull, the topsiders made up flaked tiers of towing hawsers along the decks. Hardly schooled on the activities of stranding, these deepwater sailors were getting firsthand education on its exigencies. As much muscle seemed needed on deck to rig fenders and haul lines to the freshly powered winches as engine power on the water. There was no idle time to think of their embarrassment; in the face of the heavy work at hand it had scarcely occurred to them.

Ships continued to pass on the channel a half-mile south. Harbor pilots, now well aware of the situation, exchanged gossip with ship captains—from New England the colliers *Malden* and *Tilica,* the Norwegian freighter *Fernstrom,* bound for the Far East, and the Old Bay Line night boat, with passengers for Baltimore.[17] Neither bridge nor tunnel yet crossed any part of the Chesapeake; ferries threaded up and down the Bay, several operating from a busy terminal east of the naval base. Seasoned mariners shook their heads, as much in sympathy as in awe. The last people to second-guess the misfortune of a ship and its crew are experienced seamen. In years of travel they have collected their own inventories of trouble, but they talk, and their yarns were headed around the world. The grounding of the *Missouri* would become part of seamen's lore.

Tankers worked alongside the battleship throughout the afternoon, hastening to complete their efforts before the evening tide. The intention was to pump close to eight thousand tons of black oil from the bunkers before the tugs reconvened. That amounted to more than four feet of draft. The pulling power of the tugs might make the difference.

As vessels jockeyed for positions alongside, fenders, chafing boards, spring lines, and boarding ladders were rigged, relocated, and rerigged. Operating an overcrowded parking lot at the edge of a disorderly parade, work gangs rushed to where ships came alongside, made room for arriving small craft among the service vessels, and hastened departures to allocate space for boats waiting in the distance, striving to do everything in proper sequence, all the while respecting rank and priorities.

Admiral Blandy named Rear Admiral Smith director of the salvage operation within his own command. The energetic Smith was a hands-on leader, intense in achieving naval objectives, yet very much a man of his own views.[18] At the Naval Academy, as captain of the midshipmen's basketball team, his reputation for physical agility compensated for less-than-average stature. As his career progressed, "Hoke" Smith's agility became intellectual. He served at sea in both world wars, taking the battleship *South Dakota* to fight in the Marshall Islands as its CO in 1944, thence to Iwo Jima and Okinawa. Following that he was assigned as chief of staff to Admiral Spruance, president of the Naval War College. That experience, coupled with his long interest in foreign relations, made Smith a Renaissance man within the Navy, politically adept and with a broader worldview than most of his peers. He got on well with Spruance, sharing with him the characteristics of poise, intelligent decision making, and rigorous attention to detail.[19]

Unlike the modest Spruance, who disliked publicity in any form, Admiral Smith saw great benefit in well-conducted public relations. Appointed to Commander Battleships-Cruisers Force Atlantic Fleet (ComBatCruLant) in 1949, he used that position to nudge forward his conviction that missile-carrying cruisers were better suited than big-gun battleships in support of the new, fast carriers. With only one battleship in the Navy, he felt that his title, Commander Battleships-Cruisers, was inappropriate, and changed it to the less-than-inclusive ComCruLant. He was, of course, familiar with the value placed on the last survivor. He didn't propose to give it up; instead he used it to advance another idea. Smith felt it important to broaden the training of career officers beyond regular naval requirements. They should develop a sense of the world, he contended, an understanding of the countries they could be called on to defend or to fight. Further, the Navy ought to be proud to show off its forces around the globe. From these premises, the admiral devised a plan to use the *Missouri* as his flagship on two midshipmen's cruises out of Annapolis to Europe during the summer of 1949. He was never far from that august vessel, and on the afternoon of the grounding he joined it again.

Two days before his fifty-eighth birthday, Rear Admiral Smith moved himself and part of his staff into flag quarters aboard the stranded ship. He would be far more comfortable there, he decided, some distance from his peers—ten shored-based admirals who could see the ship from the upper stories of their quarters on Dillingham Boulevard.[20] He didn't need the repartee of "Gold-Dust Row." They would be quick to remind him of how he had dropped the word "battleship" from his own title. "Hoke," they would say to their classmate and associate, "are you about to make your title precise?" They would recall his discussions at the War College about the obsolescence of current-day battleships, how they were suitable for little more than training. They knew he saw guided-missile cruisers as faster and more economical than battleships. All, that is, except the president's own. That one, Smith proposed, might continue to serve if it too were fitted with guided missiles—a convenient compromise. In the light of his expressed views, the current situation added a touch of irony to his challenge.

But Allan Smith was troubled as his white barge, with its two-starred, blue admiral's flag flying above shining brass, pulled along-side the *Missouri*'s grey hull. Blackened fenders and loose lines hung over the side, the new paint already dirty and scuffed by the craft that had hastened to work beside it; this was not the pride of the cruiser forces. Slanting steeply down the side of the hull, an accommodation ladder lowered to the extent of its falls ended high above the choppy water. Next to it hung a Jacob's ladder, enabling precarious access to the boarding ladder's lower platform.

In his long, olive foul-weather jacket, the admiral clambered from the launch onto the swaying rope ladder, swung up some ten feet and over to the companionway, and climbed hurriedly to the quarterdeck. Eight sideboys piped him aboard to the trill of a boatswain's whistle. Saluting the quarterdeck, the admiral had to feel daunted by the task he faced. Observing the distress flags at the yardarm, he noted also that the battle efficiency pennant, once flown so proudly by the war-ship, had been struck.

With all the prestige of his rank, a flag officer normally remains a passenger on his division's flagship, staying aloof from the specific operations of the ship that carries him. Salvage requirements change the circumstances. Under traditional maritime practice, when a sal-vage master comes aboard with the express intent of saving the vessel, the captain gives up operational control. But it is rare for a Navy cap-tain to relinquish command. While Captain Brown remained com-manding officer of his ship, he came effectively under the direction of Admiral Smith, not in the capacity of ComCruLant but as director of salvage operations. Thus Smith, all but nominal captain of the ship, would exercise more direct control in the latter capacity than he would have as fleet commander.

The admiral and captain maintained an agreeable silence as to the cause of the mishap. *Navy Regulations* require the convening of a court of inquiry following any incident of grounding. That was high on Smith's agenda, after more urgent matters fell into place. Mean-while he asked Brown and his staff only for those details pertinent to an assessment of the condition of the ship and the Navy's concerted efforts to refloat it.

Admiral Blandy's appointment had interesting ramifications. Smith would have time enough later to reflect on the ironies. Now he needed to sort out the relevant issues, first among them being his own lack of salvage experience. The Navy's salvaging capability, while perhaps the best in the world, was spotty. It was the nature of the beast: unpredictable needs, little focus of talent. Some skills were retained in the Construction Battalion (the well-known Seabees), and service forces included shipyards and rescue ships, but beyond the headquarters staff, support for the saving of ships was not centralized. Two small salvage schools, one for each ocean, operated out of Bayonne, New Jersey, and Pearl Harbor. Specialized equipment was widely distributed, typically housed near where it was last used. The problem with maintaining a peacetime salvage organization is one of location. How do you identify where disaster will strike? In wartime, salvage forces focused on the perimeters of battle, often entering embattled ports to start work alongside the Seabees even before the areas were fully secured. In peacetime, determination of where and how to distribute salvage vessels and to base the skills to use the equipment amounts to a costly gamble. The strategy, if there was one, was to make do when something happened. In his first, hastily called conference with Captain Brown, the CO of the *Kittiwake,* and Captain Treakle from the naval base, Smith made do by calling for three salvage ships to come down from New York and requesting the services of an Army dredge, the latter request made with some chagrin.

Brown deferred making a detailed announcement to the *Missouri's* crew about the state of affairs until after the initial meeting with his commanding officer. Before the start of the second attempt to pull the vessel free, a somber voice came on the loudspeakers with a carefully worded speech stating the obvious and outlining the work ahead. No cause was given for the mishap. There was no prediction of when the ship would be afloat. A period in the shipyard was certain, and that would determine participation, if any, in Portrex. Perhaps to imply that the ship would soon be headed to sea, no liberty was being granted. That about answered everything for the time, but failed to belay the scuttlebutt. Every word that had traveled on the talkers' wires during the morning was recounted; the scene from every angle on the brief passage across the water was described; fifty or so partial witnesses became a hundred and fifty reporters and grew to five hundred experts on recovery.

After sunset more tugs, now fourteen in number, were harnessed for the second pull.[21] The night signal for a vessel aground near a fairway, two vertical red lights, glowed from the top of the mainmast above bright lights gleaming along the *Missouri*'s decks. Nestled in a cluster of service craft, the ship had lost much of its dignity. Electricity delivered from the *Kittiwake* made line handling easier than it had been in the morning. The haul began in darkness before high tide. Towing hawsers radiated from the ship's sides and rounded stern, stretched taught as the tugs worked up to full power. Searchlights beamed along the lines, shifting from wake to boiling wake. Wide, white streams surged forward around the ship, making it seem to those peering over the side that the hull was moving sternward. For an hour the tugboats danced on their hawsers like waterborne kites, but again to no avail.

Car traffic at Buckroe Beach grew heavier as thousands of spectators flocked to the shore.[22] Boating activity increased around Old Point Comfort. Ignoring wintry weather and darkness, small craft motored out of Hampton Creek, a narrow fishing port a few miles to the west. By dawn it seemed that no one under way hesitated from cruising among the naval vessels to gain a closer look at activity around the big ship. Members of the press, newsreel cameramen, and radio reporters strove unsuccessfully to board the battleship; many visited other ships in the vicinity.[23] Early on the day after the grounding, onlookers were startled to see what appeared to be a cargo ship, tall stack amidship with housing forward, hull high in the water, steaming at full speed down the Bay and headed directly for the *Missouri*. The seagoing dredge *Comber,* a spotless 352-foot ship, was hardly distinguishable from a freighter but for wide steel pipes slung along each side. A twin-screw vessel able to make over seventeen knots when empty, the Army dredge had traversed the 150-mile route from Baltimore in a hectic nine hours. Under the civilian command of Capt. Andrew Knudsen, its crew of seventy-five men had worked it down the Bay in record time. The persistent shoaling of channels at the *Comber*'s regular station in the upper Bay would have to be tolerated or cleared by other vessels.[24]

Col. G. T. Derby, U.S. Army, the District Army Engineer, accompanied by Herbert Rice of Planning and Dredging, boarded the battleship to arrange for the *Comber*'s support. Seated at a large table, Admiral Smith outlined his first estimate of needs. A level exit channel, 35 feet deep at low water and 150 feet wide, must be dug in a straight line from the stern of the battleship to the natural channel. This would be routine work for Knudsen and his crew; he had done similar trenching off Cape Henry during the war. There, when a tanker was split in two by a mine, Knudsen had been called to dredge out the sunken stern for salvage.

Aboard his own ship, pipe clenched between his teeth, a slide rule and chart before him, the stocky Knudsen was in radio touch with the Army team on the *Missouri.* He explained that his drags could suck up thirty-three hundred cubic yards of sand in eighteen minutes: they'd need perhaps two days to do the job, working around the clock. First, said the admiral, a trench had to be dug around the hull, and that had to be done without interfering with other vessels alongside, so the drags should begin at the bow; more tankers and lighters were scheduled, and divers would be going down soon. After tunneling out the sides, work could be started on the exit channel. Whatever tensions might have existed between Army and Navy, they were eased in that first meeting as the two groups agreed on their mutual goals. The big "mudsucker" set its drags and went to work. Through the day and into the night it could be seen and heard from the shore, steadily plowing around the *Missouri* while other service craft arrived and left. Small craft carrying the curious continued to circle the site. They emerged solemnly out of the darkness, hovered nearby in the loom of lights, and just as solemnly departed.

Preparing to save a stranded ship matches in some way the preparation for warfare itself. Little will be accomplished without a positive approach to the task. There can be no wide-eyed, wishful thinking; good, solid plans must be made, adversity anticipated, contingencies thought out, a can-do attitude maintained. Inherently an optimist, Allan Smith quickly claimed the *Missouri*'s mishap presented a chance to display Navy capability in planning and executing a branch of seamanship in which few had experience. He also sensed a more significant opportunity. Gaining the cooperation of other services, as he was already doing, would directly support the new Chief of Naval Operations at a difficult time. Under congressional pressure to unify the services, the Joint Chiefs had recently been told to stop their squabbling and make unification happen. In spite of differences among the units, the salvage task called for tactful work with the Army Corps of Engineers, responsible for dredging operations in inland waters; with the Coast Guard, responsible for buoyage and free passage of ships within Chesapeake Bay; and with multiple departments of the Navy for immense and varied support on what would be a tight schedule. Smith considered and quickly rejected the possibility of putting out civilian contracts for refloating the ship, although on the next day he would be presented with that option in a curious way.

The next concern the admiral faced was that of handling the public's queries and cries during an awkward time. After four years of peace, public relations was not the sharply honed skill it had been in wartime. While forces were being reduced, military press releases were oriented more to anniversaries, interunit sports, and charitable activities. The Atlantic Fleet's public relations office issued the first brief information within hours of the grounding, along with an aerial photo, putting the disaster in full public view. The convergence of the tugboat fleet made the news wires in time for the evening papers on the day of the mishap. The *St. Louis Post-Dispatch* carried a front-page article and a Defense Department photo of the beleaguered ship surrounded by tugs. By Wednesday morning the story was on the front page of most major papers. "NAVY'S MIGHTY WARSHIP CAUGHT FAST," cried the *New York Times*. Coverage was thorough, with little left unexplained about the ship's condition. Initial public reaction was largely sympathetic; however, people's curiosity was aroused by the Navy's limited explanation of the circumstances contributing to the accident. Attribution of the cause to engine failure was quickly denied. Early news items said this was Captain Brown's first sea voyage and that he had operated without a harbor pilot. The first item was imprecise, and the second reflected common practice. The appointment of Lt. Comdr. Joe Wornom, assistant public information officer for the Fifth Naval District, to take charge of the press was timely.[25] Potential publicity about the acoustic range troubled Navy officials. The two range buoys known among Chesapeake pilots and both civilian and Navy mariners were hardly matters of public interest. Their purpose remained classified information, not fully explained even to ship captains who had agreed to pass through them. Wornom would have to do his best to divert interest. Unless the vessel was refloated soon, attention was certain to focus on the range. Add to that the current strife within the Navy, from the top

80

down, centering on massive cutbacks and the retirement of limited-use vessels. A prolonged midwinter salvage effort of this symbol of American fighting power would certainly be kept alive in the news, a situation unlikely to be to the Navy's advantage.

Smith's two top issues went hand in hand. A quick and successful salvage effort could avert bad publicity, might even become propitious. Anything but a quick resolution could undermine the Navy's interests for years. Putting America's best-known warship back to work as soon as humanly possible, and at the smallest cost, became critically important, not just to Admiral Smith but to the future of the U.S. Navy.

Safety of the vessel was not an immediate concern, nor was it urgent to restore it to service in a fleet devoted chiefly to training. One could rationalize that the salvage effort itself would enable ample training exercises. National security might justify haste, but with supercarriers eclipsing the utility of battleships that argument would be weak. The foremost reason for urgency, unspoken, was to save the face of the Navy at a time when its fleets were threatened with severe cutbacks. Since the end of the war, work to refit the uncommissioned *Kentucky* as a guided-missile cruiser—activity tactfully advocated by Admiral Smith—had been irregular. Even now, with its reconversion nearly 80 percent complete, Congress wavered on final appropriations. What of the cost to do this additional job?

After the tugs pulled away following the second attempt, a Navy diver went down from the *Kittiwake* to assess the extent of damage to the battleship's hull. When one carried an underwater torch into the deep, night or day mattered little. Hearing the preliminary report, Smith asked for a return to the seafloor and evaluation of the use of high-pressure hoses for tunneling under the flat-bottomed hull to supplement the dredge's work. Navy Master Diver Raymond Shaw descended from the *Kittiwake* with nine others.[26] Tunneling work would be risky and chilly, edging under the hull in thirty feet of murky 48° water. Self-contained underwater breathing apparatus had not yet been perfected. Divers wore suits of rubberized canvas below heavy bronze headpieces. They remained tied to their tender as they plodded in leaden boots around the long hull, drawing air from pumps on the rescue ship. The tender would have no difficulty delivering massive quantities of water through high-pressure hoses. If it were to be done, the tunneling job would set a record, becoming the largest such operation ever attempted. The divers surfaced to describe a bottom of hard-packed sand, having the consistency of loose concrete. Incidentally, they reported, there was no damage to the four giant screws; those were well above the ground. That was positive news for the salvers.

Traffic in the waters around the *Missouri* quickly became a logistical headache. Tankers, lighters, rescue and supply ships, launches, and tugs idled nearby, vying for tie-up time. Forlorn as it may have been, the big ship was never without company. A minute-by-minute schedule was drawn up for execution by the officer of the deck, who worked like a headwaiter arranging tables in an overpopulated eatery. As boats approached, their appointments were confirmed through loud-hailers or by TBS. Line handlers were called to stand by the battleship's railings with fenders, hoses, and cables rigged and ready. Messenger lines flew across the water, and within minutes the craft nestled alongside, rendering the required service. A garbage barge was needed regularly to haul away the refuse of over fifteen hundred people. Newspapers and mail were delivered twice daily, those bundles the crew's best source of information about their own ship. It rankled those with close-by families to have to correspond via the fleet post office when they were practically in sight of one another. Liberty? Not for now; there was much to be done aboard.

Smith likened his challenge to the job of moving the RCA building, as high as the *Missouri* was long, with all its people and furnishings, a half mile beyond Rockefeller Center.[27] He organized the operation into three interdependent activities: increase the ship's buoyancy, dredge an exit channel, then pull the ship off the bank into the channel. He expected that the work could be done using routine salvage techniques, even if they must resort to every method currently known. To bring that off as expeditiously as possible he established a schedule of twice-daily planning meetings, to be followed until the ship was safely afloat.

In an early discussion with Commander Zoeller, the battleship's chief engineering officer, Smith learned that the main plant would have to remain inoperative until the ship could be dry-docked for investigation and repairs to its cooling system. That eliminated his most useful salvage method. Theoretically, if a ship's plant has not used its full forward power in going aground, and if it can summon up, even briefly, maximum power astern, the possibility exists that it can back itself off. The deep-keeled Confederate ship *Virginia* had done just that in these very waters during its battle with the *Monitor.* Friction along the bottom is the major resistive force to overcome, unless the hull has been impaled on rocks. No rocks were known to exist in the vicinity, and none had been reported by the divers. A sample of gravelly sand, the "loose concrete" reported by the divers, was taken from the *Comber*'s hold for examination. Admiral Smith wanted a shoreside study of the coefficient of friction between flat steel plating and densely packed course sand, stuff later to be given the quasi-scientific name of "Missouri sand." The hull rested on a gradual slope, wedged into the crevasse it had carved. Could it be simply budged at the next suitable tide? If so, there was hope that by overcoming its inertia the ship would be started in motion, and then, with a strong pull, might slide off the slope into deeper water. The information gained from the friction study would help Smith assess his adversary, the bottom of Chesapeake Bay. Without backing power, his weapon of choice in dueling with the adversary was the pull of a yet-to-be-determined number of tugboats.

Tidal lift was his next countermeasure. Possibly enough fuel could be discharged to compensate for diminishing tidal ranges through the next ten days. Weather might be helpful if it should push extra water down the Bay. There was little early prospect for that, but winter weather often brings northeasters, the most likely source of abnormal tidal range. The rarity of seamen hoping for heavy northeast weather became a reality.

The admiral asked the Coast and Geodetic Office for more detailed tidal reports than were customarily available. After the failure of the second pull, he specified that tidal gauges able to measure changes in draft to the quarter inch be placed alongside the hull. He wanted a balance sheet, listing real and projected tidal range in one column, the ship's current and attainable gross tonnage in the other. Assets and liabilities, they would identify the extent of remaining effort in terms of weight to be removed and the window of time in which to do it. Could tidal gauges be sufficiently accurate in the Bay's normal chop? The Navy Yard must make them such that readings in fractions of an inch could be taken. One such gauge driven into the bottom forward of the ship's stem would serve as a standard to enable detection of even the slightest horizontal and vertical shifts.

In his mind's eye Smith clearly saw the dynamics of the task—offloading rate in tons moved per hour matched against a diminishing curve of rising and falling tides, every twelve hours a helpful lift, finally one that would do the job; external horizontal forces matched against the inertia of heavy metal pressing against coarse, wet sand, ultimately a force strong enough to make up any gap not met by the tide. In time the tidal curves would trend upward. Men and muscle would win over mud. It was critical to learn the effect each action would have. He intended to identify the exact minute of flotation.

A calendar before him, the admiral said that within two days he wanted the gauges in place, fuel off-loaded, the exit trench dug, and towing plans outlined in finest details, with all assisting vessels listed. The naval base and its full-service facilities were within easy radio touch. Auxiliary ships had gone to work within an hour of the mishap. The Army was cooperating splendidly. By Friday the Coast Guard would have a lighted range buoy placed forward of the ship and the exit channel astern similarly buoyed. That would help in controlling traffic, especially at night. The ship was practically upright on a smooth, predictable bottom, in generally protected waters and well clear of normal shipping lanes. Meanwhile, Commander Zoeller reported the restoration of a second turbo generator. Feed water from the ship's own supply and later that from a water tanker would supply the boilers. Clouds of steam soon issued from both stacks as the generators produced ample electricity to keep the ship habitable. The shocked and silent *Mo* had been roused into consciousness and was ready for a quick recovery.

From the beginning, Smith consulted with Rear Adm. Homer Wallin, commander of the Norfolk Naval Shipyard. It was Wallin who, six weeks earlier, had joined Admiral Smith at the installation of Captain Brown as CO of the *Missouri*. Wallin was a recognized salvage expert, conveniently nearby, and the next day he came aboard as deputy salvage director.

The sparse history of salvage parallels the history of iron warships.[28] Admiral Wallin earned a measure of fame with the work he did in World War II. Following his efforts in clearing the destruction from Pearl Harbor he became highly regarded as a salvage consultant. That work combines the ingenuity of trained sailors with the use of highly specialized equipment. They must be able to deliver where and when needed, precisely. After nearly a century, the U.S. Navy was probably the world's expert, although people like Wallin were rare in the fleet.

The development of the ironclad steamship first generated the need for formal training in salvage and the identification of specialized salvage organizations. Metal construction and steam propulsion limited a fleet's mobility by the demand for fuel, water, and mechanical repairs. Powered tugboats, operating out of naval repair centers, often rendered assistance to stranded vessels, but they could do so only within their own cruising range.

By 1860, losses and wrecks in the prosperous shipping industry exceeded the ability of skilled salvers to keep up. The work attracted opportunists, who often did more harm than good, lacking seamanship and engineering skills. Thirty-five American ships were being wrecked per month, hundreds of lives lost, millions of dollars wasted. Marine underwriters, determined to put salvage work on a businesslike basis, formed a commercial wrecking company under Israel J. Merritt, equipping his Gloucester mackerel schooner with $8,000 worth of specialized equipment. But naval salvage work developed irregularly during the last quarter of the century, the Navy relying heavily on commercial salvers. With a single exception, those companies were based on the Atlantic coast. The Merritt organization, later Merritt-Chapman and Scott, operated a salvage station at San Pedro, California, for twenty years. The Navy was fully dependent on it for its Pacific recoveries. But by 1938, with less-active naval operations, there was insufficient work to make it profitable and Merritt closed the base. Compelled to develop internal capability to sustain its Pacific Fleet, the Navy decided to establish a formal salvage school at Pearl Harbor. It was a well-timed decision. On 7 December 1941 most of the school's original candidates were awaiting transportation from San Francisco. Pearl Harbor forced the issue. A week after the attack the Navy Salvage Service was established in a tightly worded contract with Merritt-Chapman and Scott, the principal contractor.

Then within two months something happened that would lodge disdainfully in public memory. The new service took on its largest and best-known single-ship salvage job following the strange loss of the USS *Lafayette*. The 65,000-ton French liner *Normandie* had been requisitioned by the United States upon entry into the war, and was renamed *Lafayette* when the Navy took it over for conversion to a troopship. Berthed at Pier 88, passenger row on New York's Hudson River, famous for the docking of glamorous European ocean liners, in February 1942 the ship caught fire. The New York Fire Department, concerned that the fire would spread to the city, insisted on pouring water onto it. Expressing equal concern that the ship would capsize in its berth, officials of the Third Naval District pleaded with Mayor La Guardia that the fire department desist. That raised the question of who would be responsible for subsequent damage to the city. Feisty La Guardia called President Roosevelt, asking him to force the Navy to take responsibility. The president refused. The mayor, a fire-fighting buff, backed up his chief and told him to put the fire out. During the subsequent firefighting efforts, after tons of water filled the ship to its waterline, the *Lafayette* did capsize, rolling over in its berth nearly 80° into icy water. The public witnessed it all—the bickering, the failures, the loss of a famous liner, and the suspicion-charged inquiries that followed.

It was never precisely determined what had caused the *Lafayette*'s fire. In the hysteria of the nation's new state of war, sabotage was suspected, but it is more likely attributable to conversion work that had been going on throughout the ship. The work of righting, refloating, and ultimately scrapping the grand ship fell to the new Navy Salvage Service. Large amounts of manpower were needed, but such could hardly be drawn from the busy and equally inexperienced Pacific forces in Hawaii. It made sense to establish a school for both Navy and civilian salvers at Pier 88, and thus was born the Navy Salvage School. Wartime incidents had suddenly introduced formal training with actual work in both oceans. Pearl Harbor remained the base for Pacific operations, and there Homer Wallin did his first good work on saving surviving battleships. After the war the Salvage Service became effectively the staffs of the two schools. The Atlantic school gave up its high-rent space in Manhattan and moved to Bayonne, New Jersey. It was to Admiral Wallin and to the Bayonne Salvage School that the *Missouri*'s director of salvage went for help.

Comparisons were certain to be made with earlier events. Lingering in public memory was not just the fiasco of the *Normandie* but the

1939 tragedy of the submarine *Squalus,* the Navy's last major peacetime salvage effort. Those who remembered it were apt to confuse the near loss of the sub and deaths of some of the crew members with the heroic salvage efforts that followed. The sub foundered in deep water off the Maine coast while on a training cruise. Thirty-three crew members were saved by using a new rescue chamber, but the sub was too deep to raise in time to save the twenty-six men in the damaged after portion of the hull. The sub's initial depth limited the amount of work divers could accomplish in the chilly water. Day by day for nearly two months the public followed the divers' work as pontoons developed expressly for the situation were cabled to the sunken vessel. Six hundred and forty-eight dives were made, four of the divers winning the Medal of Honor for heroism. Finally, after one failed attempt to lift it, the sub was brought to the surface and towed to dry dock in Portsmouth, New Hampshire. Recommissioned as the USS *Sailfish,* it served admirably in the Pacific throughout World War II. A fickle public could well recall the losses and overlook the immense gains that were made in salvage technology.

Would the *Missouri* be a replay of naval failures in the public view? Good news is boring. Heroics command space only when histories are written. News predators thrive on tragedy, foibles, and risk. As it happened, something did occur that served to divert the public's attention. A $1.5 million Brink's holdup, the largest bank robbery on record, had taken place in Boston on the same day as the grounding, and a national manhunt was under way. The public relations office of the Atlantic Fleet gained a bit of breathing room.

What caused the *Missouri*'s grounding, and how soon would it be afloat? The task of the public relations office was to focus on the challenge of returning it to the fleet. Lt. Comdr. M. W. Ross, Wornom's counterpart on Admiral Blandy's staff, made no promises as he stood in for Admiral Smith in responding to the press. Patiently he arranged to bring dozens of reporters, newsreel cameramen, and photographers to the site aboard Navy boats, and by that won their cooperation. They had his assurance that as much information as was issued from the salvage director's daily conferences would be shared with them. Attention now was on refloating, not on contributing causes.

Opportunists emerged early. On the evening of the day Smith took charge, Thomas Little contacted the Virginia papers to announce his bid to the Navy. Identifying himself as head of the Thomas Little Ship Repair Company in Berkeley, "with an interest in the Submarine Engineering Company," he said that he had offered to refloat the grounded ship and return her to dock under a bonded $200,000 contract. He went on to say that a company diver had surveyed the vessel and discovered it stuck in "a sub-soil condition" that would make the *Mo* "a monument in Hampton Roads" unless it was properly handled. According to the diver's report, the ship sat in a mixture of sand, blue clay, and mud. Little criticized the Navy's early efforts to lighten the vessel, claiming they were doing things the wrong way. "They should be putting more weight on her to squeeze out the sub-soil."[29]

Admiral Smith ignored Little's comments. Considering the extent of traffic alongside the *Missouri* all day Wednesday, the arrival of the *Comber,* and the presence of Navy divers lowered from the *Kittiwake* still later in the day, Little's diver must have had a distant view.

The next day the owner of the Submarine Engineering Company, Capt. L. H. Barnes, submitted his own position to the press. He said that he had made no earlier statement regarding the battleship or the Navy's attempt to refloat it. Nor had he authorized any official of his company to comment on the operation. "The man in charge of the refloating probably has good and sufficient reasons for any operations they may take. My company has made no inspection and has no intention of doing so."[30]

The refloating plan gradually fell into place. Admiral Smith had reduced it to the simplest: lighten the ship, dig a trench, count on the highest available tide, then haul the ship off at its height. But he named no specific time for success. Each task had several detailed elements, many required the delivery of special equipment, and most called for strenuous labor. Smith sensed almost from the beginning that two weeks would elapse before he could bring everything together and achieve success. A review of the tables showed that the next tides matching those of the seventeenth and eighteenth would not occur until the second of February, Admiral Blandy's retirement date. A sense of urgency must be maintained—there would be no sitting around waiting for the ideal opportunity. It could occur tomorrow! He kept the preparations going, in priority order.

After scooping around the bow on Wednesday, the *Comber* started carving side trenches and an eighteen-hundred-foot channel astern of the battleship. Throughout the night its pumps sucked up a stream of gravel and sand that roared stridently into its metal hold, pausing only long enough to spread the load among the hoppers. Once filled, the dredge raised its drags and pushed off to nearby dumping grounds. Minutes later it was back, puttering like a trot-line crabber along the lengthening channel, shattering the air with the grating sound of cascading gravel. Men on the ship got little sleep. By morning the trench around the hull had been excavated as far as the dredge's drags could reach. The divers had reported favorably on the proposed plan to use high-pressure hydraulic jets to complete the tunnel. There was merit to Little's theory of squeezing out the mud under the hull. Smith's idea was to leave the wide ship on a pedestal. He hoped that, by adding ballast to the after end, the weight of the ship would lever loosened sand forward. That should raise the bow, which they now knew was tightly wedged into the sea bottom. Initially weight could hardly be added to a fully laden ship. And they remained unaware of the stresses that redistribution would put on the keel. Tidal gauges, when fixed in place, could help them measure that.

Lighters came alongside and removed both fifteen-ton anchors, along with three hundred fathoms of chain, over eighty-four tons off the bow. By Friday the ship's fuel and water would be reduced by eight thousand tons. The *Comber* would have cleared away all but a wall of sand under the counter, and the smaller, civilian dredge *Washington* would scrape that out. The salvagers raced against a scheduled tide of uncertain height. An outside chance existed that a marginally higher range in the next few days would suit the lightened ship. Twenty towing vessels were scheduled for that possibility, over two hundred people put on alert. Two maritime muscle men, the submarine rescue ships *Windlass* and *Salvager,* were added to the roster, booked to lend assistance with beach gear. The plan was for them to kedge heavy bow anchors into the seafloor far aft of the stranded ship, then take a towing position along with the other tugs at the end of thick cables extending to the ship's stern. While applying full forward power on their towing lines, they would also draw up on their anchors: the irresistible force on the immovable object. Something had to give.

Smith had asked for too much. There just wasn't enough time for everything to be in place for the massive pull-off. If things looked favorable the salvagers should be ready to attempt it. Failing that, the admiral already had an alternate plan. What concerned him was that he still didn't have a grasp on the ebb and flow of water around the hull. He was convinced that a section of the battleship lifted from the bottom with each rising tide—not enough to heave off entirely, but perhaps enough to reduce frictional resistance to the tugboats. Until he could track precisely the rise and fall of the tide, and the motion of the ship within it, he couldn't compile an accurate balance sheet. The tidal gauges would not be installed until late in the week, perhaps coincident with the hoped-for favorable tide. He needed more information on the forces necessary to overcome the friction on the bottom. He was aware that these unknowns were not apt to be offset by cooperative surges of ocean water. But the admiral kept the pressure on, insisting on daily constructive progress.

Thursday the wind shifted to northeast, blessedly dirty weather, blowing bitter and strong throughout the day. That and the arrival aboard of salvage expert Wallin heartened Allan Smith. His optimism was expressed in his 2100 report to CinCLantFlt: "Fair to good chance of earliest success to refloat . . . rainy nasty northeast wind building up favorable tide."[31] Astutely he hedged his bets, planning for the subsequent use of the *Squalus* pontoons currently stored in Boston. The tidal gauges were scheduled for placement late Friday, after the scheduled attempt to float the ship. Perhaps they wouldn't be needed.

The battleship had been stranded for three full days while derision mounted in the press. One writer had unearthed the fact that "Missouri" was the Native American term for "big muddy." It would be called the "USS Misery," the "Once-Mighty Mo," and "General Mud," with a new reputation as murky as the water in which it wallowed.

Friday's tide was predicted to be within three inches of that at the grounding. Calculations led the salvage team to assume 11,700 tons of deadweight resisted their planned efforts. The combination portended well. A heavier flood might add four inches more to what it had been on the fateful morning, each inch lifting 150 tons. The conquest of inertia and friction depended on some five hundred tons of horizontal pulling force.

Again the admiral and his staff assessed the pluses and minuses. Through the prior night divers had done their work with the high-pressure tunneling hoses. The ship sat on a broad pedestal, the edges of which were caving in. Lacking accurate vertical measurements, the extent to which this settled the ship was uncertain. The remaining broad hillock of sand might crumble if motion was started. Eight to nine inches of excessive tide was necessary to supplement a calculated horizontal force of five hundred tons, enough perhaps to budge the ship from the shoal. Up to seven inches of lift might develop, and a collapse of the sandbank could make the difference. The *Comber* had not completed the exit channel, but if the battleship floated it could be held in the trench dredged to its stern. In all it was a testy situation, but with increasing urgency for refloating Smith felt it was worth the effort.

Tide waits for no one. At 0630 the tugs were positioned. Then *Salvager* reported that it was unable to rig its beach gear in time. It could work only as a conventional pulling tug. *Windlass* fouled a towing wire and would be unable to pull. By 1000, when the pull started, nineteen vessels were harnessed to the *Missouri,* their lines extended from the after part of the ship like ribs of a broken fan, at balanced but irregular angles.[32] Hills of white water heaved up from their sterns. Wide streams of roiling water again surged along the sides of the motionless grey hull as the helpless vessel waited for an urge to move.

Crews of twenty ships and the salvage team watched tensely as tugs pushed at the warship's bow and strained hawsers astern. Sailors hung on the rails of the stranded vessel, looking aft, adding their mental English to the struggling tugs, pouring determination into every imagined tremble of the hull.[33]

Any child who has played at the seashore or along a riverbank knows the pull of wet sand. Feet sink readily up to the ankles into the muck. Extra muscle and a wiggle is needed to get free from the mud's suction. An ancient practice, sallying ship, is sometimes effective in freeing grounded vessels. By rhythmically shifting shipboard weight from side to side, providing the wiggle, the hull can be worked free of the suction holding it in place. The crew's total weight had been calculated, 102 tons. A third of them were deployed on the foredeck, as many aft, in tightly scheduled periods at half-hour intervals. On the broad fantail they were arranged in two fore-and-aft units, one amidship, one to the side. To the cadence of a CPO poised on the projection booth, they hustled half the width of the ship to port or starboard, shifting the phalanx on the rail to midship, the midship one to the opposite side. Foreward and aft, nearly sixty tons of humanity carefully orchestrated in three shifts, scurried from side to side at precisely called six-second intervals, long waves of sailors in winter clothing, swashing across the wooden deck under the massive guns, their breath in cloudy puffs. Most of the men had a rollicking good time, but the mud beneath them kept its grip.[34]

At 1145 the salvage director shook his head grimly and ordered the tug engines stopped. Immediately he called for a meeting. He would invoke his alternate plan, one that was to culminate at the high tide of 2 February, what the admiral considered his last chance for success.

Three attempts. Three failures. Admiral Blandy wanted a forecast. Rear Admiral Smith's noon report stated that he was "optimistic of refloating *Missouri* 2 February the next favorable high tide." Extraordinary effort was needed, including a plan to "unload ammunition and stores and unneeded personnel." He was determined that nothing would deter him from meeting Blandy's date.

5

Pinioned

From the hour of the grounding an uneasy mood had overshadowed the battleship's wardroom. Deck and engineering officers skipped the cold meals, arrived late, and departed early. The work they faced provided a pretext to avoid any semblance of sociability. Enlisted men, in a funereal spirit, were on their tenderest behavior. Sweepdowns and eight o'clock reports were punctually observed with meticulous attention to detail. Sailors stood watches with the rigor of a crew approaching battle. In its travail the black-shoe Navy was behaving its best.

The admiral routinely ate in flag quarters, where he was often joined by members of his staff. Captain Brown had his private mess, and unless duties required him elsewhere he secluded himself in his quarters. Commander Peckham, whose behavior as executive officer was well known to the crew, seemed far more attentive. He was all over the ship, at each quarterdeck attending to arrivals alongside, forward checking lines and chafing gear, aft seeing to the cleanliness of an easily cluttered deck, deep in the hull examining the status of watertight doors, high in the conning tower reviewing logs and notebooks, in the radio shack turning over dispatches, and persistently conferring with watch officers, chiefs, and visitors from assisting ships. It seemed impossible to avoid him, except in the wardroom, where his presence was rarely seen.

The enlisted men ate better than they might have expected. After the first meals of cold cuts, they got more fresh fruit, milk, and bread than normal sea fare, more ice cream and pies. Reducing the quantity of provisions destined for unloading may well have bolstered morale. It would hardly reduce the work ahead. Hopes had grown as the

third attempt to free the ship approached, only to be dashed following its failure. Attempting to justify the futile effort to sally ship, some
claimed they had sensed left-right motion of the hull. After all, one
sailor said, thirty tons of deadweight vectored by half the beam of the
ship was a powerful lever. "Deadweight" proved to be an inflamma-
tory word to his weary shipmates. They had off-loaded 2.25 million
gallons of black oil and 60,000 gallons of diesel oil, more than 8,000
tons of fuel in all. In the firerooms, machinist's mates and boiler tend-
ers were put to work overseeing fuel pumps that heated up as the
saltwater cooling lines routinely filled with sand. Every fifteen minutes they were forced to shut down the pumps, flush the lines and
resume pumping in a seemingly endless cycle.[1] As they sought some
return for their efforts, speculation circulated that forward and after
sections of the great hull were lifting with the tide.

In Norfolk, Admiral Blandy waited no longer for results from
Hampton Roads. While tugs struggled to free the ship, he issued an
order for Rear Admiral Smith as ComCruLant to convene a court of
inquiry.[2] Smith was in the unusual position of having to select and
direct those who would find the cause of the problem he had been
assigned to solve. The court was charged to find and sort out the facts
concerning the accident and report them with recommendations to
ComCruLant, who in turn would review and take actions warranted
by the findings. Court members were named, but the admiral
deferred formal proceedings until salvage work was completed.

Allan Smith had a problem of his own, one that grew with each
day of warship immobility. A court of inquiry might dismiss a simple
touch-and-back-off grounding as an unfortunate incident, attributing
it chiefly to the ill-defined range buoys, but each failed effort to
refloat the ship magnified the gravity of the mishap. Questions of
competence, and worse still, malicious intent, could arise. Washington lately wallowed in paranoia. Thus far most public reaction to the
predicament was supportive, but how long could that last? A lengthy
period of adverse news might well arouse wild suspicions. It was Rear
Admiral Smith who had appointed Captain Brown to command. He
had been responsible for ensuring that Brown's qualifications were
adequate. What if culpability of captain and crew were established?
The extent of guilt could well be proportional to the length of the
Comber's channel and the extent of trouble encountered in getting

the ship to deep water. Could the wrong man have been chosen? Smith would have to answer to Admiral Blandy for the effect of his selection.

Blandy made clear that he had no intention of deferring his retirement beyond the second of February. The fleet admiral would turn over his command before that appointed day. Smith, exercising some bravado, committed to that date based on his observations after the third failed pull. Although stuck fast, the ship appeared unharmed. A simple hull inspection in dry dock while the sea chests were being flushed might be accomplished in time to put the ship back in service and on its way to Guantánamo. Such had been Smith's hope until Friday, a hope that dwindled as he terminated the latest pulling attempt. Now he was uncertain whether he could free the ship prior to the arrival of the new commander of the Atlantic Fleet.

As director of salvage operations, Smith quickly established a tightly structured organization under his deputy, Rear Admiral Wallin. He temporarily assigned his own new chief of staff, Capt. Roland Smoot, to Wallin as chief of staff, to be the one to whom all salvage operations and planning officers would report directly. Smoot, who had reported for duty to ComCruLant only days before the accident, now found himself in a fully unanticipated role. Smith and Wallin were of the same rank, but it was Wallin who had the know-how and naval connections on matters of salvage. Dredging, diving, towing, laying of beach gear, intership communications, and the rigging of pontoons made up the operations activity, while Lt. J. B. Drachnik, Admiral Smith's aide, undertook the rigorous control of small-boat traffic at the site and posted continuing weather forecasts. A planning group oversaw weight and buoyancy computations and determining the logistics of making buoyancy improvements with the assistance of the Norfolk shore facilities. Lt. W. T. Coulson took up liaison with the fleet and naval district offices, a task that had grown to unexpected dimensions as thousands of uninhibited civilian suggestions poured in. Lt. Comdr. J. E. Greenbacker, Smith's flag secretary, was assigned the full-time task of coordinating and preparing appropriate replies from Admiral Smith to every such correspondent. It became important to maintain a readily available set of progress diagrams, visual aids, photographs, and summaries, not just for the Navy's top brass but also for the press and civilian liaisons.

The salvage director's staff conferences became intense. Twice daily the two admirals with their aides, a dozen or more staff officers, orderlies, and yeomen assembled in flag quarters. Captain Smoot oversaw much of the detail, but Smith was careful to let nothing pass without the stamp of expertise, either Wallin's knowledge of big-ship salvage or the agreement of two lieutenant commanders, one experienced with beach gear and the other in the use of pontoons. Captain Brown and Commander Peckham reported regularly, representing the *Missouri.* At each meeting, for over an hour the immediate problems and consequent actions were firmly framed in naval gold braid, particulars recorded in a daily log later to be summarized in ComCruLant's regular dispatches to CinCLantFlt. These, with a smattering of Smith's imagination, reflected his optimism. If some means existed to pump his buoyant outlook under the ship, he could take it to sea the next day. It veiled any concerns he might have had about the course to be taken by the board of inquiry.

At the first debriefing following Friday's failure to float, lurking suspicions were first voiced and associated. Two days earlier, during oil off-loading, three midship fuel tanks on the starboard side had resisted the negative pressure of the pumps. They were filling from the bottom with seawater as oil was withdrawn from the top. Divers had returned from one of their descents to confirm that a gash existed in the outer hull along the skin of the same tanks. Aboard the *Kittiwake,* warming up after plodding through 48° water in a strong and murky current, they described the cut. They reported it to be little more than a scratch at one end, broadening as it extended under the hull beyond their range of visibility. Sealed tanks above prevented flooding; there was little concern for the security of the rest of the hull. Precautions taken by the *Missouri*'s damage control team continued to maintain watertight integrity between all compartments below the waterline. Of 450 tanks in the outer hull of the battleship, three leaking ones were considered light damage. The immediate problem was a small one, the inability to remove the liquid within.

Wallin discussed the towing performance with senior pilot Treakle. They had observed some tugs pulling in flat seas while others churned hills of water behind them, delivering a less efficient pull. Surveying the tugs' skippers, they found that those tugs with roiling water astern had started operations with less than full fuel tanks.

Treakle assured Wallin that the tugs in the next operation would be fully fueled to submerge their screws as low in the water as possible.

Commander Peckham brought up the problem of the crew's morale. A decision was made that no corrective action would be taken until stores had been unloaded. Buoyancy took priority. Boats, skids, anchors, and three hundred fathoms of chain had been transferred with a floating crane the day before. Most of the liquids were gone. Next to be unloaded were the dry stores, followed by chilled goods. They waited only for the lighters to be secured alongside. There would go the morale-fortifying extra ice cream and pies. Turn the men to heavier labor, lugging off stores they had only recently brought aboard. No one, no matter their specialty, was excused from passing cases and cartons to the lighters. Storekeepers, yeomen, photographers, metalworkers, and gunners formed human chains with the deck men, winding up from lockers below decks. They started before sunset and kept at it through the night.

A critical alongside-space factor contributed another challenge and was addressed with the development of a time-space diagram clarifying the frequent movement of vessels on both sides of the warship. Dredging, diving, and tunneling contended with off-loading, all requiring their share of nearby tie-up time.

Through Friday night and into the morning, sailors stood in long lines, passing cartons of canned beans from one to the next, swinging sacks of flour, sugar, and potatoes, shuffling number 10 cans, six to the case, of plums, pitted prunes, pears, and peas. The goods came up from the lockers indiscriminately, sliding down chutes to the lighters, where they were sorted and stacked. On the lighters the men had to be fleet of foot lest a descending case bark their shins.[3] A sailor called back to the source to send up something light. Up came a single carton of cereal, followed by more cans of beans, peas, and potatoes. Not all goods handled got to the barges. Someone in the line would put down a carton to rest his back; someone else reached out a foot to slide the box under a gun turret, clear of the line; later a third person tidied up the deck and took the case below, midnight small stores. Later in number two fireroom they feasted on sardines and crackers.* Another compartment smelled like Hawaii for days, so

* Clarence "Skip" George reported forty-four years later that as a result of the surfeit he has never eaten another sardine.

97

plentiful was the supply of pineapple juice.[4] Occasionally someone shouted down to a sailor aboard one of the lighters, requesting a reading of the battleship's draft as if the ship were about to bob off the ground. No change, except in the tide. They kept at it, with comments. Powdered eggs occasioned a cheer, coffee brought groans, toilet paper invoked vulgarities. Where's the saltpeter, one sailor asked. Shoulders ached, arms hung heavy, mouths went dry. Someone insisted that between tides they had eased the draft by half an inch; they could relax. Let the next watch beat that, they said, slumping low against the bulkheads. Canned tomatoes, canned potatoes, canned berries, canned cherries. With grunts and grumbles the work went on. The second gang stopped when a theoretical inch of buoyancy was gained, by then too weary to watch the night's movie. By the time the third gang fell into their sacks, early Saturday morning, they had manhandled 250 tons of dry stores off the ship, with more to go; ninety-four tons of fresh fruit and vegetables, frozen food, sides of beef and pork. A water lighter took away over 209,000 gallons of potable water—650 tons. After nearly three hundred tons of provisions were removed in the all-night effort, 1.4 inches of added buoyancy was gained, hardly more than the diminishing tidal range. Not much more was movable but ammunition, 2,200 tons of it, and that was next. The crew did their share, even when at ease. Coffee consumption went from 350 to 450 pounds per day.[5] The salvage director, in his end-of-week report to CinCLantFlt, reiterated his confidence, evidently pleased at the progress.

Then early on Sunday, men from the *Comber* delivered aboard a collection of more than a dozen rocks, each the size of a football, drawn up by its scoops working around the hull. Could there be larger rocks under the sand? Unknown, was the reply, the *Comber*'s scoop would have rejected anything larger. Where were these found? Along the port quarter, bottom of the trench, some ten feet underground. That curiosity confounded all prior geological theories about the formation of the lower Bay.[6]

Wallin thought the hull might be poised on an uncharted boulder, potentially ready to be gored further if sternward motion was induced. Should that be so, it would take an immense force to tear steel plate with rock, an undesirable situation if it had to be done.

The ship must first be lifted high enough to get it off the unseen obstruction, with no more damage done to the plating.

Adding to the salvers' frustration was the realization that they could not use the four giant propellers, all in good shape and clear of mud, each with fifty thousand horsepower idle on its shaft. Was there any chance the condensers and sea chests could be flushed with high pressure from within or without? Based on what he had heard from the divers and seen within his own engine rooms, the highly respected Commander Zoeller continued to shake his head. The intake pumps and sea valves were so clogged that external efforts beyond the capacity of undersea workers would be necessary.

Admiral Smith became impatient as one thing interfered with another. Until the tugs had cleared away from the pulling effort, a pile driver couldn't be positioned beside the hull to put the gauges in place. The Coast Guard cutter *Jonquil* had positioned lighted range buoys fore and aft of the *Missouri*. Detailed recording of hull motion should have commenced with Friday's second high tide, using the specially designed measuring devices. Only with those could the admiral start his weight and buoyancy accounting. He wanted the gauges in place at once.

Casually, Admiral Smith asked Commander Peckham about maintenance of the ship's rough log. Peckham said that shortly after the grounding he had directed both the operations and engineering officers to collect and safeguard all pertinent documents and records.[7] The deck log, he said, was being kept regularly. Better to close it out and start a fresh one, suggested the admiral; the current one will be important evidence. That put the cards on the table. Legal proceedings were about to start.

As if to imply that CinCLantFlt thought the inquiry was immanent, on that same day the uncompleted battleship *Kentucky* was floated and moved out of Drydock Number 8 at the Norfolk Naval Shipyard, by that making room for the *Missouri*. Some commentators concluded that the newly designed missile carrier was being hustled into shape as a replacement for the permanent monument on Thimble Shoal.[8] But its premature launching was due more to lack of appropriations than to the intention of making space for quick repair of its sister ship. It delivered a public message that the Navy was prepared to hasten the return of the *Mighty Mo* to active service. The *Kentucky* never was completed.* The return of the stranded ship might be soon, but the men aboard could hardly anticipate their customary heroes' return to port.

Over all of this hung the specter of a further obstruction, the possibility that the damaged hull sat on rock, the extent of its resistance unknown. Wallin envisioned it not as a pinnacle but more likely a boulder on which much of the ship's weight pushed down, denting and stressing the bottom plate to the point of rupture. That focused on the use of pontoons for vertical lift, adding their effect to that of the yet-unused beach gear. The team never forgot the importance of mastering every inch of Chesapeake tide. The salvage work was beginning to tax their ingenuity, patience, and experience and the strength and endurance of the crew. Bringing to bear everything they knew how to do, sparing no efforts, disregarding no resources, they remained aware that their efforts could still fail.

At last, four six-inch solid steel pilings were driven into the seafloor around the hull, one each at bow and stern, one amidships on each side. Loosely attached to the hull's side with steel strapping, they extended higher than the main deck and were marked near the top with finely graduated scales. Pointers fixed to the deck nearby and set to the zero mark on each scale made any vertical movement immediately visible. An electric light had been fixed above the top of the forward piling, a cross between an anchor light and a marine streetlamp.[9] Parallel to each piling a narrow pipe was fastened, with holes drilled through it near the seafloor to permit influx of water. Inside that, a float sat at sea level, under a graduated scale rising above the top of the assembly. Thus at the top of each piling an indicator showed the current state of the tide, with the effect of wind and chop suitably damped. Seamen were assigned to observe and record draft and tide measurements as part of their watch duties. They didn't lack assistance; there few aboard whose interest didn't center on the gauges.

Tides rose and fell, over two feet at first. In almost live response the ends of the ship began to heave with each tide. Like a child's

---

* The bow section of the *Kentucky* (BB-66) was put to use in 1956, when it replaced the bow of the *Wisconsin* (BB-64), damaged beyond repair in a collision with a destroyer (see Stefan Terzibaschitsch, *Battleships of the U.S. Navy in World War II* [New York: Bonanza], 166).

loose tooth, easily wiggled but remaining in place, the hull refused to let go of the ground beneath it. In the face of this hopeful sign, the moon waned into its third quarter and the tidal lift decreased each day to an extent not offset by reductions in deadweight.

Break, strike, dip, and two-block . . . Navy signalmen break and strike flags for a variety of purposes and often dip the ensign in salute between Navy vessels. The junior dips her colors first, soliciting a similar action from the senior. Sailors look to guidebooks on the signal bridge to decide seniority between vessels of the same type. The signalmen of the *Missouri* couldn't care less as dawn broke Saturday morning. At that point they were moving carcasses of beef and pork, boxes of salted fish, stems of bananas, crates of oranges, and barrels of apples as they struggled toward the three-inch mark, bootstrapping the ship with their own weary muscles. Earlier the signalmen had struck the offensive Able-Peter—not required in inland waters, halyards interfering with the cranes, flown as a courtesy anyway, they said. They were in no mood to be courteous. Why boast about the situation, they said as the signals went into the flag bag. Only the two red lights at night were required, and those could be ignored with all the other illumination. No flags flew from the beleaguered ship, no union jack from the bow, no ensign from truck or stern. The ship was locked in a cluster of vessels, motionless in the water without anchor or engine.

In this sorry state, as the flow of cold goods dropped into the lighters, a fleet of nine destroyers returning from Guantánamo arrived in the channel.[10] The first of them dipped its ensign to its saddened senior, then quickly two-blocked it on realizing there would be no return. The sleek grey ships passed quickly, with a minimum of exchanges for the battleship's signalmen to handle. Three decks below the off-loading continued. As the last of the lighters pulled away, just under three more inches had been muscled away from the Chesapeake.

Sunday morning church call got little attention. Weary sailors chose not to stir from their sacks. "Now hear this . . ." came a general announcement, bringing groans from exhausted sleepers roused to wakefulness. "Liberty will be granted in four sections, starting with the first at 1200 today. Uniform of the day, dress blues."

The sailors came to life. The announcement continued. "When

you hit the beach keep theories about the incident to yourselves. A proper court of inquiry will be the official source for that in due time. . . . Expect to receive some kidding, but the men of the *Mighty Mo* would do best to take it with a stiff upper lip. Avoid fights. You've all done hard work, and deserve credit, not the brig."[11]

A quarter of the crew stopped listening and headed for the showers and the clean clothes lockers. They groveled in their ditty bags for the Kiwi. Pass the Wildroot Cream Oil, Charlie. Shape that gleaming brown pompadour into a wave before the squared white hat; check it in the mirror; shape and reposition the hat just above the eyebrows for inspection. Splash on the Skin Bracer. Morale rose faster than the waters around the ship as LSIs came alongside for the first wave of liberty men. Reporters met them at the fleet landing, eager to collect descriptions of life aboard the motionless ship, but the sailors kept their views mostly to themselves. The men of the *Mighty Mo* were spirited, loyal, and greatly uninformative. Was there a jolt when the ship went aground? Some said yes; others said no. "It sounded like we were being dragged over rocks," one wide-eyed sailor reported. Didn't hear a thing, said another; we weren't told what had happened for close to nine hours. Have they heard the jokes that are going around? Sure, newspapers and mail arrive daily. We can take the ribbing; it's still a proud and mighty ship. What do you plan to do now? Call home, get a beer, go to a show. Setting their hats to the back of their heads, they turned up their tailor-made sleeve cuffs, exposing the Oriental embroidery beneath, and rolled eagerly into town. Sailor town, ten consecutive blocks of East Main Street, was soon populated with crew members of the *Mo.* In the bars some claimed they were from the *Midway,* the *Roosevelt,* even the uncommissioned *Kentucky,* anything to avoid the derision of others in the fleet.[12] Not so at the Krazy Kat lounge. Fleet sailors there recognized a group of Missouris. "Here come the guys from the 'Muddy Mo,'" they jibed.[13] The men of the *Mo* stood their ground, insisted on a proper reference. Tempers rose, and then fists, the battle quelled before the arrival of the Shore Patrol.

In the flag quarters salvage office, graphs had been set up to track tidal motion and hull response. Allan Smith's balance sheet of displacement and buoyancy, load and lift, was calculated and checked. Graph paper, pencils, and slide rules were spread out on Admiral

Wallin's desk. He equated pulling forces to remaining weight and factored that further by a guess at the friction between steel and sand. Bottom samples were being tested at the Navy Yard's Underwater Research Division, since more accuracy was needed in the specification of a coefficient of friction. With that the precision of their computations would narrow.

The old *Squalus* pontoons were being towed down the coast from the Boston Navy Yard. Arrangements were made for additional beach gear to be delivered aboard from the Bayonne Salvage School. Ammunition lighters would soon arrive according to tightly packed time lines. Self-powered deck winches were to be installed on the battleship's afterdeck to augment the ship's own equipment during the big pull. Protective planking was being laid over the teak of the afterdeck. The powerful submarine rescue ships *Salvager* and *Windlass* were firmly scheduled to stand by; no late arrival, and ample time to rig the cumbersome beach gear. Additional officers and men came aboard, trained or untrained in salvage work, assigned to the salvage team. Smith requisitioned the Navy Yard's full fleet of tugs, small and large, for the planned pull. During the next attempt to get the *Missouri* off the bottom, if tugs were needed in the Yard they would have to be ordered from civilian sources. The *Mo* got priority.

A week after the accident, the nation's attention continued to focus on the event and its possible outcome, aided by the administration. Secretary of the Navy Matthews took an aerial view of the site to observe the salvage operations. Earlier he had stated that keeping the ship in commission would depend on what is "the best use of the money it would cost." Reminded by reporters what the president had said about keeping it active as long as he was in the White House, Matthews replied that Harry Truman's statement and his own were not "irreconcilable." The new Chief of Naval Operations, Forrest P. Sherman, discreetly canceled his planned visit, preferring to minimize the discussions on fleet reduction.[14]

Circulation of misconceptions, negative commentary, and pessimistic forecasts increased. Allan Smith left the tactics of addressing public interest to the two officers supporting him, but the strategy was entirely his own. Still rubbing the sores of the 1949 unification controversy, he would brook no more criticism of the Navy. He identified five fallacies to be corrected: that the ship was resting on soft mud; that the grounding was not as extensive as what had been computed, twelve to seventeen thousand tons of deadweight to be moved; that the ship's departure from the main shipping channel was entirely due to negligence; that the recent attempt to pull it off the shoal was a maximum effort with full expectation of success; and that there was little to do now but give up and wait for the peak tide on 2 February.[15]

Ten days of preparatory work were now fully booked. To attenuate the negative commentary, the officers of the salvage team and the grounded ship prepared for a set of press conferences. Captain Brown called quietly for a meeting with some of his officers to work up details. On Monday two conferences would be held, to follow a meeting scheduled by Admiral Blandy.

Admiral Smith went ashore in preparation. According to plan, as Smith outlined it in company with his press representative, selected members of the press would first meet briefly in Norfolk with Admiral Blandy, after which they would join their peers in larger number to be ferried out to the *Missouri*. There they would meet with Captain Brown and his staff, who would handle their questions. Following that Rear Admirals Smith and Wallin would show them about, explaining in detail their plans to refloat the ship. Preparatory work would continue on deck while the press was aboard—welding winches into place, laying out chafing gear and protective covering, flaking tow lines. At some point the anchors and chain were to be returned, their forward weight serving to lever the stern higher. Finally, a few local reporters would be invited to come aboard for the pull-off itself, even to broadcast it live.

Rumors circulated that the ship had sprung a leak when it grounded. Considering the quantity of people traveling back and forth to the ship since Tuesday and the public's urge to light on any hint of authenticity, the gossip could have come from a dozen sources. In an inadvertent breach of faith, a spokesman for the Fifth Naval District claimed that the reports were without basis.[16]

The following day at his Atlantic Fleet headquarters, Admiral Blandy acknowledged for the first time the existence of the acoustic range within deep water. Its purpose, he said, was a military secret. He confirmed that the *Missouri* had run aground after entering the range but avoided any further explanation. A prepared release gave the reporters further details of the salvage operations, deflecting interest from matters the Navy preferred to keep private.

The top men of the *Missouri* had to tread a narrow line. Any opinions or statement not openly factual made in their press conference would be subject to refutation or denial in their chief's meeting. Fealty to their seniors was due. They were obligated to support Admiral Smith, but without knowledge of what he might say. They were responsible for skirting discussions that could prejudice findings in the forthcoming court of inquiry.

For its part, the press was interested in what and why more than when or how. They had been told when the situation would be fixed. Their readers wanted to know what had caused the mishap. Their interests would focus not on how the Navy planned to fix it but on why it occurred. Captain Brown was the prime target of their inquiries.

Upon boarding, the reporters were led up directly to the captain's quarters. Brown, dressed neatly in khakis, welcomed them into a spacious, nearly windowless office adjoining his own stateroom. Enclosed by bulkheads of heavy armor plate, its exposed steel frames contrasted starkly with the warmly lit, thickly carpeted interior and comfortable furnishings.[17] Captain Brown introduced the three officers with him as Commander Peckham, the *Missouri*'s executive officer, Lieutenant Commander Morris, navigator, and Lieutenant Arnold, officer of the deck at the time of the incident. Operations officer Millett was not present and not mentioned. Photos were taken, and Brown posed uncomfortably before a seal of the State of Missouri emblazoned on a bulkhead. Mess stewards offered coffee as all took their places, the captain sitting in a brown leather easy chair next to a matching couch and low table. Tall, grim, talking in subdued tones, Brown calmly defined the limits of the conversation. He was very much in command, yet it was obvious that he was under stress in consenting to the meeting. Those who had attended the ceremony six weeks earlier when Brown took over the *Missouri* could readily discern the change in his demeanor.[18]

The mishap was the result of "an unusual and unfortunate chain of circumstances," the captain explained in making the first public statement about the grounding. Glancing at his listeners with moist eyes, he spoke in a steady, cheerless voice, clearly frustrated. His replies to questions were deliberate, carefully worded, concise. Asked exactly what did happen prior to the stranding, he declined to give details, saying that to do so would "usurp the prerogatives of the court of inquiry" and could "prejudice the standing" of officers intimately involved in the accident. Did that include others than the three gentlemen present in the room? That answer was left to the court. Yes, he would remain on board until the ship was refloated; he and the officers of the *Missouri* were taking active parts in the salvage operation. He expected that inspection and repairs could be done in time for the ship to join the Portrex maneuvers in the Caribbean in February.

Commander Peckham praised the crew for their industry. Over the weekend they had unloaded 280 tons of stores, he said, working steadily for a period of eighteen hours. Their morale was high.

Yes, the captain and his staff had navigated Hampton Roads without a harbor pilot before, during brief trials in December. And during the war he had piloted destroyers several times through these waters. No, in December the range buoys may not have been posted. Were routine navigational cautions observed in January? The captain winced, and in a faltering voice said, "There were no unusual departures from normal pilot procedures. I can assure you that the ship did not go aground as a result of carelessness."

Morris and Arnold had little to add, agreeing firmly with the captain's views.[19] At the conclusion of the interview, the reporters were conducted up two decks and into Admiral Smith's headquarters, where he and Admiral Wallin greeted them.

Smith had already given a statement to the press, adding that "Captain Brown had no illusions about what had happened. He is calm, collected and effective in the salvage operation."

Noting the absence of engineering officers from either meeting, a reporter asked if it was possible that mechanical failures had caused the accident, perhaps due to silt being taken in? The admiral recalled that in the previous summer at the start of the "Middie" cruise while in the Severn River the ship's condensers were clogged with mud from the shallows, and the battleship did not lose control.

What about last Friday's failure to refloat the ship? According to Admiral Smith, that effort was foredoomed. "Friday was too soon and we knew it. We needed a foot more tide than we had."[20] That statement deviated from the optimism a Navy representative had expressed before the tugs started their work. Smith was apparently doing some Monday morning quarterbacking.

The two admirals displayed their graphs relating the projected states of the tide to the steadily decreasing weight of the ship as off-loading continued. At some length, aided by diagrams and charts, they went into descriptions of the beach gear and plans for its use along with flotation pontoons.

Admiral Wallin predicted that before the big pull, the ship would be partially afloat, at least with the bow off the ground; pontoons would lift the stern. Neither admiral would name a date for that event. Wallin mentioned that a special lift barge was being fashioned that could be placed under the battleship's stern. That was something new, and the reporters queried him further. He hedged, saying that they had a problem finding a place for it in the already congested waters around the ship. But it would be available soon if it should be required.

Wallin was more frank with the press than the others had been. Yes, leaks were sustained in three compartments, probably caused by a submerged rock. In the sandy Chesapeake? He told them about the "footballs" found by the *Comber*'s crew. It remained for geologists to explain their natural origin.

Satisfied they would be told no more, the press people went out to the main deck. Lieutenant Arnold, as the ship's first lieutenant responsible for topside maintenance, was detailed to escort them. Two reporters queried him tenaciously, taking notes as he explained the preparations under way on the afterdeck; just as assiduously he limited his responses to the salvage plans, admitting to nothing more about the mishap than having been officer of the deck at the time. The once pristine teak appeared now as despoiled as the recently painted sides of the ship—dirty, scuffed and scratched from many hasty tie-ups. Piles of scale and rust from the anchor removal remained to be swept away. With lines, cables, chafing gear, and tools scattered about, the vessel hardly looked shipshape. Sailors were busy clearing deck space for the next heavy-duty job, the removal of ammunition. Near the fantail, additional winches were being welded into place within hatch coamings in preparation for rigging the beach gear. Before its next contest with the Chesapeake's bottom, the *Mighty Mo* looked battle-weary.

The press in 1950 was less aggressive in its search for news than it would be later in the century. Reporters worked at a slower pace, facing less competition. Radio gave them little interference; the six o'clock news hardly affected evening paper circulation. No one would have considered tracking down the shoreside relatives of the principal officers. No one would have hovered outside the high school attended by Captain Brown's daughter for today's inevitable, stupid question, "How does your dad feel?" Television was a novelty, mostly delivering wrestling matches filmed in black and white to taverns. Weekly news magazines and daily papers formed the news. The people of the fourth estate sensed their mission to be factual reporting more than investigation. Habit derived from dealings with the military and its restrictions during World War II engendered the view that when a government agent spoke it was fact; the U.S. Navy doesn't mislead. Yet reporters competed among themselves, and if someone could get a unique edge on the others, it was pursued vigorously. Nothing set them off faster than the suspicion that there was something interesting being withheld.

Blandy's vagueness about the range buoys headed some reporters out to sea to inspect the waters for themselves. Their study that afternoon found the range as described within the normal channel but in proximity to shoal water. The black-and-white spar buoys marking the Back River channel, more familiar to the area's watermen, were introduced into their investigation, the reporters readily ruling out the possibility of confusion between these and the Navy's range buoys. From a small boat they appeared markedly different and at a substantial distance from the acoustic range.

Three days later, Hanson Baldwin, military editor of the *New York Times,* divulged the details of the hydrophone buoys and the slow leaks aboard the battleship in an article supportive of the Navy's immense effort to refloat it.[21]

Contrary to expectations, Smith and Wallin in their interview encouraged speculation that the ship would float earlier than the 2 February high tide, perhaps even before the end of the current week. Local folk were becoming familiar with the daily tide, at least in their own harbors and creeks, attempting to use it as an indicator of when the *Mighty Mo* would float. After the interview, the *Norfolk Virginian-Pilot,* observing that the tidal range was improving, bet on Thursday, the twenty-sixth.[22] Bad news makes better news than good news. In the same article it reported that the barge carrying the ship's anchors sank at its naval base pier and that it, too, would require salvage.

While dredging continued, beach gear was loaded and the pontoon barges arrived to be moored nearby. It was an opportune time for President Truman's naval aide to arrive. The presentation to the press proved to be a fortunate dress rehearsal for the two admirals. Rear Adm. R. L. Dennison spent four hours in conference with the salvage leaders, reviewing progress and plans, and departed with a comforting report for the White House.[23] Yet it appeared that no one on board gave much thought to protecting the pertinent navigational records. With the press conference behind him, Commander Peckham, acting under orders from the captain, collected the documents into his own custody. He had attended to closing the rough deck log the day after Admiral Smith asked about it. Millett and Morris were responsible for the other records, but it would be some time before the exec had everything available in one place.[24]

Battleships routinely keep a post office aboard, a yeoman of the X division as designated postmaster. The *Mo's* postmaster would have been swamped with the daily volume of mail addressed to crew members, to the captain, to Admiral Smith, often just to the ship itself. Nearly a thousand letters arrived, from every state in the Union and from nine foreign countries. Atlantic Fleet Headquarters set up a facility to intercept those that weren't personal. Comments, suggestions, and queries were sorted and submitted to the flag secretary for response. Overwhelmed, the flag office needed the aid of the Fifth Naval District's public information officer to comply with the admiral's desire to respond personally to every letter received. The Bureau of Ships was called to assist. Eight hundred and thirty-seven replies went out, even to direct phone calls, each with a printed statement of factors affecting the refloating and a diagram of the planned pull-off arrangements. Firing a broadside of facts and optimistic artillery, every line flag officer, several in the staff corps, and the public information offices of the twelve naval districts received the same enclosures.[25] This grass-roots development in Allan Smith's style was to prove effective in keeping goodwill alive.

Able-Peter was up under the code flag again, flying stiffly from a port halyard in a thirty-five-knot wind. Baker flew at the starboard yard, signaling the discharging of inflammables. The crew was bringing ammunition up from the magazines. They were in for another strenuous weekend, surrounded by choppy seas and pitching craft tied alongside. Ten thousand rounds of 5-inch projectiles to be stacked on deck, 2,400 tanks of black powder, 1,220 16-inch shells destined for the lighters, nearly 2,600 tons in all. The 5-inch shells aren't passed hand to hand. Drop one and it would break a foot or roll wildly along the deck. Mistreat its thirty-pound bag of powder and there's an outside chance you would send something off. Sailors formed in single file at four magazines, like nineteenth-century coal miners carefully shouldering their fifty-five-pound cargo up to the open deck. Five hundred miners making twenty trips should do the job, or a hundred, each making a hundred trips. Earlier dry stores duty didn't get them out of ammo duty. "Skip" George found himself working what seemed like twenty-hour days, coming out of the fire-room where he still tended the clogged cooling pumps to find himself in the line carrying 5-inch shells. If liberty was offered he was too tired to take it.[26] The shells stood vertically on deck, like early spring tulips, in a buffer zone from which they were stacked on pallets destined for storage ashore. Bags of black powder for the main battery, three to a tank, each another equally tender fifty-five-pound cargo, were gingerly handled for shipping up the Bay to Yorktown. Sixteen-inch shells have been compared to compressed Volkswagens; weighing 1,900 to 2,700 pounds each, a crane is needed to get them up and out, one at a time. At one every three minutes, that's seven hours' work if something doesn't drop in the process. The wind blew up during the unloading process, causing the ammunition barges to roll ruthlessly as the big shells were lowered into place. You had to have eyes in the back of your head to stay healthy in that environment.[27] We could do this a lot faster, one wag said, if we just aimed all the guns out to sea and fired everything off. How about over the stern toward the Army fort, came the response.

A mile further astern than Fort Monroe, in Hampton Creek, Wilson Wright readied his forty-foot cabin cruiser. It was much earlier than he customarily took up the spring fitting out, but he sensed an opportunity. Wright ran an ad in the papers and found himself in business as a midwinter charter boat operator.[28] Daily from midmorning until twilight he took passengers at a dollar per person (special prices for children and parties, his ad stated) from the pier at Buckroe Beach to circle the *Missouri* and gawk at its forlorn crew. He was not alone as a nautical entrepreneur. Thousands of people partook of this once-in-a-lifetime opportunity. Coast Guard boats maintained a barrier of sorts between the tourists and the working craft. The famous warship was getting shabbier, but that was hardly visible from the vantage point of a cabin cruiser. The cranes, barges, and water tankers formed a tight phalanx about the ship. Somehow people were thrilled to get close to what today they might call a media event.

Misfortune draws an easy crowd, and good business ideas are bound to be followed by better ones. For two dollars you could get a double thrill at Peninsula Airport, up the road from Old Point Comfort—a plane ride, and assurance that you would see the *Mighty Mo* from the air. A flight around the tall towers rising above the big guns put a memorable spark into a usually dull Sunday afternoon.

Whether or not they had seen the site firsthand, the populace didn't lack for ideas on how to free the ship, all unsolicited. Suggestions flowed by the hundreds across the desk of Lieutenant Commander Wornom.[29] Allan Smith was impressed enough with one that he shared it with Admiral Blandy in a midnight dispatch. A gentleman from Illinois suggested he mount a battery of windblowers on barges at the entrance to Chesapeake Bay and blow the tide up in time for the next pull.[30] The one that tickled him the most was a postcard from Spartansburg, South Carolina: "Rock the boat—Full speed astern—Pull and let go quick—Put a man who has false teeth in charge of the Operation—he knows something about suction."[31] Wornom answered a call from a dirigible flier who told him to pump helium into the watertight compartments. An Army sergeant wrote to suggest they line up the full fleet at the mouth of the Bay and create a wave by starting all the engines at once. Dump salt in the water to improve flotation, create an artificial wave with depth charges, use giant magnets, array the Congress on deck and their hot air will blow it off.[32] Some suggestions had merit, not excluding the proposal to fire off the big guns. Every action has an equal and opposite reaction,

and at sea when the battleship is firing its main battery it can be seen
to undergo forces opposed to the direction in which it is aiming. The
problems with doing so in the Bay centered on the guns' angle of ele-
vation to get the best effect without endangering either the eastern
shore or Atlantic shipping lanes, and on the risk that reverse forces
would damage the hull.[33] It didn't seem appropriate to conduct firing
drills within inland waters, no matter what precautions might be
taken. Someone had suggested making loaded tankers fast to either
side of the bow and then unloading them, letting their increasing
buoyancy lift the battleship. That idea was given serious thought, but
there didn't seem to be a way to connect the two vessels stiffly to the
ship; it was likely they would list sideward as their buoyancy
increased, straining their fastenings to the point of fracture. Two ideas
advanced had already been under consideration—the raising of a
high bow wave from the wash of powerful naval vessels such as
destroyers, and the use of underwater explosives.

Heavy swells on the weekend sent the commercial dredge *Washington* retiring to the lee of Old Point Comfort. A shallow area
astern of the stranded ship remained to be cleared, connecting to
the *Comber*'s exit channel. There was time yet to complete that, and
the two admirals turned their attention to setting off explosives in
the ground around the hull. Conferring with an underwater demolition team, they proposed to loosen the sand base and break the per-
nicious hull contact by setting off two shaped charges, one on each
side of the hull, seventy-five feet distant, in hopes that this would
induce some settling.

It was not a peaceful Sunday. Early efforts at rigging pontoon
cables under the hull were hampered by the swells. The pontoon situation became critical, with much uncertainty as to their usefulness.
The arduous task of rigging beach gear was slowed by the need to
clear the area for the explosive shots. Creating less of a water plume
than anticipated, the noontime detonations achieved little by way of
results, but their effect on a large school of fish soon became evident.
Thousands of bent bodies floated to the surface, the carpet of fish
gore attracting hundreds of gulls.[34]

That event quickly caught the public's fancy, giving rise to the feeling that the Navy was getting desperate, grasping at straws. Commentary got back to Admiral Smith that people were beginning to fear the

ship would never get off and would indeed become a monument in the Bay. Smith became defensive. He spent the last hours of Sunday assessing progress, analyzing risks, evaluating outstanding problems, and assembling words for a special situation report to his commander in chief. There was much going for him in his continuing plan to meet the 2 February commitment. Within his circle he had scheduled an earlier coordinated rehearsal, a full effort to pull the ship off on the last day of January in the growing hope that all factors would help him achieve a dramatic earlier success. Some settling of the stern was achieved with the detonations; the bow did look higher. Admiral Wallin had hastened the shipyard's work on a pontoon barge to be placed under the stern should it be proved necessary. Ranking the loyal crew's morale as more important than the reduction of one hundred tons of deadweight, Smith decided to keep them aboard, "at least through the first try." Anticipating the next-day return of the anchors and chain and completion of off-loading operations, he turned his attention to an effective shift of weight by reloading fuel aft. With that, he prepared a well-hedged forecast of events for release by Admiral Blandy on Monday. His words suggested that things were still very much touch-and-go:

> Firstly, if the actual high tide 2 February reaches the predicted high tide for that morning then the *Missouri* will be pulled off. Secondly, if the actual high tide is 7 inches above the predicted high tide for 2 Feb then the *Missouri* will probably float off. Thirdly, if the actual high tide is 3 inches below the predicted high tide on 2 Feb there will be a struggle. . . . In the past two days preliminary planning and preparations beyond 2 Feb have taken place and the computations show that it should never be necessary to reach the point of taking out the *Missouri*'s guns or other fixed heavy weights.[35]

Allan Smith's fate floated on four inches of water in Chesapeake Bay.

6

The Big Pull

On shore Friday had been the start of a typical wet winter weekend.[1] But out on the Chesapeake bitter winds gusting up to forty miles an hour caused pontoon placement to be deferred until the waters calmed. One week remained to the deadline date, and salvage plans allowed little latitude for the vagaries of weather. Sequentially scheduled tasks fell behind, pontoon rigging being critical to the preparations. The blow abated by Sunday before the demolition team set off their partially effective explosions. Divers submerged beneath the rank cover of dead fish to find more hard-packed sand had cracked and loosened under the bottom. That weakened the suction and increased the ship's buoyancy by an estimated seventy-five tons. For several days the bow had lifted with each rising tide, reaching a peak up-and-down movement of nine inches prior to the underwater shots. The motion, absorbed in the flexibility and sag of the long keel, had little effect on the stern. The next step was to lever the bow down in its widening trench by restoring the anchors and pumping water into the forepeaks. That should add spring to the long hull and ease the pontoon-induced lift of the stern. The hull's midship portion continued to sit stubbornly on a long mound of sand that remained. While the salvers patiently manipulated this massive array of forces, unfamiliar observers could easily conclude the Navy didn't know whether it was coming or going. Force, shifted as necessary, intensive force, was ultimately what it would take, applied with unrelenting constancy for a half hour, an hour, even longer, until the Atlantic's benevolent tide lifted and drew the ship along within a fleet of pulling tugs.

Of all mechanical devices developed since the wedge and wheel—

lever, screw, piston, gear train—surely nothing is as unwieldy as that adaption of block and tackle called beach gear.[2] Common equipment among professional salvers, it is virtually unknown to most seafaring people. Properly rigged beach gear can deliver a pulling force more than double that of the Navy's most powerful tug, preventing a stranded vessel from being driven further ashore or pulling it back into deep water. Ungainly, heavy equipment must be assembled to do the job, a task to test the extremes of human effort. Specially designed rescue ships carry beach gear, and rare skills are required to rig it on a stranded vessel. The forces applied in its use threaten unpredictable danger and almost certain injury upon sudden failure.

First, for each set of gear at the *Missouri* site a four-ton anchor designed to resist dragging was planted on the seafloor, each a quarter of a mile from the stranded ship, leading close to the direction in which pulling forces would be applied. Taking precaution, the salvers put a second anchor on each rig to alleviate any possibility of slippage. No delay due to having to reset the equipment could be tolerated. The twin anchors were lowered into position with ninety feet of heavy chain attached, each link larger than a boatswain's boot. This was to keep both anchors digging with their shanks horizontal, add spring to the pulling force, and prevent sudden surges, which could loosen the grip on the ground. Two hundred and fifty fathoms of wire rope came next—high-grade plow steel, its breaking strength over ninety tons. Extending mostly underwater, the long scope flattened the triangle of forces between the warship's main deck, the bottom of the Bay below, and the distant anchors. Strong, flat shackles, able to pass through chocks and around bitts and maintain full tension without breaking, connected hundred-foot cable lengths. Finally, inside the ship's railings, the muscles were attached. Pairs of fourfold blocks, the hauling part in each nine-part purchase leading to the drum of a deck winch, 1,200 feet of wire roven through sheaves nearly a yard in diameter extended 130 feet of falls laid out on deck between each pair of blocks.

Nine sets of this beaching equipment were stretched radially from the *Missouri*'s after quarters (see fig. 4). The battleship's standard docking gear included five powerful electric winches fixed in place, two forward and three on the afterdeck. Supplementing these, four

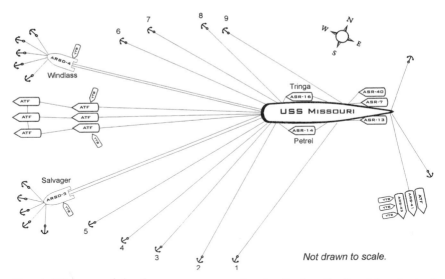

Fig. 4. Diagram of the fleet arrangement for the final pull-off, with principal vessels identified by name.

portable gasoline-powered winches, cable preloaded on their drums, were shored and welded in position behind heavy armor plate. Each could develop a line pull of nearly eight tons. In use a horizontal pulling force could be delivered double that expected of fifteen-hundred-horsepower seagoing tugs, nine powerful sinews straining at more than fifty tons of resistance.

The two large rescue craft, *Salvager* and *Windlass,* were added to this array. Each vessel planted five anchors close to the dredged channel. The Danforth Anchor Company had loaned each a 10,000-pound hook, designed for kedging ability. Added to these were the standard 8,000-pound salvage moorings and three 6,000-pound anchors, all five seafloor connections leading to a ship's bow. Then two sets of beach gear were rigged from the yoke-shaped sterns and connected by towing wires to the platform on the battleship, where they were bridled to the barbette of the after 16-inch turret. Facing the end of the dredged channel, these powerful salvage vessels would each apply three forces: drawing up on their anchors, driving their engines in normal towing fashion, and simultaneously hauling on the matched sets of beaching rigs.

The enormous amount of barely flexible wire in beach gear makes the equipment unusually cumbersome. A single kink in the best wire rope ruins it at once. In laying the cable, it must be paid off quickly without risk of bending. Stowing it on reels prevents its immediate use, so salvage ships drape it in loops along the side, each loop secured by a length of manila line, with the excess figure-eighted on the fantail. The arrangement makes the vessels easily recognized, looking far from shipshape with greasy, black rope strung over their sides from stem to stern. Three repair ships helped by tugs took two days to plant and rig four and a half miles of wire in the thirteen sets of gear the battleship would use.

A towing unit, made up of six fleet tugs positioned within the dredged channel, was added to this array. They had a dual purpose—three were to pull directly astern, and three were to surge the others to left and right of the channel, thereby producing the twist needed for pulling the hull out of the sand. Pulling vessels would also be positioned on each side of the battleship, aft of the outermost beach rigs, ready to control the freed ship's motion. Two pairs of rescue ships snugged beside the narrow bow completed the forces planned. The bow unit was supported by three more tugs to twist and surge in any direction on a 180° arc. Five harbor tugs nosing against the towing and surging units would keep them from swaying off position. Twenty-four vessels in all assembled to do the job, with two patrol boats idling nearby for observation. A model of the float plan was made up and used for explanation to the press and training of the crew. The display, a twenty-square-foot board with its miniature fleet and cables arrayed in facsimile, spoke visibly of power, like the battleship itself once did. An observer could sense that this was the muscle that would accomplish the task.

If it took only a handful of people to put the ship onto the shoal, it would take many more to get it off. With a week to go, Commander Peckham issued a notice to all hands, assigning eight officers and ninety-six enlisted men to stations on the beach gear platform.[3] In that period they would have to get the bulky equipment aboard and learn how to use it while observing rigorous safety precautions and attending to a half-dozen associated duties at tightly scheduled times. None of it was easy work, and even with the most thorough training the final activity would have its share of risk.

Dredging, diving, and lancing continued as trenches continually caved and filled. The wide hull sat on a narrower, flattened hill. As the work went on, long forward and after sections of the flexible ship heaved with the tides. Before they were finished, divers would make 367 descents, many over two hours in duration. They came to know the bottom intimately, crawling fearlessly under the edges of the hull and beneath the bow and stern. Their last task was to assist in the nearly fruitless effort of passing wire and chains under the stern to secure the big pontoons. After the chains were placed—a challenging job that called for harbor tugs to saw them into position—the bulky steel pontoons were launched from their barges and partially flooded to fit them under the counter. The task was not unlike manipulating water balloons, except that here they worked in a choppy, windblown sea with ruthlessly intolerant heavy metal cylinders and grinding chains. There was concern that the undamaged rudders and propellers would be harmed. At the bow the svelte design of the ship made it difficult to keep the long pontoons close to the hull. Hodging hooks, welded in horizontal lines along the hull's concave surfaces, were an integral part of the ship. Customarily used to secure suspended lines close to the sides, enabling placement of stagings and boatswain's chairs for scraping and painting, the hooks weren't strong enough to retain heavy pontoons. Divers struggled to pass wires under the forefoot. Ultimately this allowed two pontoons to be pulled below the surface of the water, where they floated snugly in the bow's concavities.

On Monday, the last day prior to the long pull, a discouraging sea fog formed around the ship, dispersing later in the day as strong northeast winds raised a nasty chop over Thimble Shoal. Two groundings had occurred in the Bay during the morning hours. A naval tug struck a nearby shoal, creating a measure of anguish for observers on the battleship until it worked off under its own power. Then to the south, a U.S. Lines freighter hung up near Willoughby Spit, commercial tugs anxiously working to free it before sunset. Meanwhile the twenty-knot breeze whipped the pontoons under the warship's counter, causing them to pitch wildly until one finally carried away. Divers from *Tringa* and *Petrel* worked with *Missouri* sailors to secure the pair in time for the pull, that task occupying them most of the night. The Chesapeake was being disagreeable, yet this was curiously welcome to the salvers.[4] The wind was a good omen, expected to add as many as six inches of water to the evening tide.

Ships of the pulling fleet gradually took up their positions in the misty dark. As fifty-five media representatives came aboard for the scheduled evening press conference they found the salvage director on deck, peering through the night, surveying the water, checking the status of the three tugboat units, making notes, issuing last-minute orders. He wore his customary knee-length foul-weather jacket, heavy binoculars practically a badge of office suspended from his neck. They remained strapped on his chest while he sat with the reporters gathered around his conference table. As to the outcome of the next day's event, it was difficult to discern how Rear Admiral Smith would have bet. On the one hand, he had marshaled all forces available, even holding one in reserve, its use to be decided on in the morning; he had invited a large contingency of press and radio broadcasters aboard to witness the affair at close hand; he had prepared an "almost certain" forecast of success for his commanding officer. On the other, he insisted on calling the next day's event a "coordinated rehearsal," implying it was merely a preliminary to the officially scheduled effort on 2 February. The overnight visitors were assigned observation stations. The Navy would help newsmen broadcast from high in the conning tower to a receiver placed on the roof of the Hotel Chamberlin at Old Point Comfort, and from there to the world.[5] Among the visitors, newsreel photographers, military columnists, and representatives of the major news services were carefully briefed about what they could expect the next day. No one was disabused of the probability that the ship would be freed. Following that meeting the admiral sent a dispatch to CinCLantFlt: "All factors considered it is almost certain Missouri will be refloated Tuesday morning high tide 310645R." Thirty minutes after zero hour, Tuesday, 0645 local time on the last day of January, was one hundred minutes short of two full weeks after the stranding. On balance, Allan Smith was giving an all-out effort to achieve an early and dramatic accomplishment, impressive showmanship in what he hoped would be a no-lose exercise.

The ship is 11,857 tons lighter. During the night watch dunnage was cleared, the last ammunition off-loaded, and barges moved from the sides. Officer telephone talkers at each station checked communications between ships. Command posts were established high in the conning tower at O11 fire control level, lower on the flag bridge, and aft on top of Turret 3. Although only four of the six troublesome pontoons originally planned were in place, all divers were called up. The ship was as ready as it would be.

Tuesday. A dripping fog again gathers around the cluster of ships, closing on the tail end of the biting wind. Thimble Shoal's horn can be heard to the east, the bell on Old Point Comfort occasionally clanging in the blackness astern. Passing vessels hoot as they grope through the shipping channel. A cold stationary front threatens rain and sleet.[6] Rivulets run from the *Missouri*'s decks and railings, gathering in puddles under the blocks and cables spread across the beaching platform.

0330. Dead calm, visibility 250 yards, less than the length of the ship. *Comber* and *Washington,* their dredging duties done, hover somewhere in the exit channel. Dim lights on the pulling unit astern glisten briefly, marking the route as if to beckon the big ship before they disappear in ghostly swathes of fog. Patrol boats, caught in the yellow deck lights of the battleship, maneuver quietly near the quarter units, wet clouds of diesel fumes sputtering flatly from their exhausts. From the warship's bow, two long mooring lines, slapped by a long, low swell, dip into the fog. On deck, a dozen sailors hooded in foul-weather gear keep their lonely posts along the railings. The *Missouri* rests quietly for the first time in a fortnight.

0420. *Tringa* and *Petrel* report all divers up. The bottom is clear, the ship perched for removal. Coast Guard vessels patrol to keep traffic from the operating area and clear the channel to the final berth.

0445. All hands are called to stations. The top of Turret 3 is the beach gear control station, where Lt. Comdr. James Lees, beach gear control officer, takes his position, checking the 1-JV connection with Lt. Comdr. W. R. Leonard, the talker on O11, the main conning and control station. Spot 1 and, above it, "sky control" give a full view fore and aft, to the distance the fog permits.

0515. Ninety minutes to zero hour; ComCruLant's Operation Order 1-50 goes into effect, and four individual plans are under way—communications, recovery, towing, and ship's position.

Officers and men test communications facilities one more time. Even in darkness sailors are stationed to use the flag hoists, anxious to strike the annoying Able-Peter. On the bridge a bullhorn chirps briefly as power is applied; skippers of the towing ships activate their maneuvering circuits; officers test sound-powered phones; a test message is briefly broadcast on the public-address system; on individual voice circuits, commanding officers are again reminded of proper discipline: no word of the *Missouri*'s movements is to go out over any radio voice channel without explicit approval of ComCruLant.

Five salvage rescue ships in the beach gear control group, including *Salvager* and *Windlass,* review preparations for recovery of beach gear sets, bow wires, and stern anchors. Men stand by the battleship's afterdeck with blowtorches, prepared to burn through the cables after the ship comes afloat, unlacing it from the bottom as rapidly as possible. Pontoons will remain attached until the ship is in dry dock. Temporary range and channel markers will be removed shortly after the ship clears the exit channel.

Five pulling units are on station. The bow group, *Kittiwake* to starboard, *Chanticleer* and *Hoist* nested on the port side, is ready to surge on command. *Tringa* and *Petrel,* their duties as dive stations completed, take positions on each quarter, aft of the forward pair of beach gear, deployed to pull along with the bow group. The main towing unit is made up of two sections, each a nested trio of fleet tugs. The pulling section is twelve hundred feet astern of the battleship, with *Mosopelea* (ATF-158) in the middle, designated as guide. Yard tugs will push on each side of the outboard vessels in the pulling section to keep them tightly nested with their towing hawsers parallel. Three hundred feet further out, a surging section, *Paiute* (ATF-159) in the middle as guide, will swing the six-tug unit in an arc between the anchored *Windlass* and *Salvager.* Two salvage rescue ships, *Recovery* and *Opportune,* on fifteen-hundred-foot hawsers, make up the breast group, whose tasks are to keep the battleship centered in the channel and then assist in maneuvering it to its berth. All communications with tug control are to take place through the guide ships. The towing plan is both the most critical and most detailed, requiring utmost effort on the part of each man, ship, and piece of equipment. For nearly two weeks every possibility has been considered, worked out, reviewed, and, at least in theory, rehearsed.

On getting clear the *Missouri* will anchor off Old Point Comfort until everything is ready for it to be towed to the Norfolk Naval Shipyard. Captain Brown will be in command on the bridge, with the guidance of tug and naval base pilots. Since the ship is without propulsion, the crew's task will be chiefly deck work, anchoring and weighing, and line handling with eleven tugboats.

A contingency plan anticipates several possibilities: the beach gear will be effective, allowing maintenance of an even strain until the ship floats freely; the ship will move slightly and then resist the beach gear before it has been fully two-blocked; the ship will hang up after the beach gear can no longer be effective; the ship will tend to pull out of the dredged channel; the ship will fail to move at all. Actions have been outlined for each situation.

From his station atop the turret, using a megaphone, Lieutenant Commander Lees gives the order to set taught all beach gear.[7] At this point, a bare hand stroked carefully along the lengths of cable running to the winches would have encountered no sharp, broken wires, the first signs of excessively stressed wire rope. In two hours that is not likely to be the case.

0545. All nine stations have reported beach gear taut with turns on the winch drums. Carpenter stoppers are ready, handlers standing by the long levers to press them onto the cables. These devices can force wedges against the cable to lock it in place should a winch fail. Lees eyes the rigs and gives the order to apply the first strain on the gear.

0546. Comdr. James M. Wood and Chief Pilot Treakle of the pulling tug control group survey the scene from O11. Wood issues a command for all tugs to run engines at one-third speed. Their wakes stir up a murky wash, invisible in the distance but soon swirling like a river around the hull's black boottop as the heavy hawsers rise to the strain.

0550. Forward, mooring lines are slacked according to plan, ready to be cast off upon sternward motion of the ship. The starboard line fouls on the stern of a pushing tug and is cut adrift.

Control conn asks Turret 3, "What degree of strain do we have on the beach gear?" Oily rivulets run along the cable grooves of the two foremost rigs, dripping onto wooden channels built to protect the teak deck. Grease from the cables' fiber cores, wrung out and melted by the friction within the stressed wires, collects beneath the cables like blackened sweat. The response, "One and nine have very heavy strain," their lines running to winches on the foredeck. These two sets, at greatest angle from the center line, labor under necessarily opposing component forces athwartship.

0555. Beach gear is now at 80 percent of pulling power. All men are ordered off the fantail. The backlash of a parted wire could slice a man in two. If it should split within a block, it could send three cubic feet of metal spiraling in any direction but down. Hospital corpsmen have been stationed nearby, equipped with morphine syrettes.[8] Sailors clamber to vantage points on the higher decks.

0600. *Salvager* and *Windlass* report they are exerting very heavy strain.

0601. Treakle tells the salvage director, "Tugs now making two-thirds power."

0602. Lees says, "Increase to full power on beach gear." Windlasses scream, the cables groan under the added tension.

0605. Lees urges, "Maximum strain on all beach gear." *Salvager* reports it is applying maximum power. Electric winch resistors clack in and out furiously as cables grasp and slip on slowly turning drums. Gasoline winch engines roar under full throttle. The drum on the winch at Station 6 stutters with a slipping clutch as another turn of wire is taken. Six inches gained at a windlass draw the beach gear's movable block a fraction of an inch forward on its wooden platform, that particle only an increase in the stretch of the anchor lead. The six strands in each wire seem merged into stiff steel rods, no visible sag as they angle into the water astern.

0615. A command is sent from O11 to the pulling and surging guides: "Six pulling tugs dead astern, full speed." The falls of the beach gear sing in agony, raising their chord to a higher register, sheaves turning unevenly in the blocks, eking out the last bit of resilience in the cables. A wire in one set of beach gear slips upward in its fairleads, eases its stress some small part of a ton, jumps, and with a twang becomes fouled.

0625. Again from O11, "Pulling tugs start ten-second surging." Left and right the surging unit swings the pulling unit while the push-boats press the trio between cordage-covered prows. Astern, the floating quadrille at the end of its leash drifts clockwise, northward of the channel. In the process one of the yard tugs backs over the *Windlass*'s double-wire hawser. The hawser must be slacked lest it get chopped by a propeller.

0629. On *Mosopelea* one strand of a line lashing it to *Papago* breaks. Two other strands stretch, hold briefly, then the hawser parts violently. Like a gunshot, the sound can be heard high in the tower of the motionless battleship. The report comes in on both radio circuits, shouted over the background sound of roaring tug engines: "Starboard line leading to the port tug on the inboard nest carried away."

0639. With the flood barely running, a midship tidal gauge reaches 2.6 feet, the same height as at the time of the grounding. The loosely attached gauges at midship reveal no certain evidence of hull motion. The line leading to the forward gauge remains slack.

0640. On the bridge, a sailor standing at a gyrocompass repeater hears it click. The card reads 054°. "The ship's head has come right one degree," he reports.

"Any report on motion?"

A pause. "No report on motion."

0645. Zero hour. The flood is over. Wash from the tugboats sluices between the tidal gauges and the sides of the ship. For a quarter of an hour everything remains taut, at maximum strain. Four destroyers approach through the mist from near the main ship channel and idle in formation forward of the *Missouri,* their sterns prancing in place like the backsides of chariot horses.

0700. A telephone talker reports to the salvage director, "Four destroyers are standing by for orders to pass close aboard to set up bow wave." This was to be the last refloating measure in the contingency plan, held in reserve should all else fail. The fog remains unmercifully thick, and risk of collision is too high. No order is given.

0705. All crew members not on duty are ordered to assemble on the foredeck. Rumors start at once as hundreds of men hasten forward. We're going to be shipped out to barracks on the beach. No, it's another plan to sally ship. Sally who? Hey, sailors, prepare to jump on command—if we all do it together that should get us free.

0708. Sunrise brings no more than a diffuse easterly light beyond Thimble Shoal. Wet veils of fog obscure the slender spar buoys. To the west the red towing lights of the six tugs can be found only by sighting along the rodlike lines reaching astern. Rime glazes the cables as they press through fairleads at the fantail, moistens everything on deck, runs off the grumbling blocks, their sheaves no longer moving. Men hunch at the levers of the carpenter stoppers, winch drivers peek aft under their hooded jackets, the beach control officer atop the turret shields his binoculars as he studies the wires stretched toward the shore like tines of a giant rake.

Tense, wet silence.

0732. From the bridge, an order blares from the public-address system: "The pull is over. Prepare to pull again tomorrow."

The ship's band, assembled in the shelter of the housing, strikes up not a note, returns glumly to its quarters.

The rehearsal, for now Admiral Smith is vindicated in calling it that, was precisely executed. The difficulties were minor and smoothly handled. Immediately afterward, with slide rules, tidal graphs, weight-removal tables, and lists of pulling forces and angles all spread before them, head to head the two admirals again go over their computations. The conclusion is inevitable. Some additional force of undetermined extent is resisting their effort. Homer Wallin is now confident the ship is hung on a rock that has indented the bottom plating.[9] Whatever caused the known gash, that object or something else is restraining the ship. But for the risky use of destroyers to force a bow wave, they have exhausted all orthodox means of salvage. Wallin proposes that the bow be lightened by an additional seven hundred tons in the hope that it would lift the bottom off any obstruction that might be forward. A special barge used in the study of underwater explosions, a UEB, has been under modification for several days to enable it to fit under the *Missouri*'s stern. It is compartmented for controlled ballasting and could add five hundred tons of lift to the stern. But its overall benefit is by no means certain, since its positioning will be awkward, certain to interfere with the pulling hawsers. Adding to its questionable use is the fact that it will not be ready to be put in place until Wednesday night, just before the last good tide on the deadline date. The two men don't admit it to each other, but this latest disappointment has them close to desperation.

There is nothing on record to indicate what questions Blandy might have raised, but ComCruLant's page-long situation report to CinCLantFlt, filed on Tuesday morning within an hour of the debriefing, reveals a certain testiness on Smith's part. Starting with his plan for the Wednesday pull, he turns abruptly to reasons for the Tuesday failure, "Wallin's theory that ship hung on a rock," and his own plan for "completing visual inspection of lower double bottom." Then he dwells on the weather during the pull, dodging the fact that the tide's height was equal to that of the grounding by the statement, "Tide was only one inch above predicted," shifting then to the visibility, "Fog set in which prevented seeing towing ships." After a detailed presentation of the proposed use of the modified UEB, mixed with his plans for the scheduled Wednesday rehearsal, he reverts to recent difficulties with a diver's hose becoming entangled with a propeller and a water barge going aground in the fog. Then, as to the presence of the media, "What they say or write has no effect on our plans . . . they did get a good glimpse of the problem and the difficulties. Today's pull was perhaps the greatest ever made on any grounded ship. It will be more tomorrow."[10]

Smith was an idealist when he went into battle. Through postwar reductions he kept a positive outlook on the ultimate peacetime status of the U.S. Navy. He was optimistic when he took over this task, the greatest challenge of his naval career. There was no reason now for Allan Smith to change his outlook.

Minor adjustments were made to the recovery plan through Tuesday afternoon, despite growing feelings of futility. Divers descended to inspect the area near the skegs and rudders. Another fleet tug was added to the bow unit, *Nipmuk* arriving to take up the guide position between *Recovery* and *Opportune.* Struggle with the pontoons was expedited as two more were placed under the bow. Once again a lighter took away the anchors. Toward the end of the afternoon, with the fog clearing, three destroyers were put to the test of causing a wake. This was all too effective when at twenty-seven knots the wakes fouled the pontoons and jostled three of the fleet tugs to the point of damage. The pontoons proved consistently troublesome. Divers were sent below to work on the set at the bow, while men on the fantail adjusted those under the counter. That work would continue throughout the night. It was easy to assume that this tweaking and adjusting was the exercise of floundering men grasping at straws, yet nothing was done that didn't add buoyancy.

That evening the nation opened its newspapers to read about the big rock holding the vessel fast. They read also that Fred Vinson, head of the House Armed Services Committee, fed up with the doings in the Chesapeake, was advocating the *Missouri*'s retirement. Hope for the warship's future dwindled as Smith's hope for its recovery peaked.

A northerly wind came in with the first of February, the last "rehearsal" day, reaching nineteen knots during the midwatch. By 0230 three of the four sets of pontoons were in place, one set on the stern written off as unmanageable. Two hours later the new, stronger bow-twisting unit took its place. It was clear that there would be a prolonged and generous high tide. All stations were manned by 0530, ninety minutes before the peak. Displaying a more confident attitude than on the prior day, men in undress blues were called out to stand in formation on the foredeck.[11] The operation would differ from the one of the day before by increased effort on twisting.

0545. The bow-twisting unit pulls to starboard, heavy strain taken on the port beach gear, slacking starboard gear. After ten minutes the gyrocompass repeaters start to click—056°, 060°, slowing at 064°. The salvage directors look meaningfully at one another in silence.

0600. Compass rotation stops at 066° as a strain is taken on all beach gear. Ten minutes later, Set 9 to port is slacked and a heavy strain is put on Set 1 to starboard. The tugs in the twisting unit slack their lines and cross the bow to port.

0615. The ship swings wildly to the left, compass cards ticking off the degrees like an underway change of course. They need now only to start motion and take a subsequent straight pull for fifteen feet to put the ship afloat. The beach gear is under intense strain, worn from the prior day; two cables part in rapid sequence. Slowly now the ship's head moves counterclockwise one degree a minute, hawsers of the twisting unit holding at right angles to the warship's centerline.

0626. Ship's heading is 020.5° as it rolls to a 1.5° port list. Patience is called for; no urgency, even as the time gets uncomfortably close to peak tide. The pulling tugs are ordered to one-third speed, which they hold for thirty minutes.

0644. Observers in nearby boats report the stern is down by five feet. An order is given to flood the peak tanks to regain trim. The *Missouri* is afloat. Sternward motion is hardly noticeable, although the beach gear cables begin to turn slowly with the windlasses. Sailors stand ready to cast off the wire ropes, burning through them where carpenter stoppers remain frozen. The salvagers stand and wait and watch. Twenty-five minutes elapse. No shudder, no sense of motion has been felt aboard ship. Quietly during that period, clipboard in hand, Rear Admiral Smith prepares a dispatch.

0709. The message is terse. "ComCruLant to CinCLantFlt: *Missouri* reports for duty. 7 fathoms of water under her keel. Signed Smith." In the joy of being afloat once more, Admiral Smith may be forgiven for putting seven fathoms of water under the keel rather than at the waterline.

Immense battle ensigns are hoisted to the peaks of the fore and main masts. The ship's call letters in code flags, along with the message "Reporting for duty," are two-blocked at the yards. Able-Peter has been struck. Commander Peckham, his voice strained with fatigue, unemotionally announces the good news throughout the ship. A cheer goes up on deck as the band strikes up "Anchors Aweigh." Small craft circling at a distance join in the celebration with their horns and flags as strains of "The Missouri Waltz" and "Nobody Knows the Trouble I've Seen" drift across the waters.

USS *Missouri* leaves Drydock Number 4 in the Norfolk Naval Shipyard, 9 December 1949, prior to the change of command. *U.S. Navy*

The first view from a service craft of the ship on the day it grounded. The USS *Kittiwake* (ASR-13) is tied to the starboard side. The tall structure near the battleship's stern is its aircraft retrieval crane. *U.S. Navy*

The stern after the arrival of the first fleet of tugs, revealing a draft of twenty-nine feet, nearly seven feet short of its departure draft. *U.S. Navy*

The bow showing a draft of twenty-nine feet, some six feet less than the ship's draft before it touched bottom. The *Kittiwake* is along the starboard side. *U.S. Navy*

Aerial view taken on the afternoon of 17 January as tugs hover around the stricken vessel. Steam is being produced by emergency turbo generators. *U.S. Navy*

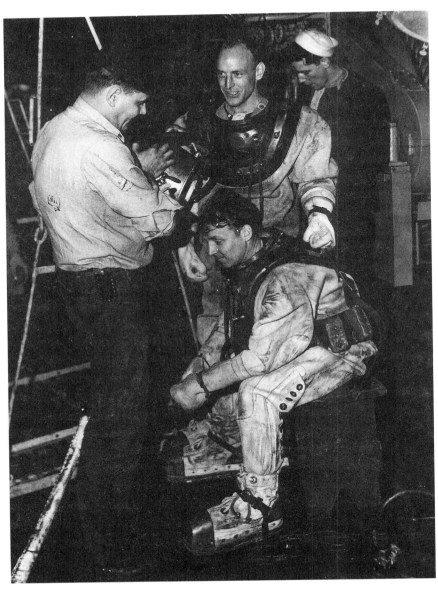

Divers preparing to descend from the *Kittiwake* to investigate the condition of the battleship's bottom. They were lowered on the suspended platform to the left of the picture. *U.S. Navy*

The Army dredge *Comber,* with a tug assisting, comes alongside to commence dredging operations. *U.S. Navy*

Aerial view of the 20 January pull. The river of water produced by the tugs extends well forward of the battleship. The yoked stern of the USS *Windlass* (ARSD-4) is visible to the left. *U.S. Navy*

Missouri crew members arriving at fleet landing for first liberty, 22 January 1950. *Norfolk Virginian-Pilot, Mays Collection, Norfolk Public Library*

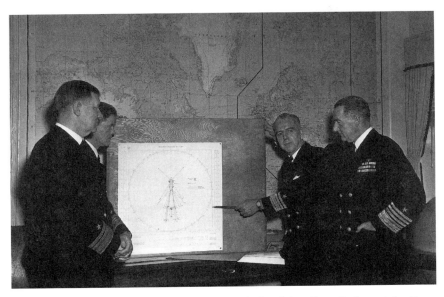

Press conference on 23 January in Admiral Blandy's office. *Left to right,* Rear Admiral Wallin, Rear Admiral Good, Rear Admiral Smith (explaining the planned pull-off), and Admiral Blandy. *Mays Collection*

The four men who were in charge at the January 23 press conference held aboard ship. *Left to right,* Captain Brown, Commander Peckham, Lieutenant Commander Morris, and Lieutenant Arnold. *Mays Collection*

Charlton Barron of the *Norfolk-Ledger Dispatch* and Helen Delich of the *Baltimore Sun* interviewing Lieutenant Arnold. Behind them can be seen part of the beach gear on a protective platform built over the ship's teak deck. *Mays Collection*

Afterdeck of the battleship as sailors prepare for the pull-off. In the foreground is one of the massive blocks making up part of the nine sets of beach gear. *Mays Collection*

Missouri returns to dry dock, floating high after the pull-off, 1 February.
Mays Collection

Court of inquiry and principal witnesses convene on foredeck, opening day of the court. *Left to right,* judge advocate Lieutenant Commander Bradbury; president of the court Admiral Miles; court members, Captains Field and McClean; defendant Captain Brown; Brown's counsel, Captain Wood; Morris's counsel, Captain Tiemroth; counsel to the judge advocate, Captain Shanklin; assistant counsel to Brown, Lieutenant Flees; first witness, Commander Peckham. The O8 level is the narrow, pentagonal structure just behind the muzzles of the number two battery. *Mays Collection*

Captain Brown demonstrates for the court how communication took place between the conn on the outer bridge and a telephone talker in the pilot-house. *Mays Collection*

Judge Advocate Bradbury receives a logbook submitted as evidence by Commander Peckham. *Mays Collection*

Navigator Morris on the right with his counsel, Captain Tiemroth, at the court of inquiry. *Mays Collection*

Commander Millett being informed that the court has designated him a defendant. *Mays Collection*

Lieutenant Carr, combat operations officer, consults with counsel, Lt. Harry McCoy, USNR, and Robert M. Hughes Jr., admiralty lawyer, during the hearing. *Mays Collection*

Commander Peckham and Ensign Harris. Peckham spoke voluntarily in Harris's defense. *Mays Collection*

7

And So to Twenty-seven Feet

Despite the flags and music there was little elation among the men in the conning tower as the ship edged into the makeshift channel. The warship had given the two salvage directors several nerve-racking minutes once it felt deep water under its keel, lurching hard to port and pressing toward the shoal. Rudders have a way of ruling vessels with sternway, causing them to do the predictably disagreeable. Finally, its motion restrained by tugs and the hull trimmed by shifts in ballast, the ship settled into place for the somber trip to the dockyard.

Captain Brown, on what was likely to be his last journey as CO of a capital ship, again stood on the O8 level at the conn of the powerless vessel, giving helm orders to maintain a balanced strain within the nest of eleven tugs. Dragging pontoons astern like tin cans behind a newlywed's car, chased by a ragtag collection of service vessels and disorderly small craft, the ship approached the naval base as the crew of the carrier USS *Franklin D. Roosevelt* mustered for Admiral Blandy's change-of-command ceremonies.[1] That the *Missouri* had successfully rejoined "all ships afloat" furnished its own crew little pride, given its forlorn state.

Allan Smith should have been jubilant, having accomplished the nearly impossible a full day ahead of his own forecast. As one of his last official acts, the warm-hearted Admiral Blandy responded to Smith's "reporting for duty" message with one of his own:

Please convey to all activities that have been under your operational control in connection with the salvage . . . my hearty congratulations and a well done for the outstanding manner in which all phases of the operation have been conducted. . . .

129

STRIKE ABLE-PETER

The skillful planning, coordination of effort, and smart seamanship displayed reflect a high degree of leadership and an excellent performance
by all officers and men who participated.[2]

Allan Smith relished the message along with an early morning salad
prepared by his steward and decorated with red peppers spelling out
the same message, "Well Done."

The refloating came as somewhat of a surprise, accompanied by
only minor flaws—one sailor with bruised shins (the only injury during the two-week salvage period), a missing pontoon believed to have
sunk, the salvage vessels *Hoist* and *Windlass* colliding with little damage, some parted lines. By nightfall the ship would be dry-docked,
and Smith and Wallin would be able to determine the nature of the
mysterious obstruction, reconciling differences they patiently maintained. But other matters pressed on the admiral, not yielding to his
fatigue. The court of inquiry was scheduled to open formally two
days hence. As convening authority he would take no active part in it,
but he had to make required personnel available and face the staffing
of the battleship once its repairs were completed. Current estimates
were that the ship would be under way for the Caribbean within a
week; the hearing was certain to extend beyond that period, and several of the officers and men were to be called as witnesses. Ten days
earlier, after the formation of the court, Captain Brown and Lieutenant Commander Morris had been informed that they should seek
counsel, being identified as "interested parties," having contributed
significantly to the events under investigation. According to the rules
of naval courts, interested parties may or may not be defendants in a
case, but in being at risk they are entitled to counsel and to cross-
examine other witnesses. Both Brown and Morris were named as
defendants.

About then Admiral Smith had tried discreetly to arrange for
Brown's immediate replacement.[3] For some months he had been cul-
tivating Irving T. Duke for big-ship command and thought him suitable for the slot. While aboard the *Missouri* Smith had told no one of
his intentions, not even his own chief of staff, but somehow the news
of possible movement got out. Brown's Naval Academy classmate and
chosen counsel, Capt. Chester C. Wood, skipper of the cruiser
Albany, picked up the name Smith had suggested, and a week before
the final pull he came aboard to see the admiral. Wood contended

130

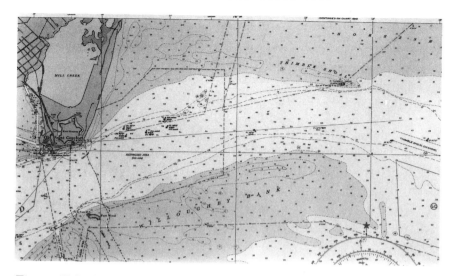

Fig. 5. U.S. Coast and Geodetic Survey Chart Number 400, Hampton Roads, dated 11 September 1950, shows the buoyage added as a consequence of the *Missouri*'s grounding. The shape of the hull and exit channel is clearly outlined by the five-fathom contour line. Twelve- and seventeen-foot spots near the "bow" are probably tailings left from placement of tidal gauges. For more detail, see back endsheet.

that unless the ship was to make a movement that conflicted with other demands on its CO, it was not fair to relieve an officer before he was found guilty. Smith sent Wood to see Blandy. Blandy sustained Wood's view, telling Wood that if there was to be a court-martial it might be held after Portrex, and promised to take the issue up with Adm. William M. Fechteler, Blandy's designated relief.[4] Rear Admiral Smith thereby lost his bid for an expeditious shift in personnel. At any rate he did not want the *Missouri* to go into Portrex with Brown or Morris aboard. Finally, when it became appropriate to relieve the two as necessary participants in the inquiry, Duke, who had been recently assigned to the cruiser *Rochester*, was no longer available to relieve. Commander Peckham, it appeared, would be called only as an early witness, responsible for turning the ship's records over to the court. So Brown could be relieved quickly, with Peckham standing in as acting CO at least until someone was found to take the ship to sea. In the meantime ComCruLant would have little time to rest.

On the afternoon of Friday, 3 February, two days after the *Mis-*

souri's return to port and the day following William Blandy's retirement, the court of inquiry came to order in the headquarters building of ComCruLant. The courtroom was a drab, high-ceilinged, government-issue meeting room on a corner of an upper floor. Pole-mounted electric fans were placed strategically between windows covered with venetian blinds. Fluorescent rectangles, interspersed with bowl-covered lights, hung over long, grey tables and rows of padded steel chairs. The only similarity it bore to a hall of justice was a raised platform at one end for the three court members. Chart racks were arranged to one side and stenographers' desks placed before the platform, near those for the defendants and their counsels. Wire recording technology was not adequately reliable for courtroom use, so yeomen in dress blues sat at stenotype machines to record the proceedings.

Rear Adm. Milton E. Miles, Commander of Cruiser Division Four and senior member of the court, took his place between the two other members, Capts. W. L. Field and E. R. McLean. Lt. Comdr. Malcolm J. Bradbury, a legal officer on the staff of the Atlantic Fleet Air Force, was designated as judge advocate, with Capt. E. W. Shanklin, commanding officer of the training battleship *Mississippi,* as his counsel. Bradbury called for order and set the stage for the forthcoming proceedings. The hearing would be open to the public, a practice that, if not instigated by Admiral Smith, certainly had his approval. He had conducted his last press conference on the salvage, or so he declared, but he adhered to his advocacy of openness in naval affairs. Photography would be allowed, limited so as not to be disruptive. The court reserved the right to clear the room and to conduct certain potentially sensitive parts of the hearing in closed session. Seats were allocated for the public, and the customary caution concerning expected decorum at all times was delivered. With that the tall, crusty Rear Admiral Miles turned to the defendants.[5]

"While you were serving as navigating officer and commanding officer of the USS *Missouri,*" he began, and went on to recount the events leading up to and including the grounding. He defined the court's role as fact-finding body, required to present its findings and recommendations to the convening authority following the hearing. Brown, who had been ill and under a doctor's care when he reported to the *Missouri*'s bridge for the final pull, appeared rested and had resumed his customary military bearing. The two defendants looked at Admiral Miles intently as he added, "You will have the rights of the accused before a court-martial."

The day's first and only witness was Commander Peckham, who handed to the court the record books and charts collected under his authority as executive officer. A note was made that some documents were classified as restricted and would not be open to the public. The quartermaster's notebook, containing orders to the wheel, was noted as containing entries up to 25 January, the day it had been turned over to Peckham. The executive officer explained that immediately after the grounding he had ordered the operations officer and engineering officer to put their charts and records under lock and key. Some days later, according to Peckham, Captain Brown ordered the documents placed under the custody of the exec. Verification was requested by Captain Wood and approved by the court that certain documents that had not been securely protected after the grounding be subject to further testimony to establish that there had been no tampering with the contents. Following these preliminaries the court adjourned to resume at the Portsmouth Navy Yard, where they would examine the ship.

The dry-docking procedure had been slow, as divers had made additional investigations before the dock was pumped. The hull still dripped as the three court members, in heavy winter bridge coats, stooped under the plating to investigate the long gash on the bottom. They were shown the damage where three fuel tanks had been ruptured, between frames 100 and 114 on the starboard side under the machinery section. A six-foot flat steel bar was found lodged in the opening, the shell plating around it torn back like the cover of a sardine can. The conclusion was that the battleship's hull had split as it passed over a portion of a submerged wreck, taking some of the wreckage with it. The mysterious boulders remained unexplained.

From the dank underpinnings of the dry dock the party repaired to the main deck, where they posed before the number one battery for a formal photo—court members, judge advocate, counsels to the defendants, Captain Brown, and Commander Peckham. They went from there to the conning tower, followed by members of the press, to survey the two navigation areas. Brown's counsel repeatedly requested that members of the court note the distances and separations between the exterior and interior portions of the bridge on O8. Captain Brown gallantly posed for press photographer Jim Mays, peering from the open bridge through an open porthole into the pilot house,* Peckham looking over his shoulder as a sailor within stood in attendance. Admiral Miles asked about the location of the magnetic compass nearest to the conning positions, raising suspicion among observers that it might fit into Brown's much-referenced "unusual and unfortunate chain of circumstances." The admiral was assured that any issue concerning the compass would be brought out in subsequent testimony. At that point the court was adjourned until Monday, taking the weekend to review the submitted documentary evidence.

Permitting the defendants to withhold their testimony until all other testimony had been presented, and calling the early witnesses in order of rank, Judge Advocate Bradbury had Commander Peckham return for additional direct questioning before calling for Commander Millett's testimony as operations officer. The story of the grounding from the executive officer's viewpoint on both conning tower levels was recounted, including the three warnings of danger he had given. With the operations officer's added testimony, a composite picture of the happenings emerged. Millett told of the manila envelope containing the request to run the acoustic range that had been received from the district commandant, how he had passed the package to navigator Morris, and his own impression that there were five buoys making up the range.

"I know now that there were two," he added.

Bradbury asked, "Was there any discussion of the multiplicity of buoys?"

"No."

The ops officer went on to describe the ship's approach to the range. "I didn't see any more than one buoy, dead ahead. . . . I pointed the buoy out to the captain and stated that we could pass it to the starboard. . . . I didn't realize that the buoy was the one that it actually was."

Following that implication, Admiral Miles cleared the court. Minutes later the room was called to order and Millett sat ruefully to hear

---

* *Pilot* photographer Mays proved prescient in arranging the pose. Nine days later, a similar scene would be described to the court.

the admiral address him. "It appears to the court that you have interesting subject matter. . . . Therefore you are designated as an interested party." The session was then adjourned until the afternoon to give Millett time to arrange for counsel. As yet not a defendant, with counsel he would have the right to cross-examine witnesses.

Reporters used the time to check with the Coast Guard on descriptions of the buoys as posted through "Notice to Mariners"— frequently issued multipage bulletins describing all changes to buoys and their charted representation. Confusion persisted in the court as to the labeling, but a spokesman told the press that the last notice had been distributed by mail and marine radio on 10 January, identifying the only two buoys in the water as N and S. Here then was a link in the "unfortunate chain of circumstances."

Commander Peckham spent most of the afternoon recounting events that led to the grounding. He revealed that he had been uninformed about the acoustic range and the plan to run the range until ten minutes before it was initiated, when he asked the CO about shifting the conn after passing Fort Wool. Following that he had a discussion with Lieutenant Commander Morris about the plan, examined the course plotted between the buoys, felt that the track as shown looked safe, and, before going below to the main navigating bridge, left Morris with the words, "For God's sake, watch it." As to the actual documents requesting the run, he did not see them until three days after the stranding.

When asked repeatedly by Brown's counsel about the practice of shifting the conn in restricted waters, Peckham conceded that it might take more than a minute to descend the four levels, but that it had been a smooth procedure under the two previous skippers. The judge advocate suggested to Wood that his concern for these matters appeared excessive, to which Wood replied that his questions were intended to "lay the groundwork for subsequent testimony by the commanding officer." Peckham maintained his composure.

Later the XO stood before a large chart of Hampton Roads to show the plotted position of the ship when he delivered the first of his warnings to the captain. The two spar buoys in the fishing area entered into the testimony only when Peckham said he had seen them dead ahead as he first became aware of the dangerous course. Questioned by Admiral Miles about the appearances of both the spars and the acoustic range markers, he asserted that the spar buoys had an "appearance entirely dissimilar, and couldn't possibly be confused with the others as being identical in appearance."

Peckham's final commentary came down heavily on the operations officer. He charged that the operations department had fallen down in its tasks prior to the mishap. Millett's newly assigned counsel, Lt. Comdr. Melvin A. Miller, objected and asked to have the comment stricken from the record. His objection was sustained. Peckham went on to state that he knew of no warnings sent to the bridge from radar navigators under Commander Millett's jurisdiction. He recalled that Captain Brown placed more faith in the operations officer than in the navigation officer, and prior to the grounding he, Peckham, had told Millett that his department "fell down" in some of its responsibilities. On that basis his charge was made to stick.

Meanwhile work on the battleship neared completion. It was scheduled to go to sea for trials on the fourth day of the hearing, and thereafter to prepare to partake in Portrex. The new CinCLantFlt, Admiral Fechteler, was cooperative. He ordered Capt. H. Page Smith, who seven weeks earlier had been relieved by William Brown, to return to command "for the time being and at least until the legal proceedings are completed." To Page Smith's satisfaction, two of his former *Missouri* officers returned aboard as navigator and operations officer. Thus the *Missouri*'s three principal officers in the inquiry were temporarily relieved of duty. Commander Peckham would remain aboard as executive officer.

Millett was called back for another day of testimony. Captain Brown, wearing glasses for the first time during the proceedings, listened intently as his operations officer admitted to having been confused on the purpose of the spars and to telling his skipper that they "may mark the range." Several in the room gasped in astonishment at the admission. Only the day before, the spars had been identified on the chart by Peckham, positioned more than a mile distant from deep water and described as being so dissimilar as to make confusion impossible. With his statement, the court judged that Millett had implicated himself and informed him that he was designated a defendant along with the navigator and CO.

Commander Millett went on to describe the encounter between the navigator and the captain in which Morris had told Brown "We must come right," causing the skipper to tell Millett, "The navigator does not know where he is; go find out." With that, Millett had repaired to the chart room, where he soon heard alarms and orders making him aware that the ship had gone aground. He failed to confirm any of the warnings sent to the primary conn from the O4 level. He said he had been at the captain's side when the last of Peckham's three orders sounded over a loudspeaker, but he neither received the orders nor knew of any acknowledgment.

Captain Wood cross-examined the operations officer on behalf of Captain Brown. Did Millett feel he got along well with the captain? Yes, he sensed a "warm, friendly" attitude on the part of his skipper, who had "turned to him as a trusted advisor." Summarizing his naval career, Millett said that he had gained "valuable experience regarding the obligations of a naval officer in command" and possibly had given Brown "some knowledge that I'd been in command of a ship."

The court then called Wallace Taylor, a scientist at the Naval Ordnance Laboratory at Fort Monroe. Judge Advocate Bradbury asked him why the written instructions referenced a 2 December "Notice to Mariners" rather than the 7 December publication with revised locations.

"I am afraid that was my error," replied Taylor. The 10 January issue described them as they were on 17 January, he went on. Also, a laboratory chart delivered to the *Missouri* showed them properly.

Questioned by Brown's counsel, Taylor said that a navigator would have no idea what the buoys looked like from the "Notice to Mariners," although their shape and color were described in the laboratory chart. Bradbury resumed questioning, and Taylor said that if the navigator had plotted his course through the buoy locations described in the 7 December publication he would have been off the range by four hundred feet. The 7 December notice stated that the buoys were labeled N and S, while the laboratory chart identified them as B and C and as having letters about eight inches high.

Bradbury brought in Lt. Comdr. C. I. Steele, USCG, chief of the Aids to Navigation Section of the Fifth Coast Guard District. Steele confirmed what most mariners already held, that one should never rely on such privately maintained buoys in harbor navigation. Asked whether his office kept a mailing list of interests requesting local "Notice to Mariners," Steele said the list included several naval vessels based in Norfolk.

"Is the *Missouri* on the list?"

"Yes, Sir."

"When was the *Missouri* placed on the list?"

"February 6, 1950." The day before yesterday.

Next to be called was Lt. Roland Hatfield, officer of the deck until ten minutes before the grounding. He reported seeing Captain Brown peering intently ahead and telling Hatfield to "keep a sharp lookout for the acoustic range." When Hatfield indicated that he didn't understand the order, Brown told him to "get yourself informed." Hatfield then went into the chart room, where an officer was apparently plotting the ship's position; he could not identify the man. Commander Millett was also in the chart room, according to Hatfield, and had pointed out four penciled crosses apparently marking the buoys. Hatfield said he was unable to find out what they looked like. When he returned to the outer bridge, Brown had told him to take the conn while he went in to check the chart. After two or three minutes the captain returned and resumed the conn "with the words 'I have it,' or words to that effect." At 0810 he had turned over his station to Lieutenant Arnold and gone below.

Was there a leadsman in the chains taking hand soundings during the episode? Hatfield explained that leadsmen take soundings only in poor visibility or briefly for practice off Fort Wool. He was then asked to identify the chart he had seen on the primary conning bridge from among those introduced as evidence. With the officers of the court and defendant counsels standing around the table, for each chart he was shown he said firmly, "That's not the one." The question of the missing chart, if any, was left unresolved.

The inquiry went into its fifth day when Lieutenant Arnold, officer of the deck when the ship went aground, was called. Arnold said he had suspected the nature of the spar buoys to be shallow-water markers, becoming the first witness to state that. He went on to relate the details of the conversation that had taken place between the navigator and the captain. Morris had recommended a course almost due east in a frantic voice, according to Arnold, at about the time the ship passed north of the northern acoustic buoy. Brown heeded him for a moment, giving a helm order to come right. As the ship turned, the engine room reported failures, probably due to sand in the intakes, at which point Arnold ordered the men in the chains to commence taking soundings.

Did he hear the leadsmen's reports? There was no opportunity to, with critical events happening so fast. The first of such events was "perplexing" to Arnold—the captain's order to "come left." The captain explained it somewhat to the effect that "I have to steer a steady course for data on the range." Arnold transmitted an order to stand by the bow anchors. Brown then ordered right rudder, followed by hard right rudder, as main control rang up "Stop" on the annunciators. Arnold relayed that information to the captain, and there followed a series of engine orders in rapid succession, before the engineer could talk directly to the skipper. Brown replied, "I understand; stop all engines," or words to that effect, according to Arnold.

Questioned by Captain Wood, the officer of the deck said he didn't think the skipper was steering for the spars. Did he recall anything about a danger line between Thimble Shoal Light and Old Point Comfort? Arnold said he did not.

As officer of the deck, shouldn't he have told the skipper of his fears concerning the ship's course? Judge Advocate Bradbury intervened, arguing that under *Navy Regulations* such responsibility applied only if Arnold had the conn, and that his duties remained secondary while the captain, with direct command of the ship, discussed the course with two other senior officers. Soon after, and with obvious relief, Arnold stepped from the witness stand.

Next on the stand was Ens. Elwin Harris, assistant navigator. He stated that his assignment on 17 January was his second at the primary plot, having been first given the duty during the trial run in December. In his testimony Harris said he had been receiving data on bearings once per minute and had experienced little difficulty plotting the ship's position. An emergency order to the chief quartermaster by Commander Peckham requesting continuous reports on bearings caused a breakdown in his plotting activity. The resultant rapid fire of bearings coming in over his headphones virtually paralyzed his chart work, Harris reported.

At several points during the lengthy questioning, without counsel,

Harris answered, "I can't remember." Shown the chart alleged to have been on the plotting table during the last few minutes of the run, Harris noted a danger bearing marked in red and the two correct range buoys similarly marked. He said he did not recall any red penciling on the day of the grounding.

What happened to the chart he worked with? It was consigned to a safe a few minutes after the mishap, without any red penciling, was the reply. Asked whether he was certain there was no danger bearing marked on the chart, Harris replied, "I can't remember."

Admiral Miles shifted in his chair, exasperated. Abruptly he ordered Harris, "Come here." The ensign approached, and the senior court member reminded him of his oath on the Bible to tell the truth, the whole truth, and nothing but the truth. He then ordered Harris to return to the witness stand on the next day and to divulge no testimony to persons outside the courtroom. Admonishing him sternly to keep his oath in mind, Miles adjourned the session.

At the time, naval law came under the Articles for the Government of the Navy, these dating back with few revisions to the birth of the republic and containing many provisions inconsistent with the Bill of Rights. Most legal minds, and certainly those in command in the U.S. Navy, felt that the framers of the Constitution did not mean the Bill of Rights to apply to soldiers and sailors.[6] Under the Articles that applied to active-duty naval personnel, all officers with command status were enabled to act as judge and jury, even concerning capital offenses. Nonlawyers were allowed to prosecute cases before a general court-martial, often did so, and could retire in closed session to reach decisions that were not required to be published. Through World War II such traditional military legal procedures were accepted for reasons of security and secrecy. Postwar, several legal cases emerged out of the transitional military environment that clashed with the sense of justice of a more enlightened citizenry. While abrogation of many civilian rights remained acceptable in the name of military control, a cry to curb command influence in legal matters was being heard. The Truman administration's drive toward armed forces unification would lead to the landmark consolidation of all military law in the Uniform Code of Military Justice (UCMJ) and bring a large measure of civilian justice into the military world.

Not signed by the president and put into effect until May 1950, the UCMJ did not replace the prior form of law in the USS *Missouri* incident. The official source document for the conduct of the investigation was the *Naval Courts and Boards* manual. To some extent the inquiry approximated a civilian grand jury hearing, with the notable difference that there was no peer review. The board, whose sole objective was to make recommendations for further action based on the facts determined, was a command group. While it is interesting how much the conduct of the *Missouri* case anticipated the new procedures, with sessions opened to the public, recourse to legally trained personnel, and notification of individual rights, it did not go far in curbing command influence. The convening authority and all court members were seagoing officers whose legal exposure, if any, came from highly specialized staff assignments. They were investigating the nautical activities of officers whose primary duties took place at sea. Defendants and witnesses with counsel were less interested in legal than in contemporary professional support. It was up to the legally trained judge advocate, Malcolm Bradbury, to keep the procedures in conformance with the Articles for the Government of the Navy. There were occasions when the limits of the Articles would be tested, yet to Bradbury's credit a sense of the new view of justice permeated the proceedings four months before such would be required by law.

On the stand for his second day as an uneasy witness, Ensign Harris was asked if he had investigated his responsibilities after receiving the navigational assignment. Not specifically; he based his notions on watching assistant navigators at work.

And what were his duties?

". . . to wear earphones, point out navigational aids and mark bearings on the chart."

For Admiral Miles this simplification was the last straw. He openly reprimanded the ensign and stated "for the record" that "the court has some doubts not only as to the competence of the witness, but also as to his ability as a naval officer." Then he cleared the courtroom for another private discussion among the members. Upon resuming the session, the admiral advised Harris of his rights and instructed him to seek counsel as an interested party. Seated among the observers was Capt. A. R. Harris, USN, a dental officer in the Fifth Naval District, the ensign's father. Later in the day, when Lt.

Comdr. Randall D. Foster reported to the court as Elwin Harris's counsel, Admiral Miles, referring to young Harris, instructed the counsel to "advise him if you will, to keep his eyes and ears open from now on."

The first enlisted man to be called was QM1 Richard Wentz, who had been in charge of maintaining the charts and aids-to-navigation records. He identified the assistant navigator's chart without hesitation and stated that he had seen a red danger bearing marked on it, recalling that he noticed the red markings a day before the battleship had gotten under way.

Captain Shanklin, the sea-wise counsel to the judge advocate, took up questioning of the quartermaster, focusing on the identification marks on the spar buoys. When the designations of buoys are changed, he asked, shouldn't the navigational records containing them be updated to reflect the changes?

"That is correct," said Wentz, who went on to explain that the spars belonged in a shallow-water category that seldom preoccupied the navigation department of a deep-draft battleship. Shanklin then produced records in evidence to show that the latest designations of the fishnet markers had not been entered in the ship's charts and records, inferring neglect on the part of the quartermaster.

Wentz's face flushed red. As to the chart, he pointed out, the failure to keep it current lay with the Hydrographic Office. Further, a separate publication dating before the official record on the ship did reflect the changes. His prompt and knowledgeable response had Shanklin, Captain Brown, and even the old barnacle Admiral Miles laughing.

At one point Captain Wood addressed the sailor, "As an expert in your field, Wentz, would you say that . . ."

Politely smiling, Wentz declined the designation.

Judge Advocate Bradbury spoke up, "Since various questions have been asked this witness assuming he is an expert in his field, I'd like the court to declare him an expert."

Admiral Miles concurred, "Yes, he is an expert."

The quartermaster had gained the deference of the court and defense officers. His testimony resolving the state of the plotting chart, clashing as it did with that of Elwin Harris, did not enhance the ensign's position. Just before Wentz stepped down, in an unusual move, Admiral Miles acknowledged the competence of the quarter-master. "The court would like to commend the witness for the straightforward testimony he has given. It was most important, accurate and painstaking."

Further conflicts in testimony arose with the questioning of two chief petty officers. Chief Quartermaster Reams, who had stood safety watch on the steersman in the wheelhouse, said that he heard "loud and clear" Peckham's warning to Brown being delivered only a few feet from the skipper. Peckham had stated that he had sent the warnings from the O4 bridge and received acknowledgment via telephone from the primary conn. Chief Quartermaster Rice, who was stationed on O4 near the plotting table, partially confirmed Peckham's account but denied knowledge of any attempt to use the 21-MC "squawk box." When the words of Peckham's warnings were read from his testimony, neither CPO remembered any recommendation for "full speed astern." As to the time the warnings were given, both chiefs seemed to believe that it was somewhat later in the ship's passage than Peckham had inferred. After the chiefs reviewed the navigational records that had been introduced as evidence, each was asked about the whereabouts of the fathometer log. Both said that it had disappeared shortly after the grounding. Reams said that Rice had reported the fathometer as working, but not working properly. Rice said he had no reports on failures in the fathometer until after the grounding. If nothing else, discrepancies in testimony tended to show that there was no collusion between the officers and men during the three weeks that had elapsed since the episode.

Even for the Navy, which customarily worked a five-and-a-half-day week ashore, this week seemed longer. On Saturday morning the inquiry went into its seventh day. George Peckham was back on the stand, having returned from the battleship's trial run under Captain Smith. His final testimony before departing with the ship early the following week was intended to present more documentary evidence: the ship's organization manual, the magnetic compass record book, engine room acceleration-deceleration tables, a fathometer chart.[7] The nature of the various duties of the principal operating officers was read into the record while most listeners leaned on their elbows, heads pressing resignedly on their hands.

"Who is responsible for the overall training on the ship?"

"I am."

"Who assigns personnel to special sea details within the operations department?"

"That is the responsibility of the operations officer to do himself or to assign as he desires."

Referring to the assignment of Harris, "Did you investigate the qualifications?"

"I considered him familiar with the existing situation."

"Did you know he would do the plotting?"

"I assumed he would, yes."

On 17 January, "Did you know he was doing the plotting?"

"I saw him there."

Bradbury asked Peckham if he remembered his words "For God's sake, watch it!" Peckham replied that he did, but that he had spoken them to the navigator, not to Harris.

Lieutenant Commander Miller, Millett's counsel, took over Peckham's questioning. Again concerning Harris, he asked, "Can you recall a conversation between you and the navigation officer?"

"Substantially. I remember that Ensign Harris was recommended and I concurred."

"Was the scarcity of officers discussed?"

"That was mentioned, yes."

"Was the appointment primarily for plotting purposes, and did not the operations officer tell you that Ensign Harris would be used for plotting only?"

"Yes. I approved his assignment as a temporary measure. I felt him very competent."

"Had you discussed the state of training in the operations department?"

"I mentioned the state of training of the COC department on two or three occasions. I wanted more coordination between conn and COC."

"Are you satisfied that the operations department could achieve satisfactory coordination in only one trip in and out of the harbor?"

"No, but personnel in navigation had made more than one trip in and out. . . ."

"What ship won the battle efficiency rating for Cru N?"

"The *Missouri*."

"What was the standing of the *Missouri* in the competition among ships?"

"Number one."

Lieutenant Commander Foster, Harris's counsel, took over the questioning. Carefully he established that Harris was only in an acting capacity since there was no qualified officer after the departure of the regular assistant navigator. Of two officers to be considered for the position, Harris had more navigation training. He had the executive officer state that he had complete confidence in Harris as assistant navigator "for straight plotting on a routine channel run."

He asked Peckham, "How about operation under the stress and strain of standing into the harbor?"

"From my observation of Harris on the bridge, I did have confidence in him . . . one of the most competent junior officers on the ship."

Foster, attempting to establish the state of confusion at the plotting table when Harris was trying to do his work, addressed the executive officer again. "Commander Peckham, is it not true that hardened navigators have even told the commanding officer to 'stand aside while I finish my plot'?"

"That is true—in fact, I have done the same thing myself," Peckham replied.

"Would you expect Ensign Harris to say anything of that sort to any of the officers who were in the room when he was making his plot?"

"No, I can't visualize Ensign Harris saying anything of the sort." Even Peckham's normally intractable face broke into the edge of a smile as laughter spread across the room.

The discussion took a hard turn as the counsels for Harris and Brown strove to delve into the competence of the young ensign. Captain Wood, seated at the table with Brown, raising questions to show that the ensign was unfit, asked Peckham, "Wouldn't you expect a young officer in the United States Navy to have sufficient intelligence—"

"I object!" shouted Foster.

The court asked that the question be rephrased.

"Upon the assignment of a young officer to an important assignment, would you, as executive officer, expect him to have sufficient intelligence and imagination to go out and learn his duties?"

"Yes, I would."

Wood questioned Peckham further, proposing that Harris could have qualified himself for the plotting role by the use of "canned" navigation problems, lacking practical ones.

Foster interjected, "Can an officer learn from 'canned' problems how to resist instructions of superior officers in the chart room?" Laughter again stirred among the listeners before Peckham answered in the negative.

The dispute became so prolonged that the judge advocate spoke up. He told the court that Wood and Foster were drifting far afield from the actual intent of the hearing.

Admiral Miles disagreed. Charges had been made against Harris that could be injurious to his naval career. In his view, the senior court member declared, all matters concerning them should be aired fully.

Finally, when the counsels had exhausted their efforts, Admiral Miles took over questioning of the exec. He referred to earlier testimony that in March of 1949 the operational readiness of the ship had been rated as "good." What would Peckham consider the ship's rating, he asked, when it started out from the naval base on 17 January?

"Satisfactory," replied the officer.

Who had made out the last fitness report of Ensign Harris? It was made out in rough by the operations officer, checked by the executive officer, and rechecked by the commanding officer, explained Peckham.

Concerning Harris as assistant navigator, "Did you assign him?"

"No."

"Was he assigned in writing?"

"No, Sir, I believe it was verbal."

"Did the captain assign him?"

"I would say that the captain assigned him."

"Did he assign him in writing?"

"I do not remember it being in writing, no."

"Who is responsible on the *Missouri* for the expeditious routing of incoming classified matter?"

"The chief clerk in the captain's office handles incoming mail."

Miles asked Peckham to retell the three recommendations he had made to the captain prior to the grounding of the ship.

"One: 'Executive officer recommends coming right, standing in to shoal water.' The recommendation was acknowledged. Two: Another recommendation to come right. This also was acknowledged. Three: A recommendation for backing full on two sets of communications. The talker said it was acknowledged on the 1-JV."

Admiral Miles asked him if, at the close of his testimony, he had anything to add for consideration by the court.

"In view of all opinions that have been heard about Ensign Harris," Peckham responded, "I feel that I should say that, without briefing on the acoustic range run, the duty of plotting the course of the ship should have been assigned a more senior officer—even myself if necessary."

This prompted the judge advocate to ask him if he had suggested asking for a more experienced plotter.

"No, everything seemed normal when I was on the bridge and I had not been let in on the secret that we were going to run the range."

The court was then adjourned until Monday, but not before Commander Peckham was told that he must be prepared to be called back from the ship if additional testimony was required. Meanwhile the *Missouri*'s successful completion of its postrepair trials found the crew returned to overly familiar work—spending another weekend loading fuel, ammunition, and stores. They would then be back to where they had been four weeks ago, prepared to depart for Guantánamo Bay. A frantic parade of witnesses was scheduled to be in court early in the week, prior to the ship's departure. Some, identified to give evidence later in the hearing, would remain behind, while most of the crew would wait for news from home to learn the outcome.

Norfolk was wrapped in fog on Monday, a fitting atmosphere for the opening of the hearing's eighth day. Three *Missouri* officers had now been named as defendants, and a fourth, Ensign Harris, an interested party, stood precariously close to having his status changed despite Commander Peckham's openly expressed support.

Lt. John Carr was aboard the battleship preparing his department in the COC for departure when he received the court's summons to

147

appear as a witness. From his first moments on the stand, being questioned by the judge advocate about the complexities of radar navigation, he did not provide many "yes" or "no" answers. Repeatedly he was admonished by Admiral Miles to "give a direct reply." On the defensive, Carr protested that such answers would not give a complete picture of the electronic problems he faced. At one point, still not complying with Miles's order, Carr refused to give an answer on the grounds that a reply would tend to incriminate or degrade him. In the course of his testimony he justified his actions or lack thereof prior to the grounding by five contributing circumstances: the radar had not been calibrated, and one set was known to have a two-hundred-yard range error; equipment failures had produced widely divergent radar fixes, making him feel that it would be unwarranted to warn the bridge; in the absence of specific requests, standard practice did not call for sending radar advice to the conn; he had been told by the XO on the day prior to departure that navigational advice would be needed only in poor visibility, but visibility had been good on the morning of the seventeenth; he was convinced that the danger indicated on the scopes was an illusion, and having heard that the bridge ordered standard speed, he felt they had the situation well in hand.

Did he warn the bridge? he was asked several times. Each time, Carr equivocated. At one point the judge advocate faced him directly and asked, "Did you or did you not warn the bridge?"

"No, Sir."

Miles called for a recess, and upon resumption of the session he informed Carr that he had been named an interested party. He was not yet excused as a witness, even though he was due to sail the next day. After questioning him further, Judge Advocate Bradbury confronted him with a printed list of COC duties, among them the responsibility of warning the bridge whenever the ship appeared to be headed into danger.

Lieutenant Carr attempted to elaborate on the order, but he was interrupted by Bradbury: "Did you sign the order?"

"No."

"Who signed it?"

"My name is printed on the bottom."

Admiral Miles's ire was raised, and once again he cleared the court. Within minutes the session resumed, and Carr was informed that he had become a defendant. The reasons cited were that he had failed to report to the bridge that his radar plots indicated that the ship was standing into shoal water and had also failed to notify the bridge of equipment failures in the COC. Carr had started the day expecting to learn the outcome of the inquiry while aboard ship in the Caribbean and ended it detained ashore as a defendant.

QM1 John Spooner, assigned to duty in the COC, later contradicted some of his superior officer's testimony. Spooner had asked Carr, "Do you think we ought to come right?" to which Carr replied, "Yes, I think we should." Then the "conversation became hot," according to Spooner, who quoted the lieutenant as "wondering what we were doing up there" headed for the shallows. Further discussions about the radar were held in closed sessions involving classified matter on the new gear, but Carr's case hadn't improved.

Chief Andrew Vargo was summoned and shown a fathometer graph taken on the day of the grounding, the only record of the fathometer's operation. It bore an inked scrawl but no time or depth markings. Vargo examined it and pronounced that the device had been operative at the time but was incorrectly adjusted. He substantiated his opinion by quoting shipyard engineers who found no problems with the instrument while the ship was in dry dock.

QM2 Bevan Travis, helmsman during the mishap, told the court that the sluggish response he had felt to Brown's right rudder order was a sure sign to him that the ship was running aground. He had reported the sluggishness to the captain in a voice audible "to the whole bridge." But he told no one but Chief Reams what he thought was the reason for the poor response. "I don't think it's my place to give the captain orders; it's my place to take orders from him."

Ens. Francis Kelly, assistant navigator to the XO on the O4 level, provided substantial support for Peckham's suggested engine orders. He had been standing beside him and recalled the words "Stop engines" and "Swing ship to right." This differed somewhat from Peckham's account, and Kelly did not admit to hearing the prompt acknowledgment from the primary conn that Peckham had mentioned, but he became the first witness to remember any suggestions regarding engine maneuvers. The chief engineering officer, Commander Zoeller, and assistant engineer Lt. James Forehan both testified that it was after they had given notice of nearly complete power failure that the bridge issued engine orders.

Thus ended an intense day of testimony from most of those familiar with links in the "unfortunate chain of circumstances." As it happened, the *Missouri* did not put out until the fog cleared, Captain Smith prudently deciding to avoid any risk of further embarrassment. It was unlikely that any detained witnesses would make pierhead jumps to rejoin their shipmates; rather, some on board were keeping their seabags packed.

In Washington, on the same day, the office of Secretary of Defense Louis Johnson announced that the *Missouri* was to become a school ship for training midshipmen and naval reservists, thereby halving its annual budget of $6.7 million.[8] If designated a "training ship" like its predecessor the *Mississippi,* it would lose its battleship classification and be consigned to the auxiliary fleet. The ship's assignments would be little altered, but even greater reduction in strength could be expected, along with decreased allotments for fuel and ammunition. The savings would enable keeping an additional carrier in service. That decision, to be carried out sometime later in the year, would put to an end some of the wrangling in Congress that had been going on since the ship went aground, dispute centered on the ship's high cost of operation. It would tarnish further whatever glow remained in the pride of the men aboard. At this point, in the courtroom, it may be that there were few who really cared.

Periodically, yeomen relieved each other at the stenotype machine to deliver the neatly folded output for typing onto mimeograph stencils. Full transcripts of the proceedings were delivered regularly to press representatives in time for the next day's evening edition. Day by day the stacked paper on the investigating officers' tables grew higher, a measure of the growing weariness within the hearing room, all this days before the two principal witnesses would have their say.

SA Arden Field stood with Judge Advocate Bradbury before the Hampton Roads chart.[9] Field was the telephone talker whose duty was to relay 1-JV messages to and from the skipper, one of three talkers called as witnesses on the tenth day. When asked to identify where the ship was located when the warning messages were delivered, he replied quietly that he couldn't say. He had been stationed in the wheelhouse of the primary conn just before the accident, speaking through a porthole near where Captain Brown stood on the open bridge. His responses to questions were so indistinct that on several occasions the court stenographer interrupted him to ask him to speak louder.

Had he ever attended telephone talkers' school? No. The court members leaned forward, cupping their ears. Speak louder, he was told again. Did he ever hear any suggestions that he be replaced by a more qualified talker? No, he replied, his voice still indistinct.

According to Field, he had attempted to relay five crucial messages to the captain, but none was acknowledged. Only once did the captain show any sign of having heard, when Field relayed the XO's second warning. And what was that?

"'The executive officer recommends we come right immediately. The chart shows we are heading into dangerous shoals,'" quoted the sailor, adding that the CO was talking to the navigator at the time.

Captain Wood spoke up, "Didn't you realize that the commanding officer would have wanted to know even though it would interrupt him?"

"No, Sir."

Asked about the weather conditions at the time, Field said softly that the wind was blowing full in his face through the porthole. Heads shook impatiently as the seaman was dismissed.

SN Arthur Cole, the bearing recorder who had been stationed beside Ensign Harris, explained entries in the log as his personal code, "220.4" as an example for a bearing of 220¼ degrees. SA John Beeman, responsible for recording water depths taken from the fathometer and for transmitting them to the bridge on request, said he had not heard such a request since he joined the ship in June 1948. Was he aware that the fathometer was inoperative? Yes, shortly after the ship left the dock, but he did not report it. What happened to the fathometer log? It disappeared.

A brief spark was introduced into the tedium with the testimony of the junior officer of the deck at the time of the grounding. After Lt. (jg) Lawrence Body reported that he had orders to stand on the starboard side of the bridge and keep a lookout for objects moving on the water, Brown's counsel expressed criticism of Body's lack of interest in the last minutes before the accident. Referring to the danger reports, Wood asked Body, "Weren't you curious to see what effect they had on the captain?"

Pausing for a bit, the officer responded, "No, Sir. But the question strikes me as peculiar." Heads lifted in attention.

Why had he failed to study the chart before assuming his watch? Because he had already kept his predecessor waiting over ten minutes for relief. How long would a study of the chart have taken? A long time, because Hampton Roads was not familiar to him, and it would have delayed even further the breakfast of the man waiting to be relieved.

"In other words, you were just kind of a high-priced lookout that morning?"

"Yes, Sir."

Two expert witnesses were called for testimony the next day. Comdr. James M. Wood (no relation to Captain Brown's counsel) had been quietly in attendance through most of the hearing. He joined Quartermaster Wentz as an expert when identified as the court navigator. Under his testimony and that of civilian docking pilot Capt. Roland McCoy, the pilot who had sent the *Missouri* on its way in January, whatever stand the battleship's navigation team may have taken on its competence began to totter. McCoy stated that under sound navigation practice regarding the range, he would "not have run the range at all." Asked about earlier evidence that the ship was making 12.4 knots, he guessed that a maximum safe speed through the range would have been 10 knots, and the 15 knots ordered "endangered the ship unnecessarily." Finally, in apparent reference to the danger bearing, he stated that while navigating "that close to shoal waters" fixed objects rather than buoys should have been used as reference points.

Commander Wood's opinions were even more damaging. The discrepancies in buoy information, he said, would have caused him to take a boat out to the range and see for himself what was there. As navigator, he would have personally taken over the plotting chart rather than delegate it to someone less experienced. Wood spent much of his time in testimony huddled over the chart with the three court members and the judge advocate. He claimed that the computed six-minute leeway to clear the shoal, based on Harris's last plot, was more like a minute and a half. He noted the lack of a turning bearing, which would have identified the point at which the ship should have commenced running parallel to the shoal. He took issue with the sharp angle of the planned courses, noting the lack of any course correction for steering inertia due to the ship's size. Navigator Morris's counsel, Capt. H. M. Tiemroth, attended to the discussions with no comment.

In a concluding sweepdown of testimony from the ship's enlisted men, SA John Watson, O4 talker with responsibility to relay lookout information to the conn, testified that he had failed to report last-minute sightings of the acoustic range because there was "too much confusion" on the bridge. SA John K. Williams, leadsman stationed in the chains, told the court that even if he had received orders to start casting the lead he could not have done so because of the speed of the ship.

Friday gave Captain Tiemroth his day in court, as he challenged court navigator Wood with a prolonged battery of questions.[10] The acoustic range was located on the left-hand side of the shoal, normally the "wrong" side, was it not? It skirted a shoal, as has been well pointed out, did it not? Taking over the plotting would have secluded the navigator in the chart room with headphones on, would it not? Elaborating on his earlier opinion, Wood suggested that Morris could have taken sights and done the plotting on a table erected on the outer bridge. The bridge dimensions that had been observed when the court visited the ship were recalled. An experiment with such a table on the outer bridge some months ago had proved to be impractical. Commander Wood conceded that under the circumstances the navigator might have chosen wisely to remain at the skipper's side.

The 15° turn planned for the ship would not have brought the stern of the ship any further from the centerline of the course than the width of the ship, would it? Steering inertia was not really an issue. As to that "sharp angle," had Wood considered the obstacle presented by Old Point Comfort? Would he agree that the real danger to the ship lay in failure to change the planned course in time, not the angle through which the course would change? Wood conceded that Morris's projected track might have involved the lesser of two calculated risks.

With focus still on the ship's track leading to the accident, Ensign Harris was called back for direct examination by his own counsel. Lieutenant Commander Foster established that Harris had been ill during a period that might have been used for practice at the plotting chart. A series of questions served to point out that the assistant navigator had accurately plotted the ship's position on its route from the Elizabeth River until he was crowded away from the table by other officers examining the chart.

The ensign was still on the stand on Saturday, long enough for his counsel to establish that while a stream of continuous bearings was being delivered without accompanying times, this by order of the executive officer, Harris had attempted to obtain three workable figures, with no success.[11] The message was conveyed that the young man was a victim of alarmed seniors. Foster's success was confirmed when Admiral Miles referred to the court's entry into the records concerning Harris's "competency . . . not only as a witness but . . . as a naval officer." Addressing the serious young officer, Miles said, "After hearing your testimony yesterday and today, the court desires to withdraw that observation and to strike it from the records." For the first time during his nine-day presence in the courtroom, Elwin Harris relaxed; long enough, indeed, to thank the admiral profusely. Miles, revealing a softened view toward the youth, told him that he would remain an interested party "for your own protection," preserving his ability to cross-examine witnesses.

After twelve tedious days of testimony, seeming to dwindle in relevance as they passed, there was expectation that much of the mystery surrounding the cause of the mishap would be swept away when William Brown took the stand. His classmate Chester Wood opened with an enthusiastic introduction, reviewing Brown's exemplary naval record and referencing his oft-quoted "unusual and unfortunate chain of circumstances."[12] The judge advocate remained unimpressed, telling Wood that the captain's record, notable as it may be, should not affect the court's decision. "Naval officers," he continued, "are required to avoid finding themselves in such circumstances if they can possibly do so."

Defense counsel quoted *Navy Regulations* on the commanding officer's responsibility for the safe navigation of his ship. Captain Brown had "no inclination to shrink from his responsibility." The captain had been led to expect a "varsity team" on board the ship, "the operations officer, the navigator, the COC officer, the assistant navigator"; he was "justified and in certain respects compelled to place faith in them." The stage was set for Brown to take the stand in his own voluntary defense.

Brown's voice was worn, dragging as he outlined his seagoing experience. He recalled that when on the bridge of the *Missouri,* his first assignment afloat in six years, he felt "extremely rusty. . . . I found my seaman's eyes playing tricks. I used to pride myself on ability to judge distances to ships and distances to the horizon. . . . I found that these were extremely difficult. . . . I didn't seem to have the awareness which I can recall having in previous commands."

Events on the postrepair run in December had caused him to "lose faith in the navigator to a certain extent" and to "lean heavily on the operations officer in navigational matters." On that first trip he was "vaguely irritated" at Lieutenant Commander Morris's failure to take a "careful departure from the Virginia Capes." He was aggravated by Morris's dependence on loran, which, Brown said, did not give good fixes in the area. The gyrocompass repeater on the primary conn had an avoidable but uncorrected error, which Brown found disturbing. The navigator's charts, which he reviewed prior to 17 January, made the captain believe the acoustic range was marked by five buoys, not the actual two. As the ship neared the range, the executive officer, whose "counsel would have been most valuable and most desired by me," left the primary conn to prepare the main navigating bridge for the captain's arrival four decks below, according to Brown. (Peckham was not present to hear that statement.) That left the captain with the counsel of three less experienced officers—the "distrusted" navigator, the operations officer, and the officer of the deck. Three buoys were sighted, one being the acoustic range marker nearest to the shoal, and farther on two spar buoys, which turned out to be fishnet stakes. He had asked his officers "whether all three buoys were not part of the range" and was greeted by silence. "Does anyone know if the spar buoys and this other buoy are part of the range?" he had demanded, and there had been no comment from the others. "Judging from their positions, I assume, then, that the spars are part of the acoustic range?" The wind was in his eyes, and he did not see the second range marker in choppy seas to the south. He believed the northern marker was an approach buoy and said, "I assume I can leave this buoy on either side." The operations officer told him there was "plenty of water" on the north side of the buoy, and it was to the north that he ordered the helm. There was no dissent from any officer present at the time.

Grimly, Brown went on: "I gained the impression on the bridge that I was utterly alone as far as any assistance from my team of officers was concerned." The spectators listened in heavy silence.

The ship was turning left. Suddenly "the navigator came running . . . waving his arms. He said 'Captain, we must come right, we must come right immediately.'" Brown then ordered a partial right helm, but "I told the operations officer, 'I don't believe the navigator knows where we are; go find out.'"

"There was no danger bearing then, though I was aware that the navigator had a danger bearing in mind. . . . any conning officer would hesitate to take a single recommendation without something leading up to it. . . . I felt like rejecting the navigator's recommendation . . . there had been no dissent earlier. . . . I felt strongly that the spar buoys were on the range and not to the north of it. I said 'If we continue to swing to the right we'll miss out on the range run.'"

"So certain was I in my own mind that the navigator was lost, I gave the helmsman a mark and told him to steady on 058 degrees.

"North of Thimble Shoal Light . . . there were no buoys, no discoloration of the water . . . nothing there that gave any indications of shoaling water; unless you were taking soundings. No soundings were reported during the entire passage." As if to reflect the emptiness the skipper had felt, the weary court adjourned for what remained of the weekend.

Brown's testimony on Saturday had not cleared up the mystery of the buoys. He introduced his concept of entrance and exit buoys to the range, considerably different from the layout on the charts that had been so frequently referenced during the two prior weeks. Evoking sympathy for the loneliness at the top, he faulted his officers and tried to share with them his responsibility for the accident. On Monday, counsels for the three defendant officers and Harris as an interested party took up their defense.

Brown had stated that he was caused to "lean heavily" on Commander Millett for navigational advice. Millett's counsel determined from Brown that he had never specifically informed the operations officer of that status; the navigator remained directly responsible to the commanding officer in all such matters. Brown himself was the first to misinterpret the nature of the spar buoys in shallow waters, with Millett later following suit.

Brown said he would have expected warnings about the dangerous course from combat operations radar observations. Lieutenant Carr's counsel brought out from Brown that he knew of certain maladjustments in the radar before the start of the trip and that positions plotted in the COC were untrustworthy.

Brown had claimed that Commander Morris had not prefaced his "frantic warning to come right" with any explanation, and that he thought by his prior silence Morris had agreed with Brown's misinterpretation of the spar buoys. But Brown admitted to Morris's counsel that Morris had made reference to the danger bearing and that it was possible Morris had not heard Brown's first incorrect assumption about the spars.

Brown had criticized Ensign Harris for failure to warn him when plotted positions showed the battleship headed for shoal waters. Harris's counsel once more established that Harris had accurately plotted the ship's position until no further fixes, accurate or not, would have given a timely warning.

Several times the beleaguered captain had been asked, in effect, who was ultimately responsible for safe navigation of the ship.[13] "The captain is responsible for the safe navigation of the ship. But the training of the team is the responsibility of department heads who are charged with the supervision of the team, and who have been sufficiently long in their job to have control," he said.

Judge Advocate Bradbury took up the questioning, wringing from the captain the admission that he alone was responsible for the final order to the helmsman. But, Brown declared, "I'd seen nothing to lead me to believe that my team of officers would fall down completely when I needed it the most."

Persisting, Bradbury asked if Brown had requested soundings. Brown admitted that he hadn't. What was the draft of the *Missouri* at the time? Thirty-six feet, six inches, was Brown's reply. Bradbury asked him to step over to the chart with a protractor and read off the water depths on the course he had ordered.

Somberly he read, "Seventy-five, fifty-nine, forty-two—and so on to approximately twenty-seven feet."

"Who was the captain of the team?"

"I was the captain of the ship."

157

8

Tragic Hero

William Brown's self-condemning testimony that, while in command of the ship, he had set a course that took it into shallow water, appeared to be enough to satisfy the court that at least one court-martial would be in order. During his testimony the captain had tried to put the onus for his error on his operational team of five officers, three of whom were also named as defendants, another as an interested party. The extent of their culpability might diminish his own. There remained unanswered questions, not the least of which was how the captain had come into such disagreement with the navigator regarding the course to the range. Now navigator Morris would take the stand voluntarily.

The lieutenant commander's counsel, Captain Tiemroth, told the court that his direct questioning of Morris would be narrowed to three parts: Morris's experience as a naval officer, his conference with Captain Brown on 14 January, and his account of the events on the morning of 17 January.[1]

At the start of what became six hours of questioning, Morris told of enlisting in 1940 in the V-7 Naval Reserve officer candidate program, of receiving his commission, and of being assigned thereafter as an instructor of navigation. During the war he was first given command of an early version destroyer escort, World War I vintage, then of the flush-deck destroyer USS *Babbitt*. In 1946 he signed over to the regular Navy and was sent to the Bureau of Ships as an oceanographer, followed by two and one-half years in what became the Research and Development Board of the Department of Defense.

Chester Wood seemed out to draw blood. On cross-examining

158

Morris his questions seemed to reflect Naval Academy aristocracy at its meanest, badgering the navigator at every opportunity. Tiemroth objected frequently while Wood continued to belittle the witness. Finally, Rear Admiral Miles warned Captain Wood, "if you persist in heckling the witness, he can heckle back." The counsel's face reddened as he apologized to Morris and turned to the next phase of testimony.

Led by his counsel, Morris declared that before the ship got under way he was confident that only two buoys identified the acoustic range. He left five range buoys marked on the chart, three lightly in pencil, the two about which he felt confident in red. He did not tell Brown that there were only two buoys in the range. "It never entered my mind," he explained, that the captain thought there were more than two. During the conference with Captain Brown and Commander Millett on 14 January, the navigator had pointed to the two red marks and told his superiors, "Here is the range." The other three buoys were not mentioned in that conversation. They had not been erased because no written authority superseded the information given in the original packet.

How had he reached the conclusion that there were only two buoys? It came from his study of the laboratory chart delivered by the Fort Monroe Naval Ordnance Laboratory. Morris assumed that Captain Brown was familiar with the descriptions in the packet. Wood asked him if he had described the color and shape of the buoys to the captain. No, Morris replied, but he believed until the ship went aground that he had entered their description on the pilothouse chart, where any of the officers could review it.

According to Morris, when the *Missouri* was off Old Point Comfort, as they approached the range he made four recommendations to the captain that the ship "come right," and Brown replied to three of them. Morris's testimony contradicted Captain Brown's statements that he had received only one such recommendation, just before the ship struck bottom.

When Brown had told his officers that he assumed the two spar buoys were part of the range, why had Morris remained silent? The navigator declared he did not hear the captain say anything about the spar buoys.

At the conclusion of cross-examination the court recessed for Washington's Birthday, returning to take up detailed questioning of Morris about his relationship with the commanding officer.[2] "A warm personal relationship did not exist," he said, although when Captain Brown first came aboard he was "affable" toward the navigator. The frequency with which that word was used among Brown's top officers could make one wonder to what extent they had shared views on their skipper prior to giving testimony. Morris "subconsciously believed" Brown did not "think me at home in my job." He had the impression that the skipper felt the navigator's "rustiness" was nothing that "a little seagoing would not cure. . . . all of us were somewhat rusty." How did Morris feel the skipper rated his performance as a navigator? At the end of the trial run he thought he "would be satisfactory" to the new skipper. He was not asked specifically how he came to that conclusion. How, then, did the "lack of harmony" arise between him and Captain Brown? He explained that "certain navigational pieces of information were not asked of me. I felt I might have been called on for these." The navigator remained consistently self-confident.

Commander Millett testified next in his own defense. He claimed that in his view the decision to run the acoustic range was solely a navigational matter, not an operational one. When asked the same question put to Morris—Why did Brown encounter silence when he asked about the spars?—Millett said he had not heard Brown mention them. The operations officer had sighted the two spar buoys and remarked that they might be part of the buoy system marking the range.

Delving into the tensions existing between the officers, the court asked Millett if he had been aware of the CO's "distrust" of Morris. He replied that he had not, but Brown had told him that he was not "completely confident the navigator was as competent" as Brown desired. The difference in views seemed semantic, hanging on the word "distrust." Counsel for Lieutenant Carr asked Millett about Carr's performance as combat operations officer in Millett's division. The operations officer thought that Carr was "highly satisfactory" in his duties. After two hours on his second day of testimony, John Millett rested his case.

Captain Brown's senior counsel was absent from the hearing room during most of that morning session. Until this time, Wood had actively cross-examined each witness as he sought to refute every damaging statement made. Brown, paying little attention to the proceedings, remained busy at his table writing and editing his work. For sixteen days he sat stiffly in place, riveted to the words of each witness, grimacing at conflicting evidence, intent on every element reported. Now it appeared that the captain was preparing a closing statement.[3]

Counsel for Lieutenant Carr, who earlier had shown reluctance to respond to direct questioning, took up his defense by calling Lt. Richard Bagg Jr. as a witness.[4] Bagg, a combat operations officer on the *Mississippi,* was qualified as an expert witness after it was explained that he had taught in COC school for two years and had experience as a COC officer on two capital ships. Asked to examine the chart used in combat operations on 17 January, Bagg told the court that he would have notified the bridge sooner that the plot showed the ship standing into shallow water. But he said that the area in question was the worst in the channel for getting radar fixes, adding that radar is not always dependable when the ship is near large land masses. Challenged by Judge Advocate Bradbury, Bagg said his views were based on the *Mississippi*'s modern instruments, implying that the *Missouri*'s gear may not have been as accurate.*

Carr, on the stand, developed his own credentials as a COC officer, pointing out that in 1949 the *Missouri*'s COC team was rated first among Atlantic Fleet units, for which he had been given a letter of commendation. He was rated "excellent" on the last fitness report prepared by Captain Smith.

The combat operations officer testified that he had known the ship's radar was not perfectly adjusted and had so notified both Commander Peckham and electronics officer Lt. (jg) Harold Gibbs. Adjustments could not be made while the ship was docked. His failure to recommend to the bridge that the ship come right was a matter of timing; he was about to do so when the talker announced "Right full rudder!" The day prior to the sortie the executive officer had told Carr to be prepared to make course recommendations because poor

---

* It is interesting to note that Captain Shanklin, Judge Advocate Bradbury's counsel for technical support, was Bagg's commanding officer on the *Mississippi.*

visibility was expected, but then he thought it unlikely that the COC would be asked because visibility was "good for that time of day and was improving."

Under Bradbury's cross-examination, the lieutenant admitted that there may have been a lack of coordination and poor liaison with the bridge. The ship's organization called for sixteen radarmen, but he had only four in his section. Rear Admiral Miles asked him about the training status of his men, and Carr replied that he did not think they were "particularly well trained." They had been sent to COC schools in Norfolk and Boston and had been given "canned" practice problems while the ship was in port.

The court then asked counsel for Elwin Harris if he had anything more to add. Randall Foster replied on Harris's behalf that the ensign had already spent two long periods on the stand and chose not to take the stand again, since a third period would add nothing and only lengthen the record. With final testimony gathered, the court allowed an extended break in the inquiry for the counsels to prepare their closing statements.

After seventeen days of testimony from nearly fifty people, with nearly twelve hundred pages of mimeographed proceedings now stacked on the tables, at the end of February the inquiry came to its last day.[5] All that remained was for the four defendants and their counsels to make their closing remarks, followed by the judge advocate's summation. The tedious process was brought to a dramatic peak when Captain Brown stood to take full blame for the stranding of the *Missouri:* "I, and I alone, bear sole responsibility for the grounding. . . . As captain of the ship, it was my duty to keep her safe and secure. And I didn't do it." In this surprising reversal of the attitude marking his defense throughout the month-long process, he asked the court to view the conduct of his subordinates "in the light of day-to-day practice, and not in any sense connected with the grounding of the ship."

Everything that followed was anticlimactic. Morris and Carr elected not to make statements. Millett, in a brief presentation, spoke of his sincere desire that all the necessary facts be presented to the court. He did not wish to avoid giving any information or to color his testimony in any way. "I believe that I have gained through my experience in the Navy a thorough understanding of my responsibilities as an officer, as operations officer and as a witness before this court, and that I have lived up to those responsibilities," he said.

Judge Advocate Bradbury in his summation said he did not want to point the guilty finger at anyone, but that there were certain pieces of evidence that could be marked as sins of omission and commission. Listing these, he gave instances when each of the defendants might have acted differently.

Chester Wood gave the closing arguments for his associate. Three complex issues contributed to the mishap, he said: first, the strength of the structure assigned to assist Brown; second, "sheer circumstance" affecting the course of events; and third, the "amazing and tragic" mixture of circumstance and personal failure surrounding the event. Wood directed the court's attention to failings of ten members of the ship's company, from seaman and chief petty officer to the captain's three top-ranking subordinates.

The hearing ended somberly, and the court withdrew into closed session to assemble its report. Facts, opinions, and recommendations ensue from a court of inquiry, these delivered to the convening authority to respond with appropriate action. Not uncommonly, with matters being serious enough to justify undertaking an inquiry, recommendations include the courts-martial of implicated parties under the jurisdiction of the convening authority. The convening authority, while not obligated to act on anything presented, carries the action from there. The charges in a court-martial are brief and straightforward statements of possible offenses. They are supported by detailed specifications, often based on the opinions formed by the original court of inquiry. Each charge must be found either proved, drawing a verdict of guilty, or not proved, resulting in acquittal. Extenuating circumstances may mitigate a guilty verdict, usually because of failure to prove all specifications associated with the charge. The court makes a recommendation for sentencing in accordance with its verdict, the penalty subject to review for possible reduction, but not for increase. To protect an accused individual, a reviewing authority oversees and endorses or takes exception to the final action. Justice in a military environment is rendered swiftly and, with rare exception, free of prejudice.

The three court members labored for over a week to present 142 statements of fact, 23 opinions, and 6 recommendations.[6] On 8

March, Milton Miles, as president of the court, and Malcolm Brad-bury, as judge advocate, affixed their signatures to the long document and submitted it to the convening authority, Rear Admiral Smith, as ComCruLant. Smith took another week to formulate his opinion, identify his concurrence or disagreement with each recommendation, and list the actions to be taken. His report went with the court's original documents to Smith's superior, the new CinCLantFlt, Adm. William Fechteler.

The court's recommendations included the following: that four officers—Brown, Millett, Morris, and Carr—be brought to trial by general court-martial; that a letter of reprimand be addressed to Commander Peckham; and that no further action be taken against any other person in connection with the grounding.[7] A general court-martial, the Navy's highest court, is the only one that can try a commissioned officer. A letter of reprimand is the most severe document of criticism that may be entered in an officer's service record and is generally considered a barrier to promotion.

Admiral Smith did not concur with the recommendation on Lieutenant Carr, stating that there was insufficient evidence for general court-martial.[8] The omissions with which Carr was charged consisted largely of errors of judgment rather than culpable inefficiency. Smith went on record that when piloting in good visibility, the passing of radar-based navigational information can and does create doubt and confusion. Instead he addressed a letter of reprimand to Carr for failures cited in the report.

Nor did Smith agree with the recommendation that a letter of reprimand be addressed to Commander Peckham, since Peckham did exert himself to save the ship and during the hearing did not have the opportunity to present his case. (Peckham was at sea when some statements were made in court to which he would certainly have taken exception.) It was Smith's intention to address a letter of caution to Commander Peckham. Such a document does not technically bar promotion, but it remains in the service record, thereby influencing reviews until mitigated by subsequent commendatory letters.

The admiral agreed with the court's opinion that "there is no serious blame in connection with the grounding of the USS *Missouri* that is attached to Ensign Harris." He wrote that he intended to instruct the commanding officer of the *Missouri* "to see that Ensign Harris takes more interest in his assignments, and prepares himself better to handle a situation which is more than routine."

Finally, Smith concurred with the court's opinion that the engineering plant of the battleship was secured in a commendable manner without serious damage, and addressed a letter of commendation to the engineering officer, Commander Zoeller.

On 16 March, Admiral Fechteler ordered that Brown, Millett, and Morris be brought to individual trials before general courts-martial on 27 March. "The formal charges and specifications to be served on the officers will not be made public prior to the convening of the respective courts," the Navy said in its release. "The individual officers concerned, however, may release the charges and specifications in their respective cases at their own discretion." The privacy of the individuals charged was being respected. No statements were forthcoming from the three defendants.[9]

Three separate seven-member courts would convene, all under the jurisdiction of ComCruLant. A court-martial in itself is not a disciplinary action. As a court of inquiry corresponds to a grand jury, so a court-martial parallels a civilian trial, with the potential decision of the court, as both judge and jury, ranging from acquittal to an order for severe punishment.

After a requested delay, on 30 March, with the two other trials already under way, Captain Brown appeared before the four rear admirals and three captains making up his court.[10] He had taken leave after the inquiry[11] and returned tanned, looking well rested, his voice clear and firm. Three charges were presented by the judge advocate, who acts in a court-martial as prosecuting attorney: "through negligence suffering a vessel of the Navy to be stranded . . . through negligence suffering a vessel of the Navy to be hazarded . . . neglect of duty."[12]

To each charge Brown answered "Guilty."

His counsel, Captain Wood, spoke emotionally in Brown's defense: "The court cannot impose any sentence which will be greater in effect than the self-inflicted punishment which has already resulted from this tragic occurrence. Needless to say, the scars of this punishment will long outlive any action taken by this court." Wood hoped for the court's recommendation of clemency and asked for true compassion in its final action. Four flag officers under whom

Brown had served during his twenty-six years as a naval officer were
called as character witnesses, and a ten-year compilation of Brown's
fitness reports was entered as mitigating evidence.

Standing with his papers before him, Brown read:

> May it please the Court: Mindful of the importance of my own posi-
> tion here before you . . . I wish to make this statement.

> . . . I am not concerned with the legal technicalities of my position. I
> only recognize that I was responsible for the safe navigation of the ship.
> My orders put the ship aground. Therefore, any culpability involved in
> the grounding is mine. That is my position.

> . . . The evolving of my present position has been a painful process amid
> a great ordeal. . . .

> The mental shock which accompanied the grounding, the nervous strain
> placed upon me in the salvage operations, and my resulting weakened
> physical condition unfortunately militated against clear thinking as
> regards my personal position. In fact, I refused to consider it until after
> the ship was refloated. . . . I can only say that throughout the entire pro-
> ceedings, I have had no other thought than to carry out my duty with
> the same conscientious sincerity which has motivated me throughout my
> entire naval service.

> I very much regret the harm that has been done to others by the
> grounding of the ship. . . . I only trust that as a required aftermath of the
> unfortunate occurrence, officers of the Navy, wherever stationed, will
> more than recognize the grave responsibilities which go with their duties
> and carry them out accordingly.[13]

In less than ninety minutes the trial of William Drane Brown was
over. When the news reached his former command, the crew's reaction was one of sadness for the man they had known for but three
months and only at a distance. There was no feeling of recrimination,
of justice being served for the difficulties he had brought upon them.
He was, after all, a shipmate, and that makes a difference among
sailors. Brown became a tragic hero, forgiven for his errors, admired
for his honesty, lamented for the uncertain career he faced.[14]

Meanwhile the other *Missouri* officers were already facing their
own uncertainties. The separate courts-martial of John Millett and
Frank Morris opened on schedule, prior to Captain Brown's. Commander Millett's counsel, Lt. Paul F. Borden, new to the hearings,

asked for a continuance to prepare his case and achieved from the seven-member board a one-day postponement. Delay could prove beneficial in light of Brown's final statements. Following their commanding officer's dramatic admission before the court of inquiry, both officers may have sensed a better chance of survival in the fight to save their own careers. With his statement "I . . . alone bear sole responsibility for the grounding," the captain had given them each a source of hope.

Morris, too, had a new counsel for his trial, Lt. Comdr. Herbert E. Ost. The navigator was being court-martialed for "culpable inefficiency in the performance of duty" and "neglect of duty," each with four specifications.[15] To both charges he pleaded not guilty. Ost was plainly prepared to wage a long battle. Asked routinely after the opening formalities if the defense had any objections to the appointed court members, he replied, "The defense has objections to each and every member of the court due to publicity given not only to the grounding but to the entire proceedings of the court of inquiry."[16] He referred to the "mountainous articles" of the local press, praising them for their excellent detail but raising the question of whether it would be possible for his client to get a fair trial. Each of the seven judges claimed he was unprejudiced by newspaper accounts and had no opinions as to guilt or innocence. Ost had done his homework, and he asked to examine one court member in more detail. Comdr. E. R. King Jr. admitted that he had read detailed accounts of the grounding, considered that the work of the court of inquiry was complete, and conceded that he was a classmate and friend of Commander Millett. However, he denied that there was any conflict of interest in Morris's case or that he had formed any conclusions as to the guilt or innocence of the defendant. Ost stood his ground, holding to his objection. This caused the court to go behind closed doors with the *Naval Courts and Boards* manual. Upon their return the presiding judge, Capt. John F. Madden, whom Ost had also challenged, stated that the court had overruled his objection, pointing out that according to current law, a court member making "a positive declaration that he is not prejudiced against the accused, in the absence of material evidence in support of the objection, will justify the court in overruling the objection."

Ost objected to each accusation made by Judge Advocate Malcolm Bradbury* against the defendant, claiming the specifications were "defective, duplicitous, ambiguous, vague and indefinite." In some instances, he said, the specifications failed to cite a violation and failed to support the charge. All objections in the course of the day were overruled. It was going to be a long trial. Herbert Ost wanted not only to be certain that proceedings were clearly followed but also to protect his client in the eventuality that a higher naval authority would review the court record.[17] The barrage of objections would continue throughout the trial.

On the second day, Ensign Harris returned to the stand to testify in defense of his superior, stating that Morris had informed him of the existence of only two buoys in the acoustic range. Ost raised the question of self-incrimination when it appeared that the witness was once more being put on the defensive.

QM1 Richard Wentz, recognized expert witness on navigational charts, spent nearly a full day on the stand, further extending his expertise by showing his familiarity with the contents of several navigational texts introduced as authoritative references. He explained again how he had plotted five buoys, only two of which were marked in red to indicate certainty about their presence. He said it was not standard practice on the ship to put descriptions of such range buoys on the charts.

By now Captain Brown had wrapped up his own trial, and, after multiple requested delays, Commander Millett's court-martial started, with several witnesses being called almost at once. Morris was among them, thus requiring the recess of his own nearby trial. With the same parade of witnesses called for each of two concurrent hearings, it became necessary to coordinate the testimony. No new evidence was delivered until Commander Peckham was called by the prosecution in the Morris hearing.[18] Then, for the first time, the executive officer revealed that Captain Brown had effectively relieved him of his navigational duties on 23 December, and that he had told that fact to both the navigator and operations officer. He was called the next day as witness in the Millett trial, at which he related the same story, that

---

* Bradbury's assignment as judge advocate in the Morris court-martial, following a similar role in the court of inquiry, was not unusual. As a legal officer in the Atlantic Fleet staff he could expect to be called for any legal duty for which he was qualified.

he had been admonished to keep his hands off the *Missouri*'s navigational matters. The only other one who could attest to the discussion between Brown and Peckham was Captain Brown himself, who had told the court of inquiry that his executive officer's presence on the bridge would have been "most valued and desired."

Early in April, Admiral Smith sent Peckham a letter stating his intention to issue him a formal letter of caution.[19] This was a routine procedure called for when the individual has had no chance to defend himself in court. As Peckham had earlier been recommended by the court of inquiry for the most serious censure, a letter of reprimand, and now was not yet the recipient of any damaging judgment, his circumspect behavior might yet save his career. Much depended on the acquiescence of William Brown. As Peckham gave testimony in both trials, he was in the process of preparing an official response to Admiral Smith, explaining in detail why he should not be censured.

The prosecution in the Morris trial brought Captain Brown to the witness stand, where he spent the entire day, much of it under arduous cross-examination.[20] There were discrepancies between Brown's testimony and the navigator's earlier statements before the court of inquiry. According to Brown, Morris had never given him descriptions of the size, color, or markings of the buoys; he had made no recommendation for course changes after the only buoy sighted had been passed; if Morris had given the warnings he had testified to, "they were given so ineffectually they might just as well not have been made"; the skipper had received no reports from the navigator about the depth of the water; and the navigator had failed to comply with a request the captain had made in December that a conning officer's tactical plot be provided on the open bridge. Challenged by Ost, Brown repeatedly admitted to his own "rustiness." That word was becoming so overused that one might have looked for an accumulation of scale on the blue sleeves of the officers. Finally, Brown stated what every officer involved must have thought, "We all share some culpability within our own minds."

Commander Wood, court navigator for the court of inquiry, was called by the prosecution as an expert, only to have him surprise both prosecution and defense by stating that the ship would not have run aground if it had turned right when Morris first recommended the course change.[21] In his usual manner, Ost had challenged Wood's qualifications, but he was overruled, the ruling helping his client's case. The prosecution rested, and Ost indicated he would call seven witnesses for the defense, including the defendant himself.

The first three witnesses suffered somewhat at the hand of Judge Advocate Bradbury, who openly acknowledged he was trying to impeach their testimony.[22] In over two hours at the stand, Lieutenant Arnold, officer of the deck at the time of the grounding, made statements that disagreed with his earlier statements to the court of inquiry. He now claimed that Morris gave the second of several recommendations that the course be changed to the right when the ship was five to seven hundred yards from the sighted buoy, whereas at the inquiry he had said that the first warning was given when the ship was two to three hundred yards from the buoy. Wallace Taylor, scientist in the Naval Ordnance Laboratory, gave a detailed history of the acoustic range, listing forty-one ships that had successfully passed through it over a seven-month period. Bradbury objected to the introduction of new and apparently irrelevant evidence, but the court overruled him when Ost explained that he would show that the skippers of those vessels operated without explanations of the buoys' arrangement. Lieutenant Bland, communications officer at the time of the grounding, claimed that Morris had given a specific course to the captain with his recommendation to turn right. Again Bradbury objected and was overruled. The judge advocate resigned himself to hearing the evidence presented by the day's remaining witnesses, who tracked the route of the packet requesting the range run from the Naval Ordnance Lab to the planning meeting between Brown, Millett, and Morris.

Both trials plodded tediously to an end as witnesses crossed from one hearing room to the other. Ost seemed determined to stretch out Morris's trial. Meanwhile, after several continuances, the Millett trial picked up its pace. Millett was charged with neglect of duty, two specifications, and through negligence suffering a vessel to be hazarded, one specification.[23] He pleaded not guilty to both before his counsel, Lieutenant Borden, submitted several charts and documents in evidence. The judge advocate, Lt. Comdr. Randall Foster,* quickly

---

* Foster did double duty in the hearings, serving first as counsel to Ensign Harris during the court of inquiry, then as judge advocate in Millett's court-martial.

called six witnesses, including the watch officers above and below decks at the time of the grounding, and the executive officer, the only person to introduce new testimony, as he had done hours before in the Morris trial. Foster indicated that he would attempt to introduce into the trial Millett's testimony before the court of inquiry by having it read by the custodian of the records. Borden asked the court for a ruling, and the court declared that all testimony Millett had given before he was made a defendant was inadmissable. Millett's subsequent defense was as brief as it was inconsequential. Three character witnesses, including his former skipper, Captain Smith, spoke of his reliability and straightforwardness. Smith, again in command of the *Missouri,* told the court, "I would be very happy to have Commander Millett with me in any capacity."[24] Millett did not take the stand in his own defense, while elsewhere in the building his former shipmate Frank Morris was preparing to do so. The adversaries in the Millett trial each took more than an hour to summarize their cases before Millett made a brief statement to the court. "Regardless of the decision," he concluded, "my sincere desire to discharge these responsibilities [his obligations as a naval officer] to the best of my ability will not diminish." The following day, in a statement preliminary to announcing its verdict, the court announced that it found "not proved" one of the three specifications, the allegation that Millett had failed to read papers containing instructions for running the acoustic range.[25]

Meanwhile, as the Morris trial drew to a close, Admiral Smith announced two developments of interest. He would not issue any letter of reprimand to Commander Peckham, nor would he take any other disciplinary action. He recognized that George Peckham was never made a defendant or an interested party in the court of inquiry. And, after reviewing Peckham's report of the discussion Captain Brown had held with him at the conclusion of the December trial run, Smith agreed that the executive officer had been excluded from navigational responsibilities. Interestingly, in his statement the admiral made no mention of Peckham's multiple attempts to avoid the disaster.

A few days later the admiral was able to announce what he had tried to achieve shortly after the grounding. Capt. Irving T. Duke was taking command of the *Mighty Mo.* In a brief ceremony aboard ship he relieved Captain Smith, with Rear Admiral Smith looking on. No reference was made to the mishap besides the admiral's indirect comment, "I feel she still is the outstanding ship of the fleet."[26] Duke, also a personal friend of Captain Brown, became the battleship's tenth skipper in its six-year history.

The Morris court-martial dragged on, delayed further by the illness of the presiding judge. Morris, in his own defense, attempted to explain why he did some things and did not do others on the day the ship went aground, but he seemed to lack conviction. At one point his testimony caused the judge advocate to put an entry in the record that Morris answered some questions in a "confused and hesitant manner."[27] Ost rose to the occasion, charging Bradbury with prejudicial error. Bradbury again tried to impeach the testimony of Lieutenant Arnold and of Morris himself. Ost objected to the admission of testimony that contained no contradiction of any sort by either witness in the meaning or significance of their statements. He was overruled, but went on to object to each question and answer as it was read to the court, each time being overruled. After Bradbury completed his rebuttal, Ost said he had no rebuttal to make.[28] Nothing remained but final arguments from both parties, and those took four more days.

Judge Advocate Bradbury put a copy of the charges and specifications before him and called the court's attention to every element of evidence supporting each specification. "According to the evidence the court can return one verdict alone: That the specifications are proved and that the accused is guilty of the charges," he concluded.[29] Lieutenant Commander Ost took the entire next session to identify eight critical points the judge advocate had not addressed, to enumerate the events leading up to the grounding, and to present arguments against each of the specifications of charges. He focused on the contradictory testimony given by Brown and Morris, the latter's supported by a number of witnesses while Brown's stood alone. He suggested that the captain "was preoccupied with something else," giving "intense concentration" to the spar buoys, and that this explained why Morris's warnings were unheeded by Brown.[30] One month after it started, the trial of Frank Morris concluded in a thirty-minute session during which Malcolm Bradbury countered Ost's request for a full acquittal by asking for one verdict, "the accused is guilty."

9

The Navy's Problems

Rear Adm. Allan Smith's desk was stacked with facts, opinions, recommendations, verdicts. In mid-March when he had ordered the three courts-martial he drew up a summary letter to cover the long and thorough record of proceedings prepared by the court of inquiry.[1] In it he ventured his first views to be sent to higher authorities on the problems currently plaguing the U.S. Navy, this even before the court-martial verdicts were handed down:

> The grounding of the USS *Missouri* disclosed personnel problems with which the U.S. Navy has been struggling since World War II. These problems may be divided into two parts. The first part has to do with the individual and collective failures of the personnel in the *Missouri;* the second part concerns the effect, which the broad personnel policies determined for the Navy as a whole, had upon the individuals and organization within the *Missouri.*

He would undertake additional study on the second part, he promised, but went on to express already formed opinions in naval bureaucratese. There was no teamwork among the officers and men, nor was there a well-formed "operational navigating group." His judgment was based on an opinion expressed by the court of inquiry: "There appeared throughout the testimony of a great majority of the witnesses who were personnel of the USS *Missouri* (BB-63), both officers and men, an intangible and elusive strain of avoidance of responsibility, and a belief that someone else was taking care of the task at hand."[2] Smith attempted to explain Captain Brown's behavior by suggesting that the captain was drawn to the collection of accurate data,

173

conditioned perhaps by his earlier assignments, to the point that he ignored readily available "navigational security features." The admiral made sure to include in his report that he himself had covered matters of morale, discipline, and ship security with each new commanding officer, both in personal conferences and in pamphlet form. Even before the completion of the court of inquiry, Smith claimed, he had looked into the question of whether any other heavy ship had similar outstanding weaknesses, and uncovered none, the implication being that his coaching efforts had been effective. If Allan Smith was adroitly sidestepping any possible suggestion that he might have selected his captain unwisely or been inadequate in preparing him, he need not have been concerned. Brown's staunch admission of guilt and consideration of his fellow officers followed the most respected naval traditions. Considering his stated "impression on the bridge that I was utterly alone," Brown was being generous with them. The question of Brown's capability as a naval line officer was never raised.

When the verdicts were reported, Frank Morris was found guilty on seven of the eight specifications under two charges: neglect of duty and culpable inefficiency in the performance of duty. John Millett was judged guilty on one specification in each of two charges: neglect of duty and through negligence suffering a vessel of the Navy to be hazarded. A recommendation of clemency accompanied the finding. Earlier, William Brown's court had recommended clemency after he pleaded guilty to all charges. There remained for Admiral Smith one last task, that of handing down sentences for the three convicted officers. He did it within a week.

Naval officers are routinely ranked for promotion within their grade, promotion points positioning them on seniority lists. Brown was reduced by 250 points on the list of captains, from a ranking of 399 among 1,786 line officers holding captain's rank to 649. Brown's court had recommended a reduction of 300 points, but Admiral Smith, in reviewing the unanimous recommendation for clemency, set the sentence at 250. John Millett was reduced by 100 points, from a ranking of 1,295 among 3,127 commanders on the list to 1,395. Frank Morris was reduced by 350 points, from 830 to 1,180 among 4,838 lieutenant commanders.

The Navy, like most seniority-based organizations, has its share of promotion-list analysts. They would find it difficult to rank the severity of the sentences meted out. Because there are fewer officers in higher grades, the loss of a single point in the captain's grade had roughly twice the effect as the loss of one point in the commander's grade and about three times that of a one-point loss in the grade of lieutenant commander. Captain Brown dropped from the upper 22 percent of his grade to the 40 percent slot, Commander Millett from 42 to 45 percent, and Lieutenant Commander Morris, in the top 17 percent of his grade, fell into the top 24 percent. Whatever the severity, the sentences made clear that the grounding was an inexcusable occurrence of a grave nature.

But questions remained unanswered as to how things got to such a state that the inexcusable came to pass, and why responsible men let those things happen. To answer that, one would have to read carefully through twenty-nine pages of findings and opinions, meticulously peruse the charts and logs maintained, perhaps delve into the fifteen hundred pages of accumulated testimony and arguments. Even then the feeling persists that something is missing, that all the loose ends have not been tidied up.

Admiral Fechteler, CinCLantFlt, was more to the point in his endorsement of the ComCruLant letter.[3] "It is doubtful if a major unit of the United States Navy ever went aground under circumstances less excusable than in this case," he opened. "That she went aground can be attributed to only one factor—personnel failure. The record of proceedings is long, thorough and complete. From start to finish it is a story of lack of coordination, cooperation, and initially a story of apathy, negligence, and incompetence of both officers and enlisted personnel of the Operations Department." The Chief of Naval Personnel concurred, as did Forrest Sherman, Chief of Naval Operations. Finally, the judge advocate general approved the report, closing the casebook on the USS *Missouri* incident in Chesapeake Bay.

Here were the men who had been recognized for efficiency at sea in the summer of 1949, and their skipper, a man who arrived with the potential for admiral's rank. How had they become "incompetent" by January 1950? If they were negligent and apathetic, what had happened? More important, what would it take to correct the situation? Reports were undertaken, but these said little more than what Fechteler had observed. The key issue was never identified by those in the line of authority, although there is evidence that it was not unknown to them. It lurks in the hindsight often applied to what William Brown called an "unusual and unfortunate chain of circumstances." For years, mariners—particularly those of the U.S. Navy—would discuss the astounding details that in less than a month brought about the strangest mishap in the history of the peacetime Navy. Rhetorically they would ask, "Why didn't they . . . ?" Those with a tad of nautical expertise might pose an action and say the accident would not have happened "had they only . . ." After-the-fact insights fit into four categories—shipboard organization, conning, navigation, and operations.

The court of inquiry held the opinion that the captain failed to take his senior subordinates into his confidence after finding that the executive officer was unaware of the CO's plan to run the acoustic range.[4] The conversation between the captain and his exec on 23 December, which Peckham reported to Millett and Morris, telling them the captain had "bawled me out," came to light in Peckham's response to Admiral Smith's letter of intent. Circumspect as always, the executive officer didn't make that incident public until he had good reason. What strange chemistry arose between the ship's two top officers in the one month they worked together remains unknown. It was never explained why Captain Brown excluded Commander Peckham from navigational matters, an exclusion that became even more curious when Brown referenced his XO as one on the bridge whose "counsel would have been most valuable and most desired." Further, although Brown leaned heavily on the operations officer for navigational advice, he had never specifically informed Millett of that status. It is likely that Brown took for granted the supremacy of the operations department, and navigation within it, and saw the executive officer as a sort of staff captain, an administrator unconcerned with the details of ship movement. It was not an uncommon attitude, nor was it explicitly contradicted by *Navy Rules and Regulations,* but it limited the ability of the next in command and cut the skipper off from timely counsel. Peckham might have pushed further when, four decks below, he asked the captain if the northern range marker had been sighted. When Brown affirmed that it had, would the exec have been out of order to ask that a bearing be taken on it from the skipper's higher level? By such a challenge the fatal left turn might have been avoided. Both men were victims of an organizational misconception.

The court found that the O8-level bridge was "normally staffed."[5] It is possible that under the Navy's tables of organization it was heavily overstaffed. Too many people with too little to do added to the confusion when the pace of message activity picked up. There was little sense of active participation or display of interest in anything beyond narrowly defined tasks, although many were in a position to observe what was happening. Quartermaster Travis may have spoken for several others who were on the bridge during that crucial period when he told the court, "I don't think it's my place to give the captain orders; it's my place to take orders from him." It was contrary to any accepted practice that someone, particularly an enlisted man, should raise a voice, even if addressed to no one in particular, to say, "Thimble Shoal Light isn't where it's supposed to be—those sticks aren't meant for big ships—ask the bow lookout if anyone sees the buoys— the helm isn't answering." That would have been more likely if only a half-dozen people were on duty. Men stationed on each level monitored the activity of others. Yet the telephone talkers, the "nervous system of the ship," were not relaying messages and in some cases were using the wrong circuits, such that some messages did not get through.[6] A well-put grumble ("Speak up, sailor!") from a chief listening in on the interchanges might have clarified the risks for the skipper early enough to avoid disaster.

Conning is not an activity to be taken lightly, particularly for a ship the size of the *Missouri,* yet when it came to ensuring an adequate understanding of the Thimble Shoal channel and the experimental passage within it, there was little planning and less involvement of the responsible people. In its opinion the court blamed Morris for not having taken proper and adequate steps to ascertain definitely the correct number, description, location, and arrangement of the buoys marking the acoustic range.[7] It cited twelve facts concerning frequently changed descriptions, and by the testimony of a scientist in the Naval Ordnance Laboratory, one description was incorrectly dated. The navigator was aware of the confusion and had ample time to get an accurate picture of what they would encounter east of Old Point Comfort. It would have been a simple matter, a day or two before getting under way, to lower a ship's boat or requisition a launch from the naval base and send a trio of sailors out to survey the site—no more than a half-day's work to get a firsthand description. Knowing specifically what to look for would have made the ultimate search for the buoys easier, enabling the conning officer to focus on tracking the planned course.

Nothing in the regulations requires that the captain himself take the conn in restricted waters. Article 880 of the regulations then in effect held him responsible for the safe conduct of the ship, and the next article specified that he shall "pilot the ship under his command under all ordinary circumstances." Therein lies the authority for a tactic undertaken by some skippers, often when they find themselves among others who are apt to be more familiar with the circumstances. It is particularly useful to those new to their commands, as Brown was. A pilot acts strictly as a guide to the person at the conn.* Brown could have designated the officer of the deck as conning officer and stood nearby to act as his pilot, possibly learning something while he observed, making suggestions as needed, and, if he felt it necessary, taking over the conn at any time. That might have given the younger officer a sense of pride to be so trusted; the captain would be no less responsible, but freer to observe the ship's operation in tracking the plotted courses. Lieutenant Arnold would have been a good choice for conning officer, being the first one to recognize the fishing stakes for what they actually were.

No conning officer's tactical plotting station was maintained on the O8 level,[8] ostensibly for good reason—there was little room on the crowded open bridge for a chart table. Nautical charts are expendable items. Additional ones could have been kept in a vertical rack like the hymnal rack on the back of a pew, folded like a road map, readily available and easily referenced and marked as desired. Trips to the chart room would have been fewer, and the designated plotting officer would not have found himself as frequently crowded away from his work. That no one thought of such an expedient illustrates the casual attitude toward piloting and navigation that often prevailed in the Navy.

---

* The Panama Canal is the only exception to this. There the canal pilot legally relieves the commanding officer of all navigational and ship-handling responsibility. Skippers have been known to retire to their quarters to read their mail or nap during the passage through Gatun Lake and the locks.

Depending on a navigator's perspective, the twenty-minute passage from Fort Wool to the lighted buoy south of Thimble Shoal
Light was either a demanding situation with very limited support or a
simple matter of buoy-hopping. Few navigational marks were available, none for good cross bearings after Old Point Comfort fell aft of
the beam. It was a case of peering ahead for the lone nun buoy on the
route to the channel south of Thimble Shoal Light. Bearings on the
most obvious landmark, the white lighthouse on Old Point Comfort,
helped somewhat until a bearing could be taken on Thimble Shoal
Light, that mark nearly in line with and beyond the channel buoy,
properly located off the port bow. By closely watching the true bearings on Old Point Comfort Light as the ship turned around the point,
the navigator could determine when to turn eastward. That turning
bearing, 255°T to 250°T nominally, then became the western or after
end of a danger bearing on Thimble Shoal Light, drawn on the *Missouri*'s chart as 075°T, slightly to the left of the desired course. Buoy-
hopping with a known fixed speed of, say, ten knots, would bring the
ship up to the next mark in fifteen minutes; the buoy, conical and red,
should be sighted by sharp lookouts in perhaps eight to ten minutes.
This was no place to vary the ship's speed. It was an appropriate
locale to listen to reports from someone watching the fathometer, not
because of shoaling but as another means of positioning. Certainly
that person should have been told to report all readings less than nine
fathoms, the middle of the channel. With those aids at hand and well
watched, the slender spars intended to mark a narrow northbound
channel through a fishnet area would be of no concern. So little of
this was done it appeared that these deep-sea sailors were bent on
getting to Little Creek as soon as possible and then off into the Gulf
Stream. Piloting as done in small craft just didn't interest them.

Some would say the passage itself was risky, particularly if the
attractive but ill-defined route through the acoustic range on the left,
shoalward side of the natural channel was to be followed. Captain
Brown either saw no added danger or was intent on complying with
the request in spite of it. He seems to have paid little note to the fact
that compliance was optional; no response in either case was
required. There was no traffic, the ship had the passage entirely to
itself, and the visibility was good. Well before they reached it, Brown,
Millett, and Morris planned to pursue the route, conforming to what

Brown may have taken to be orders. ("I have to steer a steady course for the data on the range," may have implied obligation in his mind.) The junior officer of the deck (Chester Wood's "high-priced lookout") and the bow lookouts could have been put to the explicit task of finding and identifying the spherical white-and-orange range markers, ones considerably different from the upcoming nun, but no descriptions of the range buoys were made available to them. It seemed to be the captain's own project, one he shared reluctantly. Had the junior officer of the deck known what to look for, and had he maintained a continuing conversation with lookouts on the bow and O4 wings and the COC plotters, the people in the COC could perhaps have discerned one or more of the buoys on their PPI scopes. They could have gotten a start on calibrating the radar and shared in any observations of courses deviating from a safe route. The lack of initiative to coordinate fire control, radar, and visual fixes led to the operations officer's early confusion at the time he advised the skipper to leave the northern buoy to starboard. If his men below had doubts, they failed to share them with the conn.[9]

Ironically, when Millett thought he was doing what his skipper expected of him he was a victim of the negligence of his own department. Brown's December conversation with Peckham, which may have encouraged Millett when it was relayed to him, brought a curse on all the top men of the *Missouri*. It certainly contributed to the apathy of the other officers, as they sensed that their skipper didn't welcome volunteered advice, even from his next in command.[10] When, minutes before his ship struck ground, three of his top men stood by him in silence, unresponsive to his questions about the spar buoys, they preferred to shelter their doubts rather than risk invoking his displeasure. Brown was in error in his understanding of the buoys in the area, and there was no one with the courage to tell him, or even to raise doubts. The navigator was using the danger bearing as a more reliable guide than the confusing and poorly identified buoys, but he was late in sharing his knowledge. Even then, in the court's opinion, the captain ignored the repeated urgent recommendations to bring the ship right.[11] The officer of the deck suspected the true nature of the fishnet stakes but chose to say nothing rather than counter what might be on the minds of his superiors. They were all victims of myopic conformity, perhaps even the captain himself.

If Brown did put the contributions of the operations department higher in his esteem than the duties of the executive officer, he was not alone among large-ship commanders. The position of operations officer came to be on capital ships when efforts were made to reduce the number of department heads reporting to the executive officer. Typically a senior officer answering directly to the exec, the operations officer had the navigator, communications officer, and combat operations officer reporting to him for purposes of administration. On navigational matters, based on long tradition, the navigator stepped out of that chain and reported directly to the captain. The confused structure within operations tended to reduce the navigator in experience, rank, and prestige. Hanson Baldwin expressed this view in his *New York Times* column as the *Missouri* defendants concluded their cases.[12] After the mishap very little was done to emphasize the navigator's significance. Later some commands did a better job of isolating the position and putting the focus where it belonged, largely due to the *Missouri* incident. But Brown was not entirely out of place in sending Millett to check on Morris's estimate of position. He lost sight of the importance of the navigator's role, and much earlier, when he was first piqued by Morris's shortcomings, he passed up an opportunity to enhance it.

In this sad litany of failings, all symptoms of the "unfortunate chain of circumstances"—avoidance of responsibility, negligence, apathy, the attitude that someone else was taking care of things— there was one common thread, the failure to risk speaking out, to say "Something's wrong." George Peckham had the courage, but until the ship was standing into danger he found himself torn between navigational matters he had been told to avoid and his sense that something was indeed not right. Then, in the last minutes during which the grounding could have been avoided, lack of coordination got in the way.

Military organizations cannot operate like town meetings. Authority must be recognized, conformity with leadership must be expected, in battle more than in peace, at sea more than in the lecture hall, in crisis more than in routine. But when people put too high a price on conformity, it can develop into the attitude that command authority confers infallibility. Captain Brown's behavior only reinforced that view, and he may well have been a victim of it himself.

Allan Smith knew better. In an article on his accomplishment published a year later in the Naval Institute *Proceedings,* he wrote, "All members of my staff understood that they must speak up if they had a worthy comment or needed a question answered, and that the discussions were helpful to the decision."[13] Even when on the receiving end, when he knew that President Truman and the Secretary of the Navy were watching the affairs in the Chesapeake, he enjoyed the benefits of latitude in action. "The main factor in refloating the *Missouri* was the efficient organization of the United States Navy and the splendid mutual understanding inside the Atlantic Fleet. I received no orders or suggestions from any senior officer and all the support and assistance needed."[14]

But a proposal for broader application of this concept never was put forth. Nowhere in the letters on the incident that traveled through channels to the Navy's top command did anyone recommend that the apathy the reports so readily identified could be overcome by empowering men to participate in their leaders' decisions. The feeling was strong that rank is right and that the key to career progress is conformity to the wishes of the next higher in command. Well it may be. Louis Denfield had expressed his views on rapid demobilization and got thrown out by the president, and lesser men in the top ranks shuffled quietly into line. To do otherwise was risky. In addition to requiring a solid position, it took tact and timing, the stuff that makes outstanding naval officers.

Leaders build teams by recognizing people as essentially capable and anxious to cooperate. They create an environment in which those people can develop the courage to speak out should they see things clearly going wrong, one that revels in their leader's success. Call the spirit it generates empowered participation or call it carefully generated teamwork, it was the unrecognized solution to the problems the Navy faced. Some time later, after the events that brought those problems to light had faded from the public's interest, when world events diverted the attention of the Navy's top leaders, who did little about the problems they identified, the one person best suited to recognize the solution would identify it in most colorful language.

10

As You Were

Even after the *Missouri* returned under tow to the dockyard, work remained to be done at Thimble Shoal. The tidal gauges were quickly removed lest they be mistaken for additional spars leading to the fishing grounds. The Coast Guard reclaimed its anchorage buoys, and a search was put out for the lost pontoon. Like any derelict craft, it would be a hazard to navigation if it remained afloat on the Chesapeake. The wide search proved fruitless, and ultimately it was assumed to lie somewhere on the bottom. Tugboats returned to the naval base to dump on a service pier tons of twisted and broken cables retrieved after the battleship was freed. The wire rope had been so stressed it was useless, with strands snapped, burned through, unraveled, and snarled. Metalsmiths were put to work breaking up and bundling the lengths onto barges to be deep-sixed in the Atlantic. Heavy leather gloves issued to the workers wore out in half an hour, so many broken wires had sprung from the cabling.[1] Somewhere today in the ocean's depths there exists a steel reef, once some four miles of muscular sinews used in the final pull.

South of the shoal, the bottom area with its narrow dead-ended channel had to be sounded anew for the next release of nautical charts. Forty years later a mariner lacking visual bearings in a fog could follow a five-fathom contour line with a depth finder and accurately determine position above the hull-shaped crevasse remaining on the bottom. Buried beneath there lies the wreckage of a railroad barge known to have been lost in the 1920s and almost certainly the source of the steel bar that cut into the battleship's bottom. After the barge sank it was recognized as an obstruction to navigation and was dynamited to level it to the area's charted depth.[2] Quite likely the football-size boulders brought up by the *Comber* were ballast carried by that barge. Shortly after the findings and recommendations of the court of inquiry were released, the Naval Ordnance Laboratory arranged to place a set of privately maintained lighted buoys along the hydrophone route, providing much-improved guidance for mariners.

Cost studies of the salvage operation were hurried to completion and found to be surprisingly low, less than $225,000 to get the ship afloat and approximately $48,000 for dry-docking and repairs, the latter offset by a $32,000 savings in fuel not used during the period. All costs were absorbed within current appropriations. There was justification in multiple training benefits derived from the suddenly needed all-out effort. Many young officers and enlisted men gained substantial experience in staff work, logistics, and salvage. Morale among the crews of the often idle salvage fleet improved remarkably.[3]

The Portrex operation in March was a disappointment. While the assault on the beaches of Vieques landed a maximum force in a minimum time, the only opposition was the surf and the terrain. There was no air cover for the marines streaming ashore, due to a ship-plane "communications breakdown." As a consequence the joint Army–Navy–Air Force invasion was considered unrealistic, and observers of each of the military units verbally sniped at one another.[4] The armed forces were not yet acting in unison.

Publicity died down quickly once the battleship put to sea, but within the Navy there was wide interest in what would happen to the disciplined officers. Would Captain Brown, not yet forty-eight, "swallow the anchor," in Navy lingo, and take retirement after twenty-six years, or would he continue his career with the stigma of conviction following him wherever he went? He would never command another ship. Although few but friends would discuss his difficulty with him, he knew he could never walk into an officers club or naval facility again without the feeling that behind his back people were nodding toward him, talking in suppressed voices about the man who drove the *Mighty Mo* aground. The severity of his sentence actually worked in conjunction with the procedures of naval selection boards to encourage his continued active service. Being dropped 250 places removed him from consideration for promotion for several years, allowing him to build up longevity, thereby increasing his ultimate retirement pay. If, instead, he had been reduced by only ten or twenty points, he would have come up routinely for review by the selection board, and with the general court-martial conviction on his record he would have just as routinely been passed over. Automatic retirement would have followed the second instance of being passed over.[5] The Navy was his life, and Brown did in fact continue in a much subdued career. Returning to his home state, he was assigned as commander of a sub group that was to be closed down within a year, from there to chief staff officer in the Florida group of the Atlantic Reserve Fleet. He became commander of that unit in June 1953, and two years later he retired gracefully with the "tombstone rank" (an honorary promotion sometimes given on retirement) of rear admiral. During World War II Brown was awarded the Legion of Merit, with a later gold star for his service in the South Pacific. He died in January 1991 at the age of eighty-eight.

Commander Peckham remained on the *Missouri* as executive officer until it returned to Norfolk in July 1950 at the end of an abruptly terminated midshipmen's cruise. He was then sent to Stanford University, where he achieved a Master of Arts degree in personnel administration. Much of his subsequent career was spent in various personnel assignments—as a branch head in Washington, briefly in command of a cruiser, then a policy assistant in the Bureau of Naval Personnel. Promoted to captain, he closed out his career as chief of staff in an amphibious training command. He retired in 1959 with the tombstone rank of rear admiral.

There is indication that George Peckham was held high in Admiral Smith's esteem, in spite of Smith's briefly considered intention to censure him. Allan Smith was an intellectual person, not always content in social circumstances with the shallow Navy-only dialogue of his military associates. Try as he would at dinners and cocktail parties, he found it difficult to steer the conversation away from the subject of the Navy. Ultimately he learned how to survive the boredom by seeking people of interest who might be standing aside from the main group, and challenging them with the question, "In your view, what is the most important thing that has happened in this world? You have ninety seconds to think it over and respond." Over time he collected some four hundred replies from university deans, foreign ministers, newspaper editors, priests, politicians, and many naval personnel.[6] It is evident from his list of respondents that these were people he admired. Among them were two men of the *Missouri,* Capt. H. Page Smith and Comdr. George Peckham. Their answers seemed to reflect their current circumstances; Smith's was apropos of the social occasion, something to do with the emancipation of the British Empire, and Peckham cited the development of disease-curing drugs, penicillin having recently been discovered.

Rear Admiral Smith, who opened this tale by returning in the fall of 1950 to the ship he had pulled off the shoal to take it again as his flagship, had expected to assume command of the Thirteenth Naval District in Seattle.[7] While waiting for that billet to open he couldn't give up his interest in good naval public relations. Shortly after the battleship was repaired and off to sea, the admiral was invited to tell his story on a popular national radio show. He accepted gladly, and one more time gave his "final" report to the public on the salvaging of the *Missouri,* the account told with his customary enthusiastic inflections.[8] His accomplishment was one for the records—he had successfully directed the salvage of the heaviest single unpowered object ever moved by man. The Korean War ended Smith's public relations campaign when he was assigned as Commander of the United Nations Blockade Force in Korea, Task Force 95. There he initiated a three-year east coast blockade, becoming known as the Duke of Wonsan. At the end of the Korean War he took retirement, completing forty-three years of service with the tombstone rank of vice admiral. During his retirement he wrote two books, toured the world, and continued as an active spokesman for American military policy. He died in 1987 at age ninety-five.

Harold Page Smith belongs in this group of heroes. Twice captain of the *Missouri,* he next took up several staff assignments, was promoted to rear admiral before taking command of a transport squadron, and after that became Chief of Naval Personnel. Twice more promoted, his last assignment, CinCLantFlt, found him also as Supreme Allied Commander of the NATO fleet. Upon Smith's retirement in 1965, President Johnson pinned the Distinguished Service Medal on the beaming admiral's beribboned chest.

It was aboard his flagship in Amphibious Group Two, Atlantic Fleet, that Smith identified the solution to the problems troubling the pre–Korean War Navy.[9] Lt. Edmund Butler, a naval reservist and World War II veteran recalled to active duty during the Korean War, was navigator of the USS *Mount Olympus,* the amphibious force command ship. The afternoon the ship sailed out of Hampton Roads with Rear Adm. H. P. Smith aboard as its new flag officer, the lieutenant received an invitation to dine in the admiral's mess. Surprised, he reported this to his CO. The skipper had also been invited, not an uncommon situation, but was equally surprised that this young fellow would be joining him.

Admiral Smith, a button-eyed, jowly southern gentleman, welcomed the two men to flag quarters and proved to be a genial host at a delightful dinner. The conversation was light and unconcerned with ship's business. When the table was cleared, coffee poured, and cigars lit, the admiral leaned back with a twinkle in his brown eyes and addressed the captain of the *Mount Olympus:*

"I suppose you're wondering why I invited your navigator to dinner on our first evening at sea. The following story will make the invitation clear to you.

"I had command of the *Missouri* in 1948 and 1949. Captain Brown relieved me and within a few weeks drove the ship aground on Thimble Shoal. While I had no legal responsibility, I felt a deep sense of moral responsibility for the grounding. All the officers involved, except Captain Brown, had served with me. I trained them, so I felt at least partly responsible for their actions.

"I was ordered back to the ship, relieved Captain Brown, and retained command until the *Missouri* was proven seaworthy. While the board of inquiry and subsequent courts-martial covered all the facts concerning the incident, none of the testimony disclosed what I believe to be the true reason for the piloting error—the navigator didn't have the courage to contradict the operations officer and the captain, and forcibly point out to them that the ship was standing into danger. All he did was call out the ship's position, course, and speed. Until too late, he left it up to the captain to discover that the course put them out of position for a safe transit.

"This is where I felt a deep responsibility for the events that transpired. I failed to impress upon the navigator that rank has no privilege where the safety of the ship is concerned. If he knew the ship was standing into danger, he should have got the conning officer's attention any way he could to provide him with timely advice in order to correct the course and speed."

Seconds elapsed in silence. Facing the navigator, the admiral went on, "So, young fellow, if you learn anything from my story, remember this. You, as navigator, are responsible for knowing the ship's position at all times. If the course or contemplated course change will head the ship toward dangerous waters, it is your bounden duty to bring this fact to the attention of the conning officer, the captain, and, in the event a flag officer is aboard, to that individual. I don't care if you have to swing at us with a wet swab—you are to get our immediate attention."

His point that the Navy needed swab-swingers when leadership is approaching trouble was not lost. Looking steadfastly at the navigator, he closed his advice with one more charge, "Just make sure you're right!"

Page Smith's jargon never became colloquial. Then no phrase in common usage identified people who deviate from hierarchical protocol. Today someone who calls public attention to harmful practices, attempting to protect broader interests, is known as a whistle-blower and is given protection under federal law.* But whistle-blowing can be a risky activity. Rank in error may be without privilege, but it is not without power. Discretion is often seen as the individual's safer alternative. Who does not have faults to overcome before broadcasting the errors of others? But that misses the point. "Remove the plank from your own eye first; then you will see clearly to take the speck from your brother's eye" (Matthew 7:5). Nothing in the biblical adjuration tells one to keep quiet; rather, it encourages self-improvement. When circumstances exist to encourage swab-swingers, they are more likely to be sure they speak from an unassailable position. The organization thereby gains tougher team players. Even the leaders improve, lest they suffer criticism. Page Smith was not concerned with Brown's distrust of his navigator, or with Morris's casual approach to navigation. It was the fact that Morris hesitated when he knew trouble was developing that disquieted the admiral, and for that he took some of the blame on himself. His lecture in the flag mess was at once an example in self-improvement and an effort to put military discipline

---

* The term "whistle-blower" was first used in John Hamilton's article, "Blowing the Whistle on 'The Bosses,'" *New York Times,* 23 March 1970. See also Clarence L. Barnhart, Sol Steinmetz, and Robert K. Barnhart, *The Barnhart Dictionary of New English since 1963* (New York: Barnhart/Harper & Row, 1973).

in perspective. Page Smith died in 1993. Would his message live after him, to the end-of-the-century Navy?

> His average age is 22. . . . clearly a product of prosperity . . . he romped through adolescence . . . with more money and less parental supervision than his [predecessors]. He came of age in an era of full employment. . . . Frequently he was the child of itinerant parents . . . younger. . . healthier, better schooled, and more adept at learning. . . . he is also plainly undisciplined, jealously aware of his rights but not his responsibilities. Moreover, he is mercenary and antagonistic to authority in almost any form.

These words were not written to describe the children of the permissive seventies, the naval officers who year after year frolicked in Las Vegas to the ultimate embarrassment of even the Secretary of the Navy. They are not referring to the Naval Academy football players who put grades above honesty, to be staunchly defended by faculty members in that school's worst scandal. The words are those of Gen. Omar Bradley, Chairman of the Joint Chiefs, speaking of the postwar soldier in 1949.[10] They could have been written by Plato. Human behavior has no new traits, only new needs for reminders, from whistle-blowers, swab-swingers, or prophets, in cases of ineptitude or iniquity. Lack of individual responsibility, innate professionalism, and pride in one's position may be a result of the times. The pressures of one period do seem to have a way of recycling later on. Yet the presence of people with the courage to send out a propitious warning could have made the difference in convention corridors, in examination halls, or decades ago on the bridge of the *Mighty Mo.* The ramifications of a single inept act can usually be offset by a single competent act. The consequences of a single immoral deed are often more difficult to dispel. Fortunately, honest, moral people are inclined to stay that way and to outnumber their opposites in most respectable organizations.

The men of the *Missouri* had their chance to recover after H. P. Smith's brief return. In mid-April Irving T. Duke relieved him to take the ship on two scheduled midshipmen's cruises. Then on Saturday, 24 June, the North Koreans invaded South Korea. After two tense days of emergency sessions, Harry Truman decided to provide air and naval support to the South Korean forces.[11] The *Missouri*, in Boston on the first of its cruises, was called back to Norfolk. Inadvertently,

Truman had avoided having to renege on his promise to keep his favorite in commission. The ship would remain in the battleship class and be outfitted for transfer to the Pacific Fleet, with its complement increased to 2,184 officers and men, battle efficiency level.[12] The admiral's resolution to investigate and modify the Navy's personnel policies was put aside when, for the third time in the century, the Navy called on its reservists to help fill its needs. More than a third of the crew headed for the Far East would be new to the ship. Sailors who had taken for granted their spacious living quarters found themselves with much tighter accommodations.[13] Sure indication that they would be on extended deployment in distant waters, the Washington, D.C., Navy Band was assigned aboard.* Newcomers asked almost at once about the experience and reactions of those who had been aboard in January. The old-timers soon tired of the questions, preferring to put the events behind them. New and old alike soon were challenged in working together. Finally under way for the Pacific, southeast of Cape Hatteras the ship drove through a hurricane, suffering moderate damage. Nearly all the lightbulbs on deck were broken by the combined forces of wind and water; waves rolled aboard and stove in the admiral's barge and captain's gig; two helicopters were lost off the afterdeck.[14] The warship plowed on, cleared the Panama Canal, and headed to Pearl Harbor for repairs and additional armament. To test the mettle of the newly assembled crew further, on arrival in the Sea of Japan a typhoon swept up from the south to confront them on station. Adversity was pulling the third crew of the *Mighty Mo* together. The siege of Wonsan, initiated under Admiral Smith, restored their fighting spirit. The battleship was later joined by the *Iowa,* which ultimately relieved it, but not before the men of the *Missouri* were visited by Syngman Rhee, president of the Republic of Korea. The infamy of Thimble Shoal became dim in memory.

The *Iowa* class remained active in the evolution of naval warfare. While their big guns prevailed in shore bombardment, it was as guided-missile carriers that they took up their final assignments. Naval strategies, envisioned and shelved before events in Korea put a

* Members of that original band have stayed together for more than forty years, performing for special events associated with the battleship, including the annual meeting of the USS *Missouri* Association.

harsh spotlight on the Cold War, became justified in a world of sporadic aggression and terrorism. The *Iowa* class continued to serve—the *New Jersey* in Vietnam, the *Missouri* and later the *Wisconsin* in the Persian Gulf, forty-five years after the last ship in the class was launched. The incentive to modernize the ships in the manner planned for the never-completed *Kentucky* didn't occur until the 1980s, when trouble developed in the Middle East, and then with much-advanced equipment—Harpoon and Tomahawk missiles. Still, the big guns weren't stilled. They were used in 1991 to break up an Iraqi command bunker during Desert Storm.[15]

In its fifty years of life the *Missouri* has shipped aboard four crews. These are not crisply defined, static organizations. Personnel turns over continuously with expiration of enlistments, reassignments, illnesses, and deaths, but the men identify with events coinciding with their period of service. The "plank owners," those who came aboard in 1944 when the ship was first commissioned, think of themselves not as sailors in the last stages of battle but as veterans of Tokyo Bay. The second crew, those who took over on the ship's return to the Atlantic in 1945, was the most loosely defined and longest lived—some four or five years. Theirs was the least heroic purpose, subsistence through training, with the glory of battle in Korea going to the latecomers, those who were trained to become the third crew. The second group looks on the ignominious month in 1950 as a mere blemish in a splendid history, one not without its humorous elements, but the shame is largely forgotten. The fourth crew, the men who took the ship around the world, served in the Persian Gulf and fought in Desert Storm, see the event of the stranding as a footnote in history, if they are aware of it at all. It has been eclipsed by so much that was honorable and heroic.

After basking in their fame for a period in the Reserve Fleet, all four ships were struck from the Naval Vessel Register in January 1995. The cost of operating them outweighed their value to the fleet. As the world changes politically, so it must in warfare. The last sea battles were fought in World War II. Shore bombardment as done in Korea and Vietnam is better undertaken by smaller ocean vessels or from carrier-based aircraft. Faster and more adept ships are available for fleet escorts. The fifty-year old *Iowa*s may continue to serve as memorials, periodically opened to the public for conducted tours of their magnificent main decks. Reenlistments and retirements have regularly taken place on board the *Missouri,* typically a dozen retirement and three times as many reenlistment ceremonies every year. It was the most popular ship on the West Coast for such purposes. Navy men continue to revel in its renown. In recounting the glorious elements in the history of the *Mighty Mo,* they would do well to include both the tribulation and the message of Thimble Shoal.

A

Men of the USS *Missouri*

Some fifteen hundred officers and men were aboard in January 1950, contributing to the ultimate saving of the ship. The following have been mentioned in the narrative as active participants and surviving witnesses.

Officers

Capt. William Drane Brown	Commanding Officer
Comdr. George E. Peckham	Executive Officer
Comdr. John R. Millett	Operations Officer
Comdr. R. A. Zoeller	Engineering Officer
Lt. Comdr. Frank G. Morris	Navigator
Lt. Edward E. Arnold	First Lieutenant, Watch Officer
Lt. Paul N. Bland	Communications Officer
Lt. John A. Carr	Combat Operations Officer
Lt. James N. Forehan	Assistant Engineering Officer
Lt. Roland B. Hatfield	Watch Officer
Lt. (jg) Lawrence G. Body	Junior Watch Officer
Lt. (jg) Harold B. Gibbs	Electronics Officer
Ens. Elwin R. Harris	Assistant Navigator
Ens. Francis Kelly	Assistant Navigator

Enlisted Men

John L. Beeman	Seaman Apprentice
Arthur J. Cole	Seaman
Arden A. Field	Seaman Apprentice
Ward Folansby	Seaman
Clarence George	Machinist's Mate Third Class

Angelo Goffredo	Electronic Technician Third Class
James Happenny	Seaman
Robert Hess	Seaman
Oscar T. Hood	Seaman First Class
Gene D. Jensen	Seaman
Harry A. Kimble	Quartermaster Third Class
Warran Lee	Fire Controlman Third Class
Robert Marks	Seaman
Patrick McGough	Radioman Third Class
Vincent McGrath	Ship's Cook Third Class
L. R. Reams	Chief Quartermaster
Harold A. Rice	Chief Quartermaster
John C. Smith	Metalsmith Third Class
John W. Spooner	Quartermaster First Class
Bevan Travis	Quartermaster Second Class
Andrew Vargo	Chief Radio Electrician
John Watson	Seaman Apprentice
Richard Wentz	Quartermaster First Class
John Williams	Seaman
John K. Williams	Seaman Apprentice

B

History of Modern American Battleships

TABLE 1 Battleship Service in World War II

Hull	Name	World War II Service	Status, 1941–50
33	*Arkansas*	Atlantic Fleet; Normandy; South of France; Iwo Jima; Okinawa	Nuclear target, 1946
34	*New York*	Atlantic Fleet; Normandy; South of France; Iwo Jima; Okinawa	Nuclear target, 1946
35	*Texas*	Atlantic Fleet; North Africa; Iwo Jima; Okinawa	Decommissioned, 1948 Relic
36	*Nevada*	Atlantic Fleet; North Africa; South of France; Iwo Jima; Okinawa	Nuclear target, 1946
37	*Oklahoma*	Sunk at Pearl Harbor	Scrapped, 1941
38	*Pennsylvania*	Damaged at Pearl Harbor; Attu; Kiska; Marshalls; Saipan; Guam; Palau; Leyte; Surigao Strait; Lingayen; Wake Island; Okinawa	Nuclear target, 1946

APPENDIX B

Hull	Name	World War II Service	Status, 1941–50
39	*Arizona*	Sunk at Pearl Harbor	War Memorial, 1941
40	*New Mexico*	Pacific Fleet; Southwest Pacific; Attu; Aleutians; Makin; Kwajalein; Kavieng; Saipan; Guam; Occupation of Japan	Decommissioned, 1946 Scrapped
41	*Mississippi*	Southwest Pacific; Attu; Makin; Kwajalein; Kavieng; Palau; Leyte; Surigao Strait; Mindoro; Lingayen; Okinawa; Occupation of Japan	Auxiliary training ship, 1946; Reclassified to gunnery test ship (AG-128)
42	*Idaho*	Aleutians; Attu; Kwajalein; Saipan; Guam; Palau; Iwo Jima; Okinawa; Occupation of Japan	Decommissioned, 1946 Scrapped
43	*Tennessee*	Damaged at Pearl Harbor; Aleutians; Kiska; Tarawa; Kwajalein; Eniewetok; Kavieng; Saipan; Tinian; Guam; Palau; Leyte; Surigao Strait; Iwo Jima; Okinawa; Occupation of Japan	Decommissioned, 1947 Scrapped
44	*California*	Salvaged at Pearl Harbor; Saipan; Tinian; Guam; Surigao Strait; Leyte; Lingayen; Okinawa; Occupation of Japan	Decommissioned, 1946 Scrapped
45	*Colorado*	South Pacific; Tarawa; Kwajalein; Eniwetok; Saipan; Guam; Tinian; Marcus I.; Leyte; Mindoro; Lingayen; Okinawa; Occupation of Japan	Decommissioned, 1947 Scrapped

Hull	Name	World War II Service	Status, 1941–50
46	Maryland	Damaged at Pearl Harbor; Southwest Pacific; Tarawa; Kwajalein; Saipan; Palau; Leyte; Surigao Strait; Okinawa	Decommissioned, 1947 Scrapped
48	West Virginia	Salvaged at Pearl Harbor; Leyte; Surigao Strait; Mindoro; Lingayen; Iwo Jima; Okinawa; Occupation of Japan	Decommissioned, 1947 Scrapped
55	North Carolina	Guadalcanal; Tulagi; Solomons; Gilberts; Kavieng; Kwajalein; Truk; Marianas; Palau; Yap; Ulithi; Waleai; Hollandia; Truk; Satawan; Ponape; Saipan; Philippines; Leyte; Luzon; Formosa; China Coast; Nansei Shoto; Iwo Jima; Honshu; Okinawa; Occupation of Japan	Decommissioned, 1947 Relic
56	Washington	Scapa Flow; Guadalcanal; Solomons; Gilberts; Kavieng; Kwajalein; Marianas; Philippines; Palau; Leyte; Formosa; Luzon; China Coast; Nansei Shoto; Iwo Jima; Honshu; Okinawa	Decommissioned, 1947 Scrapped
57	South Dakota	Guadalcanal; Gilberts; Kwajalein; Truk; Marianas; Palau; Ulithi; Yap; Satawan; Ponape; Hollandia; Philippines; Saipan; Okinawa; Luzon; Formosa; China Coast; Iwo Jima; Honshu; Occupation of Japan	Decommissioned, 1947 Scrapped

197

Hull	Name	World War II Service	Status, 1941–50
58	*Indiana*	South Pacific; Marcus I.; Gilberts; Kwajalein; Truk; Satawan; Ponape; Philippines; Marianas; Yap; Ulithi; Palau; Luzon; Iwo Jima; Honshu; Nansei Shoto	Decommissioned, 1946
59	*Massachusetts*	North Africa; Southwest Pacific; Gilberts; Kwajalein; Truk; Marianas; Palau; Yap; Ulithi; Waleai; Hollandia; Satawan; Ponape; Okinawa; Luzon; Cape Engano; Visayas; Formosa; China Coast; Nansei Shoto; Iwo Jima; Honshu	Decommissioned, 1947 Relic
60	*Alabama*	North Africa; Southwest Pacific; Gilberts; Kwajalein; Truk; Marianas; Palau; Yap; Ulithi; Waleai; Hollandia; Saipan; Guam; Bonins; Philippines; Okinawa; Luzon; Visayas; Leyte; Formosa; Occupation of Japan	Decommissioned, 1947 Relic
61	*Iowa*	North Atlantic; Casablanca with FDR; Kwajalein; Truk; Marianas; Palau; Yap; Ulithi; Saipan; Philippines; Luzon; Formosa; Guam; Tinian; Okinawa; Occupation of Japan	Decommissioned, 1949 Reserve Fleet

Hull	Name	World War II Service	Status, 1941–50
62	*New Jersey*	Kwajalein; Truk; Palau; Yap; Ulithi; Waleai; Hollandia; Satawan; Ponape; Saipan; Philippines; Guam; Okinawa; Formosa; Luzon; Visayas; China Coast; Nansei Shoto; Iwo Jima; Occupation of Japan	Decommissioned, 1948 Reserve Fleet
63	*Missouri*	Okinawa; Iwo Jima; Honshu; Nansei Shoto; Surrender Site, Tokyo Bay; Occupation of Japan	Active
64	*Wisconsin*	Luzon; Formosa; China Coast; Nansei Shoto; Iwo Jima; Occupation of Japan	Decommissioned, 1949

Source: Adapted from Stefan Terzibaschitsch, *Battleships of the U.S. Navy in World War II* (New York: Bonanza Books, 1977).

TABLE 2 *Iowa*-Class Battleships since 1950

Hull	Name	Date	Major Activities
61	*Iowa*	August 1951	Recommissioned
		1952–53	Korea
		February 1958	Decommissioned
		April 1984	Recommissioned
			Fitted with missiles
		August 1984	Nicaraguan surveillance
		February 1985	Central America
		January 1988	Strait of Hormuz
		April 1989	Explosion in #2 turret
		October 1990	Decommissioned
		January 1995	Struck from Ship Register
62	*New Jersey*	November 1950	Recommissioned
		1951–53	Korea
		August 1957	Decommissioned
		April 1968	Recommissioned
		1968–69	Vietnam
		December 1969	Decommissioned
		December 1982	Recommissioned
			Fitted with missiles
		1983	Central America
		1984	Lebanon
		February 1991	Decommissioned
		January 1995	Struck from Ship Register
63	*Missouri*	September 1950	Korea
		1951–53	Korea
		February 1955	Decommissioned
		May 1986	Recommissioned
			Fitted with missiles
		1986	Circumnavigation
		August 1987	Persian Gulf
		January 1991	Desert Storm
		March 1992	Decommissioned
		January 1995	Struck from Ship Register

64	*Wisconsin*	March 1951	Recommissioned
		1952–53	Korea
		March 1958	Decommissioned
		July 1988	Recommissioned
			Fitted with missiles
		January 1991	Desert Storm
		September 1991	Decommissioned
		January 1995	Struck from Ship Register

Source: Adapted from Robert F. Sumrall, Iowa-*Class Battleships: Their Design, Weapons and Equipment* (Annapolis, Md.: Naval Institute Press, 1988). Activity subsequent to 1988 is drawn from Ship's Histories Branch, Naval Historical Center, Washington, D.C., and articles in the *New York Times, Washington Post,* and Navy Wire Service.

Notes

CHAPTER 1 Last of the Best

1. John Keegan, *A History of Warfare* (New York: Knopf, 1993), 38; Warren Tute, *The True Glory* (New York: Harper & Row, 1983), 29. The ship has a sparse history. Keegan cites M. Lewis, *The Navy of Britain* (London, 1948), 76, and dates the origin of the *Mary Rose* as 1513. Tute puts its end in 1545.

2. Robert K. Massie, *Dreadnought: Britain, Germany and the Coming of the Great War* (New York: Random House, 1991), 468.

3. James M. McPherson, *Battle Cry of Freedom* (New York: Oxford University Press, 1988), 376.

4. Stefan Terzibaschitsch, *Battleships of the U.S. Navy in World War II*, translated and adapted by Heinz O. Vetters and Richard Cox (New York: Bonanza Books, 1977). The history of American battleships presented in appendix B is drawn chiefly from this book.

5. Chalmers M. Roberts, "Enola Gay: The Okinawa Factor," *Washington Post*, 23 August 1994. Roberts, during the war an Army Air Corps statistician who was responsible for following the movements of the kamikaze units, states that "kamikaze attacks sank 30 vessels and damaged 368 including 10 battleships and 10 aircraft carriers."

6. An eyewitness report of Navy correspondent F. N. Fuller, specialist first class, aboard the *Guam;* other details from the *Missouri*'s official history (*Dictionary of American Naval Fighting Ships*, vol. 4 [Washington, D.C.: Navy Department, 1969], 393–94) and from Andy Conrad of Pittsburgh, Pa., interviewed by author in San Antonio, Tex., on 3 September 1994. Conrad was part of the *Missouri*'s original crew.

7. Extracted from the deck log of the *Missouri* and summarized in the files of BB-63 by Ships Histories Branch of the Naval Historical Center, Washington, D.C.

8. David McCullough, *Truman* (New York: Simon & Schuster, 1992), 474.

9. "'Big Mo' Aground in Bay," *Norfolk Virginian-Pilot* (hereafter cited as *Pilot*), 18 January 1950.

CHAPTER 2 The Wedge

1. Paul Johnson, *Modern Times: The World from the Twenties to the Nineties,* rev. ed. (New York: HarperCollins, 1991), 683.
2. Allan E. Smith, letters of 2 December 1948, 9 February 1949, in private collection of Allan E. Smith Jr. of Medina, Wash. (collection hereafter cited as Smith Papers).
3. Allen Harper, *The Politics of Loyalty* (New York, 1969), cited in Johnson, *Modern Times,* 457.
4. Johnson, *Modern Times,* 439–50.
5. McCullough, *Truman,* 741.
6. Allan E. Smith, letter to Adm. W.H.P. Blandy after an informal poll of five fellow officers, 30 April 1949, Smith Papers.
7. "Rowboat Sailor," *Time,* 23 May 1949.
8. *Congressional Record,* 81st Cong., 2nd sess., 1950, vol. 96, pt. 1, p. 746.
9. Allan E. Smith, notes for a speech given at Type Commanders' Conference, 5 April 1949, quoting Gen. Omar M. Bradley, Chairman of the Joint Chiefs of Staff, Smith Papers. Bradley had commissioned a study of Army personnel and circulated the findings widely among all military leaders.
10. Robert F. Sumrall, Iowa-*Class Battleships: Their Design, Weapons and Equipment* (Annapolis, Md.: Naval Institute Press, 1988), 182.
11. Allan E. Smith, notes for speech given at Atlantic Fleet Type Commanders' Conference, 5 April 1949, Smith Papers.
12. *Manual of the Judge Advocate General, basic investigative report concerning the grounding of USS* Missouri *(BB-63), in Chesapeake Bay, on January 17, 1950,* 8 March 1950, Record of Proceedings (hereafter cited as *Proceedings*), Finding of Facts (hereafter cited as *Findings*), paragraph 140.
13. C. B. Allen, "Exercise Portrex: The Kibitzers Attack," *New York Herald Tribune,* 12 March 1950.
14. "Captain Brown New Skipper of USS *Missouri,*" *Pilot,* 11 December 1949.
15. This profile of Captain Brown was compiled from the following sources: curriculum vitae submitted to the Naval Academy Alumni Association; Gordon Newell and Allan E. Smith, Vice Admiral, USN (Ret.), *Mighty Mo, The USS* Missouri: *A Biography of the Last Battleship* (New York: Bonanza Books, 1969), 69; and various articles in the *Pilot* contemporary to the narrative.
16. Austin Stevens, "*Missouri* to Become School Ship for Midshipmen and Reservists," *New York Times,* 16 February 1950. Various figures have been given for the size of the *Missouri*'s crew after it completed its overhaul, ranging from 1,200 to 1,500 men, tending toward the latter as news of the ship developed. Appendix A in Sumrall, Iowa-*Class Battleships,* identifies the 1949 complement as made up of 151 officers and 2,255

men, certainly much higher than the numbers aboard late in the year, and specifies the minimum complement for the *Missouri* in 1988 as 65 officers and 1,450 men, reflecting peacetime staffing.

17. Allan E. Smith, ComCruLant summary letter, 15 March 1950, in *Proceedings.*

18. Oral reports of six enlisted members of the 1949 crew interviewed by author at the twentieth anniversary of the USS *Missouri* Association, San Antonio, Tex., September 1994.

19. Most details on Commander Millett are based on articles in the *Pilot* contemporary to the narrative.

20. "Millett Ends Court-Martial Defense," *Pilot,* 12 April 1950.

21. Terzibaschitsch, *Battleships of the U.S. Navy,* 158–59; Sumrall, *Iowa-Class Battleships,* 182; Allan E. Smith, memo of 2 December 1949, Smith Papers; *Findings,* paragraphs 73, 74.

22. Benjamin Dutton, *Navigation and Nautical Astronomy,* 9th ed. (Annapolis, Md.: U.S. Naval Institute, 1948), 187.

23. Tony Devereux, *Messenger Gods of Battle* (London: Brassey's, 1991), 189–91.

24. Hanson W. Baldwin, "Dilemma of the 'Big Mo,'" *New York Times,* 26 January 1950.

25. *Findings,* paragraphs 31ff.

26. Devereux, *Messenger Gods of Battle,* 151.

27. Dutton, *Navigation and Nautical Astronomy,* 201ff.

28. "Court Doubts 'Competence' of Ensign," *Pilot,* 11 February 1950. Most of the details of this voyage and descriptions of the officers are based on contemporary newspaper accounts. Corroborating information is in Newell and Smith, *Mighty Mo,* 69–79.

29. Jesse Glasgow (hereafter cited as Glasgow), "Ship Skipper Contradicted by Navigator," *Pilot,* 22 February 1950.

30. "Ensign, Twenty-Three, Blames *Missouri* Superior," *New York Times,* 10 February 1950. The *Times* states that Harris attended Roanoke College. Ralph Winnett of the *Pilot* (10 February 1950) correctly identifies Villanova College as the location of Harris's NROTC training.

31. W. M. Fechteler, CinCLantFlt, 17 May 1950, First Endorsement, with amplification, on ComCruLant cover letter, 1 May 1950, to *Proceedings;* amplification references Commander Peckham's reply to routine letter warning of possible letter of caution from the convening authority.

32. Glasgow, "Navigation Duties Not His, Peckham Says He Was Told," *Pilot,* 4 April 1950.

CHAPTER 3 Raise Able-Peter

1. Newell and Smith, *Mighty Mo,* 69.

2. Vice Adm. Forrest Sherman, Chief of Naval Operations since November 1949, helped write the unification plan (*U.S. News and World Report,* 11

November 1949, 40); Ralph Winnett (hereafter cited as Winnett), "*Missouri* in Portsmouth Drydock after Freeing," *Pilot,* 2 February 1950, included comments of Admiral Blandy, CinCLantFlt, at his retirement; according to Allen, "Exercise Portrex," "top military men . . . maintained . . . the joint Army–Navy–Air Force 'invasion' . . . afforded invaluable training for the troops involved."

3. William S. Ellis, "Hampton Roads, Where the Rivers End," *National Geographic* 168, no. 1 (July 1985): 87.

4. *Findings,* paragraph 37.

5. Letter from the Office of the Judge Advocate General to the author, 13 July 1993, states that the original court transcripts, once stored in the National Archives, have been destroyed or lost. Conversational details have been transcribed from newspaper reports on the hearing of the court of inquiry, many of which directly quoted the transcripts distributed to the press.

6. *Findings,* paragraph 26.

7. Dutton, *Navigation and Nautical Astronomy.* The paragraphs quoted are found on pages 703, 166, and 483, respectively.

8. Maneuvering the *Missouri* out of its Pier 7 slip is well illustrated by aerial photographs in the U.S. Navy's USS Missouri *1952–1953 Far Eastern Cruise Book.*

9. *Welcome Aboard,* U.S. Navy publicity brochure for the *Missouri.* These numbers do not differ significantly from the 1949 strengths given by Sumrall in Iowa-*Class Battleships.* Shipboard strengths change to some extent every time the ship returns to port, with reassignments, discharges, etc.

10. *The Bluejackets' Manual,* 13th ed. (Annapolis, Md.: U.S. Naval Institute, 1946), 562ff.

11. Oral report of Angelo Goffredo of Schenectady, N.Y. (ET3 in 1950), interviewed by author in January 1994; later confirmed by Robert Marks of Rochester, Minn. (SN striker in 1950), interviewed by author in September 1994.

CHAPTER 4   A Magnificent Sight

1. Oral report of John Williams of Shelby, N.C. (SN in 1950), interviewed by author in September 1994.

2. Glasgow, "Sailors on Liberty from *Missouri* Keep Theories on Mishap to Themselves," *Pilot,* 23 January 1950.

3. Marks and Goffredo, interviews.

4. Oral report of Clarence "Skip" George of Largo, Fla. (MM3 in 1950), interviewed by author in September 1994.

5. Oral report of Patrick McGough of Dallas, Pa. (RN3 in 1950), interviewed by author in September 1994.

6. Glasgow, "Sailors on Liberty."

7. George, interview. He was stationed in lower number two fireroom at the time.

8. Glasgow, "Sailors on Liberty."

9. Austin M. Knight, *Modern Seamanship,* 11th ed. (New York: D. Van Nostrand, 1950), 430ff.

10. Samuel Eliot Morison, *The Two-Ocean War* (Boston: Little, Brown, 1963), 516.

11. Newell and Smith, *Mighty Mo,* 79. Many details that follow are taken from USS Missouri *(BB-63) Salvage Report* (hereafter cited as *Salvage Report*), published for circulation within the U.S. Navy by ComCruLant, 15 March 1950.

12. Williams, interview.

13. *Findings,* paragraph 8.

14. Knight, *Modern Seamanship,* 431.

15. Oral report of Vincent McGrath of Waterford, Conn. (SC3 in 1950), interviewed by author in September 1994.

16. Ibid.

17. Shipping News, *Newport News Daily Press,* 17–18 January, 1950.

18. This profile of Allan Smith is based on several sources. The author is indebted to Allan E. Smith Jr. for some of the early material and to the U.S. Naval Academy Alumni Association for an official biography.

19. Morison, *The Two-Ocean War,* 334, 513, 530.

20. Newell and Smith, *Mighty Mo,* 78.

21. *Salvage Report.* Daily summaries were dispatched to CinCLantFlt (Enclosure 1 in the report), and a daily log was maintained (Enclosure 13) (hereafter cited as *Summaries* and *Log*). Where differences in minor details exist between these and newspaper reports, the ComCruLant report is considered authoritative.

22. Winnett, "New Channel Will Be Dug to *Missouri,*" *Pilot,* 19 January 1950.

23. *Summaries,* 18 January 1950.

24. Jacob Hay, "She Helped Free the 'Big Mo,'" *Baltimore Evening Sun,* 10 February 1950.

25. Charles McDowell Jr., "Navy Flooded with Plans to Refloat 'Mighty Mo,'" *Richmond Times-Dispatch,* 29 January 1950.

26. Winnett, "New Channel Will Be Dug."

27. Allan E. Smith, "Refloating the USS *Missouri,*" U.S. Naval Institute *Proceedings* 77, no. 2 (February 1951): 181.

28. Most of the following history has been extracted from C. A. Bartholomew, *Mud, Muscle, and Miracles: Marine Salvage in the United States Navy* (Washington, D.C.: Government Printing Office, 1990).

29. Winnett, "New Channel Will Be Dug."

30. "Twenty-One Tugs Try *Missouri* Job on High Tide," *Pilot,* 20 January 1950.

31. *Summaries,* 19 January 1950.
32. "Blandy Calls Navy Inquiry in Court Case," *Pilot,* 21 January 1950.
33. Ibid.
34. Ibid. The event was amply photographed and reported by the press across the nation.

CHAPTER 5 Pinioned

1. George, interview.
2. "Refloating Attempts Fail," *New York Times,* 21 January 1950.
3. Williams, interview.
4. Oral report of Warran Lee of Pleasantville, N.Y. (FC3 in 1950), interviewed by author in September 1994; George, interview.
5. Cameron Gregory, "Too Many Gags Told Too Often," *Pilot,* 26 January 1950.
6. "*Missouri* Adds to Geological Annals," U.S. Army Engineer's photograph, *Pilot,* 3 February 1950.
7. *Findings,* paragraph 142.
8. *New York Times,* 20 January 1950.
9. *Refloating the USS* Missouri (Washington, D.C.: Department of the Navy, Bureau of Ships, 1950) (hereafter cited as *NAVSHIPS*), 15. This document describes all but the light. Winnett, "Rock Holding Vessel Fast, Admiral Says," *Pilot,* 1 February 1950, mentions the light.
10. Shipping News, *Newport News Daily Press,* 21 January 1950.
11. Glasgow, "Sailors on Liberty"; Charlton Barron, "No Unusual Departures from Normal Piloting Procedure," *Norfolk Ledger-Dispatch,* 24 January 1950.
12. Goffredo, interview.
13. McGrath, interview.
14. *Newport News Daily Press,* 25 January 1950.
15. *Salvage Report,* Enclosure 12 (Public Relations).
16. Glasgow, "Sailors on Liberty."
17. Interior descriptions are based on photographs taken at the time and on the author's visit to the *Missouri* in the Reserve Fleet, August 1993. There seemed to be little difference over forty-three years.
18. Winnett, "Big Mo Unmoved; To Try Again," *Pilot,* 24 January 1950.
19. "Captain W. D. Brown Denies Carelessness," *New York Times,* 24 January 1950; Barron, "No Unusual Departures."
20. Winnett, "Big Mo Unmoved."
21. Baldwin, "Dilemma of the 'Big Mo.'"
22. Winnett, "Big Mo Unmoved."
23. *Summaries,* 24 January 1950.
24. *Findings,* paragraph 142.
25. *Salvage Report,* Enclosure 12 (Public Relations).
26. George, interview.

27. Lee, interview.
28. Advertisements in *Newport News Daily Press*, 26, 29 January 1950.
29. McDowell, "Navy Flooded with Plans."
30. *Summaries,* 25 January 1950.
31. Allan E. Smith, letter to Preston Hotchkis, 8 March 1950, Smith Papers.
32. "Everyone Has an Idea on How to Free *Missouri,*" *Pilot,* 27 January 1950.
33. Harry Nash, "Big Mo's Guns Might Aid If She Weren't So Fast," *Pilot,* 27 January 1950.
34. Photo, *Pilot,* 30 January 1950.
35. *Salvage Report,* ComCruLant dispatch to CinCLantFlt, special situation report, 29 January 1950.

CHAPTER 6 The Big Pull

1. Weather Report, *Pilot,* 27–28 January 1950; "Weather Halts Work," *New York Times,* 28 January 1950.
2. *NAVSHIPS.* Readers with a professional interest in the technical aspects of the *Missouri*'s salvage operation are referred to this Navy Department publication for details beyond descriptions given here.
3. USS *Missouri* Executive Officer's Notice 5-50, 23 January 1950, included in *Salvage Report, Log.*
4. "Refloating Attempt Set," *New York Times,* 31 January 1950; Winnett, "Rock Holding Vessel Fast."
5. *Newport News Daily Press,* 31 January 1950.
6. Charlton Barron, "Vessel Might Be Rockbound, Admiral Says," *Norfolk Ledger-Dispatch,* 31 January 1950, and inside weather detail.
7. Harry Nash, "Men of Steel Appear as Ghosts," *Richmond Times-Herald,* 31 January 1950. Times of events and quoted words are supported by the official log.
8. Williams, interview. Williams was in the sick bay, recovering from a hernia operation he had elected to have on board so as not to leave his ship in its crisis.
9. "Refloating Attempts Fail," *New York Times,* 1 February 1950.
10. *Summaries,* 31 January situation report.
11. George, interview.

CHAPTER 7 And So to Twenty-seven Feet

1. Hanson W. Baldwin, "*Missouri* Pulled off Shoal with Help of Unusual Tide," on board the *Missouri, New York Times,* 2 February 1950.
2. Winnett, "*Missouri* in Portsmouth Drydock."
3. Irving T. Duke, letter to Allan E. Smith, 31 October 1949; Allan E. Smith, letter to Rear Adm. R. L. Dennison, 27 January 1950; Allan E. Smith, letter to Capt. H. Page Smith, 27 February 1950; all in Smith Papers.

NOTES TO PAGES 131-65

4. Allan E. Smith, letter to Rear Adm. R. L. Dennison, 27 January 1950, Smith Papers.
5. Winnett, "Navy Opens Its Court of Inquiry into Grounding of *Missouri*," *Pilot*, 4 February 1950.
6. Joseph Bishop Jr., *Justice Under Fire: A Study of Military Law* (New York: Charterhouse, 1974), citing Henderson, "Courts-Martial and the Constitution: The Original Understanding," *Harvard Law Review* 71, no. 2 (December 1957): 293.
7. Richard Gonder, "Ensign Harris Is Defended by Peckham," *Pilot*, 12 February 1950; "*Missouri* Inquiry Focuses on Ensign," *New York Times*, 12 February 1950.
8. Glasgow, "*Missouri*'s 'New' Status Not Much of a Change," *Pilot*, 16 February 1950.
9. Winnett, "Did Alarms Reach Brown on *Missouri?*" *Pilot*, 16 February 1950.
10. Winnett, "Counsel for Navigator Scores at 'Mo' Hearing," *Pilot*, 18 February 1950.
11. "Remark on Ensign's Ability Stricken from Inquiry's Record," *Pilot*, 19 February 1950.
12. Winnett, "*Missouri*'s Skipper Tells Court His Subordinates Stood Silent," *Pilot*, 19 February 1950.
13. "Captain of 'Big Mo' Gave 'Final Order,'" *New York Times*, 21 February 1950; Winnett, "Mo's Skipper Infers Blame Not His Alone," *Pilot*, 21 February 1950.

CHAPTER 8 Tragic Hero

1. Glasgow, "Ship Skipper Contradicted by Navigator."
2. "'Mo' Navigator Says Officers Were 'Rusty,'" *Richmond Times-Dispatch*, 24 February 1950.
3. Glasgow, "Four *Missouri* Defendants Conclude Their Cases," *Pilot*, 25 February 1950.
4. Ibid.
5. Glasgow, "*Missouri* Captain Takes Full Blame for Its Grounding," *Pilot*, 1 March 1950; Hanson W. Baldwin, "Tragedy of Command," *New York Times*, 1 March 1950.
6. *Proceedings*, general introduction.
7. Ibid.
8. Allan E. Smith, ComCruLant summary letter, 15 March 1950, in *Proceedings*.
9. "Three Top *Missouri* Officers to Stand Trial for Grounding," *New York Times*, 17 March 1950.
10. Glasgow, "Captain Brown 'Guilty,' He Pleads, in Grounding of Battleship *Missouri*," *Pilot*, 31 March 1950.

11. Harry Nash, "'Somebody Didn't Get the Word' Is Story of Big Mo's Grounding," *Newport News Daily Press*, 12 March 1950.
12. ComCruLant letter to Rear Adm. Stuart S. Murray, USN, 16 March 1950, Smith Papers.
13. Glasgow, "Captain Brown 'Guilty.'"
14. Undoubtedly the views of crew members have softened over the decades, but those interviewed some forty-four years later collectively recalled their disappointment on Brown's behalf. This feeling seemed borne out by contemporary newspaper editorials (*Pilot*, 31 March, 4 May 1950) and letters to the editor.
15. Allan E. Smith, memo to Capt. John F. Madden, USN, 20 March 1950, Smith Papers.
16. "Challenges and Objections Ring Out as Court-Martial of Morris Opens," *Pilot*, 28 March 1950.
17. "Morris Aided in Testimony from Ensign," *Pilot*, 29 March 1950.
18. Glasgow, "Navigation Duties Not His, Peckham Says He Was Told," *Pilot*, 4 April 1950.
19. Glasgow, "Peckham Told to Explain Why He Not Due Censure," *Pilot*, 5 April 1950.
20. Glasgow, "Morris Told of Five, Not Two, Buoys—Brown," *Pilot*, 11 April 1950.
21. Glasgow, "Ruling, Witness Help Cases of 'Mo' Officers," *Pilot*, 8 April 1950.
22. Glasgow, "Millett Ends Court-Martial Defense," *Pilot*, 12 April 1950.
23. Allan E. Smith, memo to Capt. John F. Madden, USN, 20 March 1950, Smith Papers.
24. Glasgow, "Millett Ends Court-Martial Defense."
25. Glasgow, "Court-Martial Clears Millett on One Count," *Pilot*, 14 April 1950.
26. "Capt. I. T. Duke Takes Helm of USS *Missouri*," *Pilot*, 20 April 1950.
27. "Illness Delays Morris Trial by Navy Court," *Pilot*, 18 April 1950.
28. Glasgow, "Morris Court-Martial Reaches Argument Stage," *Pilot*, 20 April 1950.
29. "Morris Trial in 'Mo' Case Draws to End," *Pilot*, 25 April 1950.
30. Glasgow, "'Fully Acquit' Morris, Navy Court Asked," *Pilot*, 25 April 1950.

CHAPTER 9 The Navy's Problems

1. Allan E. Smith, ComCruLant summary letter, 15 March 1950, in *Proceedings*.
2. *Proceedings*, Opinion 14.
3. W. M. Fechteler, CinCLantFlt, 17 May 1950, First Endorsement, with amplification, on ComCruLant cover letter, 1 May 1950, to *Proceedings*.

4. *Findings,* paragraphs 72, 105; *Proceedings,* Opinion 1(d).
5. *Findings,* paragraph 50.
6. Ibid., paragraphs 133, 134.
7. *Proceedings,* Opinion 5(a).
8. *Findings,* paragraphs 48, 87.
9. Ibid., paragraph 114; *Proceedings,* Opinion 6(d).
10. Newell and Smith, *Mighty Mo,* 76–77.
11. *Proceedings,* Opinion 2(h).
12. Baldwin, "Tragedy of Command."
13. Smith, "Refloating the USS *Missouri,*" 181.
14. *Summaries,* ComCruLant dispatch to CinCLantFlt, 1 February 1950.

CHAPTER 10 As You Were

1. Oral report of John C. Smith of Barnegat, N.J. (MEG3 in 1950), interviewed by author in September 1994.
2. Rear Adm. Henry Williams, letter in response to Rear Admiral Smith's February 1951 article ("Refloating the USS *Missouri*"), U.S. Naval Institute *Proceedings* 77, no. 10 (December 1951): 1340–41.
3. *Salvage Report,* Enclosure 14 (Costs).
4. Allen, "Exercise Portrex."
5. "Severity of Brown's Sentence Could Prove Ultimate Benefit," *Pilot,* 4 May 1950.
6. Allan E. Smith, *Navy Humor and So Forth* (Lawrenceville, Va.: Brunswick Publishing, 1985).
7. Allan E. Smith, letter to Preston Hotchkis, 8 March 1950, Smith Papers.
8. Allan E. Smith Jr. of Bellevue, Wash., interviewed by author in January 1994.
9. Edmund J. Butler Jr., written recollection delivered to the author in January 1993. The conversation that follows is of the author's creation, but it conveys essentially what was said that evening.
10. Allan E. Smith, notes for a speech given at Type Commanders' Conference, 5 April 1949, quoting Gen. Omar M. Bradley, Chairman of the Joint Chiefs of Staff, Smith Papers.
11. McCullough, *Truman,* 780.
12. Newell and Smith, *Mighty Mo,* 95; Sumrall, Iowa-*Class Battleships,* Appendix C.
13. George, interview.
14. Ibid.
15. *New York Times,* 5 February 1991.

Bibliography

Chesapeake History

Besse, Sumner B. *C.S. Ironclad* Virginia *and U.S. Ironclad* Monitor. Newport News, Va.: The Mariners Museum, 1978.

Davis, William C. *Duel between the First Ironclads.* Garden City, N.Y.: Doubleday & Co., 1975.

Ellis, William S. "Hampton Roads, Where the Rivers End." *National Geographic* 168, no. 1 (July 1985): 72–107.

Fisher, Allan C., Jr. "My Chesapeake, Queen of Bays." *National Geographic* 158, no. 4 (October 1980): 428–67.

McPherson, James M. *Battle Cry of Freedom.* New York: Oxford University Press, 1988.

Rouse, Parke, Jr. *The Good Old Days in Hampton and Newport News.* Richmond, Va.: The Dietz Press, 1986.

Battleships

Dulin, Robert O., and William H. Garzke Jr. *United States Battleships in World War II.* Annapolis, Md.: Naval Institute Press, 1985.

Fahey, James C. *Ships and Aircraft of the U.S. Fleet.* 3 vols. Annapolis, Md.: Naval Institute Press, 1958.

Garzke, William H., and Robert O. Dulin Jr. *Allied Battleships in World War II.* Annapolis, Md.: Naval Institute Press, 1980.

Groppe, Alexander J. "The Question of the American Battleship, 1895–1991." Navy Department Library, 1991.

Grove, Eric. *The Future of Sea Power.* Annapolis, Md.: Naval Institute Press, 1990.

Hough, Richard. *Dreadnought.* New York: Macmillan, 1975.

Jordan, John. *An Illustrated Guide to Battleships and Battlecruisers.* New York: Arcor, 1985.

Mack, William P., and Thomas D. Paulsen. *The Naval Officer's Guide.* 9th ed. Annapolis, Md.: Naval Institute Press, 1951.

Massie, Robert K. *Dreadnought: Britain, Germany, and the Coming of the Great War.* New York: Random House, 1991.

Morison, Samuel Eliot. *History of United States Naval Operations in World War II.* 15 vols. Boston: Atlantic Monthly Press, 1947–62.

———. *The Two-Ocean War.* Boston: Little, Brown, 1963.

Morison, Samuel L., and John S. Rowe. *Warships of the U.S. Navy.* London: Jane's Publishing, 1983.

Muir, Malcolm, Jr. *The* Iowa-*Class Battleships:* Iowa, New Jersey, Missouri, *and* Wisconsin. New York: Sterling, 1987.

Newell, Gordon, and Allan E. Smith, Vice Admiral, USN (Ret.). *Mighty Mo, the USS* Missouri: *A Biography of the Last Battleship.* New York: Bonanza Books, 1969.

Reilly, John C., Jr. *Operational Experience of Fast Battleships: World War II, Korea, Vietnam.* Washington, D.C.: Naval Historical Center, 1989.

Stillwell, Paul. *Battleship* New Jersey: *An Illustrated History.* Annapolis, Md.: Naval Institute Press, 1987.

Sumrall, Robert F. Iowa-*Class Battleships: Their Design, Weapons and Equipment.* Annapolis, Md.: Naval Institute Press, 1988.

Terzibaschitsch, Stefan. *Battleships of the U.S. Navy in World War II.* Translated and adapted by Heinz O. Vetters and Richard Cox. New York: Bonanza Books, 1977; originally published by J. F. Lehmanns Verlag.

Young, Filson. *With the Battlecruisers.* Annapolis, Md.: Naval Institute Press, 1986.

Naval Law

Bishop, Joseph W., Jr. *Justice Under Fire: A Study of Military Law.* New York: Charterhouse, 1974.

Wiener, Frederick Bernays. *The Uniform Code of Military Justice: Explanation, Comparative Text, and Commentary.* Washington, D.C.: Combat Forces Press, 1950.

U.S. Navy Publications and Documents

The Bluejackets' Manual. 13th ed. Annapolis, Md.: U.S. Naval Institute, 1946.

Dictionary of American Naval Fighting Ships. Vol. 4. Washington, D.C.: Navy Department, Office of the Chief of Naval Operations, Naval History Division, 1969.

International Code of Signals, 1931 Code: Hydrographic Office #87. Washington, D.C.: Government Printing Office, 1943.

Manual of Commands and Orders. United States Navy. Navy Department Library.

Manual of the Judge Advocate General, basic investigative report concerning the grounding of USS Missouri *(BB-63), in Chesapeake Bay, on January 17, 1950,* with endorsements, 1951.

Refloating the USS Missouri *(BB-63).* NAVSHIPS 250-694-3, renumbered as NAVSHIPS 0900-004-8000. Washington, D.C.: Department of the Navy, Bureau of Ships, 1 June 1950.

U.S. Navy Regulations 1920–1944. Washington, D.C.: United States Navy, 1944.

USS Iowa *1952–1953 Far Eastern Cruise Book.* United States Navy.

USS Missouri *1952–1953 Far Eastern Cruise Book.* United States Navy.

USS Missouri *(BB-63) Salvage Report,* with enclosures, 15 March 1950. A report from Commander Cruisers, Atlantic Fleet, to the Chief of Naval Operations. (FF13-5/01)

Navigation, Seamanship, Marine Electronics

Devereux, Tony. *Messenger Gods of Battle.* London: Brassey's, 1991.

Dutton, Benjamin. *Navigation and Nautical Astronomy.* 9th ed. Annapolis, Md.: U.S. Naval Institute, 1948.

Kelly, Thomas J. *Damage Control: A Manual for Naval Personnel.* New York: Van Nostrand, 1944.

Knight, Austin M. *Modern Seamanship.* 11th ed. New York: D. Van Nostrand, 1950.

Political and Social History

Barnhart, Clarence L., Sol Steinmetz, and Robert K. Barnhart. *The Barnhart Dictionary of New English since 1963.* New York: Barnhart/Harper & Row, 1973.

Ferrell, Robert H., ed. *The Twentieth Century: An Almanac.* New York: World Almanac Publications, 1984.

Johnson, Paul. *Modern Times: The World from the Twenties to the Nineties.* Rev. ed. New York: HarperCollins, 1991.

Keegan, John. *A History of Warfare.* New York: Alfred A. Knopf, 1993.

McCullough, David. *Truman.* New York: Simon & Schuster, 1992.

Tute, Warren. *The True Glory.* New York: Harper & Row, 1983.

Urdang, Laurence, ed. *Timetables of American History.* New York: Simon & Schuster, 1981.

Salvage

Bartholomew, C. A. *Mud, Muscle, and Miracles: Marine Salvage in the United States Navy.* Washington, D.C.: Government Printing Office, 1990.

Smith, Allan E. "Refloating the USS *Missouri.*" U.S. Naval Institute *Proceedings* 77, no. 2 (February 1951): 181–195.

Newspapers

Baltimore Evening Sun, January–March 1950

Boston Herald, January, February 1950

Kansas City Star, January 1950

New York Herald Tribune, March 1950

New York Times, January, February, July 1944; January–March 1950

Newport News Daily Press, January–March 1950

Norfolk Ledger-Dispatch, January 1950

Norfolk Virginian-Pilot, December 1949; January–May 1950

Philadelphia Inquirer, February 1950

Richmond Times-Dispatch, February 1950

St. Louis Post-Dispatch, January 1950

Washington Evening Star, January 1950

Washington Post, January–March 1950

Index

About the Author

John A. Butler is president of Halcyon Group, Inc., a consulting firm that offers business and technical education. Before embarking on a thirty-five-year career with IBM, he served as a communications officer aboard a U.S. Navy troopship and as a deck officer for American Export and United States Lines. He holds degrees in nautical science from the Massachusetts Maritime Academy and in physics from Holy Cross College.

The **Naval Institute Press is** the book-publishing arm of the U.S. Naval Institute, a private, nonprofit society for sea service professionals and others who share an interest in naval and maritime affairs. Established in 1873 at the U.S. Naval Academy in Annapolis, Maryland, where its offices remain, today the Naval Institute has more than 100,000 members worldwide.

Members of the Naval Institute receive the influential monthly magazine *Proceedings* and discounts on fine nautical prints and on ship and aircraft photos. They also have access to the transcripts of the Institute's Oral History Program and get discounted admission to any of the Institute-sponsored seminars offered around the country.

The Naval Institute also publishes *Naval History* magazine. This colorful bimonthly is filled with entertaining and thought-provoking articles, first-person reminiscences, and dramatic art and photography. Members receive a discount on *Naval History* subscriptions.

The Naval Institute's book-publishing program, begun in 1898 with basic guides to naval practices, has broadened its scope in recent years to include books of more general interest. Now the Naval Institute Press publishes more than seventy titles each year, ranging from how-to books on boating and navigation to battle histories, biographies, ship and aircraft guides, and novels. Institute members receive discounts on the Press's nearly 400 books in print.

For a free catalog describing Naval Institute Press books currently available, and for further information about subscribing to *Naval History* magazine or about joining the U.S. Naval Institute, please write to:

Membership & Communications Department
U.S. Naval Institute
118 Maryland Avenue
Annapolis, Maryland 21402-5035
Or call, toll-free, (800) 233-USNI.